00965213

D0298384

39.50

Practical Sociology

Practical Sociology

Post-empiricism and the Reconstruction of Theory and Application

Christopher G. A. Bryant

Polity Press

Copyright © Christopher G. A. Bryant 1995

The right of Christopher G. A. Bryant to be identified as author of this work has been asserted in accordance with the Copyright, Designs and Patents Act 1988.

First published in 1995 by Polity Press
in association with Blackwell Publishers Ltd.

2 4 6 8 10 7 5 3 1

Editorial office:
Polity Press
65 Bridge Street
Cambridge CB2 1UR, UK

Marketing and production:

Blackwell Publishers Ltd
108 Cowley Road
Oxford OX4 1JF, UK

Blackwell Publishers Inc.
238 Main Street
Cambridge, MA 02142, USA

ISBN 0-7456-14922
ISBN 0-7456-14930 (pbk)

A CIP catalogue record for this book is available from the British Library and the Library of Congress.

Typeset in 10.5 on 12 pt Sabon
by Best-set Typesetter Ltd, Hong Kong
Printed and bound in Great Britain by
Hartnolls Limited, Bodmin, Cornwall
This book is printed on acid-free paper.

In memory of my father,
Gordon Bryant

Contents

Preface and Acknowledgements

Older versions of social science – often conceived as quasi-natural sciences of society – have claimed more than they can deliver. They have left a difficult public legacy. The social sciences are all too often disparaged for failing to provide laws, theories and research findings as reliable as those the natural sciences are deemed able to offer. The only escape from expectations which are variously unfulfillable and dismissive is for social scientists to reconsider what the social sciences can and cannot do and to try to re-educate publics, politicians and purseholders accordingly. This book is a small contribution to that big task. It seeks to help define a social science that works, that claims to offer only such explanations and understandings as it is capable of delivering and that has a practical value outside the academy.

Definition and promotion of a social science that works are, to a greater or lesser degree, a project for all the social sciences. My discussion is centred on sociology because that is the social science I know best, but much of what I have to say applies to other social sciences too. Also, many of the figures whose arguments I consider – Bhaskar, Habermas, Hesse and Rawls for a start – would not identify themselves as sociologists, and many of the debates I examine – such as those associated with the Committee on Conceptual and Terminological Analysis, the numerous writers on agency and structure, or the work of feminist epistemologists – have involved scholars from different disciplines. It would thus be particularly gratifying if this work proved of some value beyond sociology.

For good reasons and bad this is a book which has been a long time in preparation. Two consequences require comment. First, about a third of the book reworks material already published (not always in very accessible places). Some of these reworkings stick closely to the originals, but others do not. Chapters 1 and 6 contain material derived with modifications from an essay, 'Theory, metatheory and discourse', in Robert Burgess (ed.), *Sociology: Where Are We Now?* (London: UCL Press, 1995) and here reproduced with the permission of the publishers. Chapter 2 contains material, sometimes much revised, first published in 'Sociology without foundations', *Polish Sociological Bulletin*, no. 3–4 (87–88), 1989; and in 'Conceptual variation and conceptual relativism in the social sciences', in Diederick Raven, Lieteke van Vucht Tijssen and Jan de Wolf (eds), *Cognitive Relativism and Social Science* (New Brunswick NJ: Transaction, 1992). Consent to the first has been given by the Polish Sociological Association and permission for the second by Transaction. The discussion of the work of Bhaskar in chapter 3 includes comment developed from the *Polish Sociological Bulletin* article, and the discussion of Giddens includes comment developed from 'Coming to terms with Anthony Giddens', the introduction written jointly with David Jary for the book we edited on *Giddens' Theory of Structuration* (London: Routledge, 1991). Chapter 4 opens with some comment on Weber drawn from my *Positivism in Social Theory and Research* (London: Macmillan, 1985). Chapter 5 includes material reworked from my chapter for the book on Giddens and from 'Sociology without philosophy? The case of Giddens's structuration theory', *Sociological Theory*, vol. 10, 1992 – the latter with the permission of the American Sociological Association.

The second consequence of taking a long time to do something is the receipt of a lot of help which I can at last acknowledge with gratitude. I have benefited from comments on drafts of different bits of this book made by Henk Becker, Ira Cohen, Rob Flynn, David Jary, Stephen Mennell, Ray Pawson, David Sciulli and Greg Smith; from responses to seminar presentations at the Universities of Leeds (1989) and Utrecht (1990) and to conference presentations at the ISA Methodology Conference in Dubrovnik (1988), the ISA World Congress in Madrid (1990), the BSA Annual Conference in Manchester (1991) and the ASA Annual Meeting in Cincinnati (1991) (Bryant, 1991). I especially wish to thank Ragnevald Kalleberg and his colleagues in the Graduate School of Sociology at the University of Oslo for inviting me to give four seminars there in the autumn of 1993 which enabled me to test responses to many of the arguments of the book. Finally, I started and finished writing during leaves granted by the University of Salford in 1986–7 and 1994; I am grateful to the university for this support and to hard-pressed colleagues who covered my absence, especially Pat Walters in 1986–7 and Steve Edgell in

1994, who generously took over my responsibilities as Chairman of the Department of Sociology and Director of the Institute for Social Research respectively.

Figures 2.1, 2.2 and 2.3 are composites or reproductions of figures which first appeared in G. Sartori's 'Guidelines for concept analysis' in the volume he edited, *Social Science Concepts* (Beverley Hills and London: Sage, 1984), pp. 23, 26, 27, 29 and 33, and are used here with the permission of Sage Publications, Inc. Table 3.1 comes from Habermas's reply to his critics in J. B. Thompson and D. Held (eds), *Habermas: Critical Debates* (London and Basingstoke: Macmillan, 1982), p. 279, and is reproduced with the permission of Macmillan Press Ltd. Figures 3.1 to 3.4 come from R. Bhaskar, *The Possibility of Naturalism* (Brighton: Harvester, 1979), pp. 40 and 46, and are reproduced with the permission of Roy Bhaskar; figures 3.5 and 3.6 are taken from his *Scientific Realism and Human Emancipation* (London: Verso, 1986), p. 126, and are reproduced with the permission of the publishers. Figure 3.7 is a modification of combined figures from A. Giddens, *The Constitution of Society* (Cambridge: Polity, 1984), pp. 5 and 7, and figures 3.8 and 3.9 come from the same book, pp. 29 and 32; all are used here with the permission of Anthony Giddens. Figure 6.1 is modified from J. C. Alexander, *Theoretical Logic in Sociology*, vol. 1 (Berkeley: University of California Press, 1982), and is used here with the permission of the University of California Press.

1

Introduction: Theory, Metatheory and Discourse

'Theory building' carries with it an imagery of the careful construction of layers of generalizations about the social world, firmly cemented together by accumulated empirical observations . . . It is naive to suppose that it has much relevance to social science.

Giddens, Social Theory and Modern Sociology (1987)

[F]rom the most specific factual statements up to the most abstract generalizations, social science is essentially contestable.

Alexander, 'The new theoretical movement' (1988)

Sociology: crisis or opportunity

This is an optimistic book about sociology, and thus perhaps an unfashionable one. Ever since Gouldner published *The Coming Crisis of Western Sociology* in 1970, there have been those who, with greater or lesser relish, have proclaimed sociology to be in crisis. Most such writings also recommend their own way out of the crisis. Jonathan Turner's and Stephen Turner's 1990 account of the development of sociology in America, still the society with more academic sociologists than any other, extends the genre by concluding that sociology is condemned to remain *The Impossible Science,* forever betraying all those naive enough to seek from it reliable knowledge of practical value. What gives the notion of sociology in crisis heightened resonance in the 1990s is its association with postmodernity. Modernity, reason and societal self-reflection or 're-flexivity' went hand in hand; likewise the current exhaustion of modernity, the distrust of reason and the disillusionment with sociology – or so we are told.

I do not intend to add yet another book on modernity, late modernity or postmodernity. Instead I want to make the case for a sociology without foundations, which is nonetheless a rational endeavour of practical value. If that makes this a sort of constructive tract for, or perhaps against, our times – so be it; but it is sociology, rather than our times, which I shall primarily address. American sociology may be an impossible science, but sociology does not have to be like that. We can do better than proclaim the need to go *Beyond Objectivism and Relativism* as Bernstein did in 1983. Thanks to profound work by many scholars on the constitution of society and the making and accepting of both knowledge claims and value judgements, we can discern, at least in outline, the contours and constituents of a new practical sociology – a social science that works. As a consequence, we now have an opportunity, perhaps for the first time, to promote a sociology which can realistically expect to live up to its claims.

Many of the problems with which sociology has grappled are shared by other social sciences, and many of the ways of dealing with them which are discussed in this book owe much to contributions from writers who would not identify themselves as sociologists. Although my aim is to indicate how the reconstruction of theory and application in sociology can proceed, arguments I shall deploy often apply to social science more generally. Others seeking a social science that works may have in mind a social science other than sociology – political science, economics or perhaps political economy, or human or social geography, for example – and if this book helps them with their quests too, so much the better.

In this Introduction I shall situate some of the issues explored at length in subsequent chapters, and in the concluding chapter (6) I shall return to the specification of the new pragmatic sociology.

Theory and theory proper

Argument about theory, metatheory and discourse in sociology lies at the heart of the debate about the character of sociology itself and its claim to be a social science. I shall begin reflection on the broad range of activities which have been practised in the name of sociological theory over the last half-century by recalling Merton's conception of theory proper and the conception of science which went with it. I shall then consider the challenge to both presented by the linguistic turn, anti-foundationalism and post-empiricism. I believe this challenge has largely succeeded among specialists in sociological theory, though not necessarily sociologists generally, but I will also address the deep anxiety of those, such as Jonathan Turner in America and Peter Abell in Britain, who fear that in the process metatheory has triumphed over theory proper. I shall then recommend the term 'discourse' as a way of superseding the unprofitable theory–metatheory distinction.

Merton's view of what properly counts as sociological theory was exceedingly influential (1957a).[1] He listed six types of work which have gone by the name of theory in sociology – methodology, general orientations (for example Durkheim's generic hypothesis that 'the determining cause of a social fact should be sought among the social facts preceding it' (1895, p. 110)), analysis of concepts, *post factum* interpretations (finding an interpretation to fit the facts, such as the plausible constructions placed on documents by Thomas and Znaniecki in the *The Polish Peasant in Europe and America* (1918–20)), empirical generalizations (isolated propositions summarizing observed uniformities between two or more variables, such as Engels's law of consumption which states that as household income increases the proportion spent on food declines), and the formulation of scientific laws (statements of invariance derived from a theory) – and implied a seventh: the codification of scientific laws. Of these only the last two – deduction of propositions to be empirically tested (for which the formalization of Durkheim's explanation of differential suicide rates provides an example) and their codified cumulation (which Merton illustrates in his essays on continuities in the theories of social structure and anomie and of reference group behaviour) – are deemed to constitute theory proper (Durkheim, 1897; Merton, 1957b, 1957c).

The growth of theory proper is central to Merton's conception of sociology, which Crothers has aptly characterized as 'an advancing, accumulative science generally based on a "natural science" model and sharply demarcated from "common sense" social knowledge' (1987, p. 51; also see Sztompka, 1986, ch. 2). This is the theory in the theory-building promoted by Lazarsfeld and Rosenberg (1955) or Stinchcombe (1968) or Dubin (1969) or Blalock (1969). It is also the theory for which Wagner (1984) makes claims of growth, whose achievements Wallace (1988) celebrates in Smelser's weighty *Handbook of Sociology* (1988) and which Jonathan Turner (1989b) lauds in a volume derived from theory papers given at the 1987 meeting of the American Sociological Association. I have discussed it elsewhere in terms of 'instrumental positivism' and have declared it the prevailing tradition in American sociological theory (Bryant, 1985, ch. 5).[2] Many of its protagonists prefer to speak of the 'analytical tradition' of sociology (cf. Henk A. Becker, 1990, ch. 2). It is not, however, the whole story – even in America – as we shall see.

There were, of course, differences in the programmes for sociology put forward some four decades ago by Merton, Parsons, Lazarsfeld and Stouffer (Turner and Turner, 1990, ch. 3), but there was also a broad consistency in so far as they were all modelled on natural science. As a consequence they were all doomed to disappoint. A comparison between Merton and Parsons reveals why. Parsons differentiated four levels of conceptual systematization (Parsons and Shils, 1951, pp. 49–52; Mulkay, 1971, ch. 3). The progressive achievement of a scientific sociology requires movement from the first to the fourth. The four are: first, *ad hoc* classifications; second, a categorial system (an interdependent system of classes and definitions); third, a theoretical system (a categorial system plus laws which specify relations between its elements); and fourth, an empirical–theoretical system (which affords predictions under real, as distinct from experimental, conditions). Parsons thought that economics and psychology were beginning to establish themselves at the third level, as evidenced by the theory of marginal utility and the stimulus–response theory of learning, but that other would-be social sciences had not even got beyond level one. This Parsons believed he could remedy by establishing for the first time nothing less than a categorial system, not just for sociology, but for all the social sciences. His failure to do so cannot leave us unmoved in so far as routine, but systematic, comparison and cumulation of social research findings – what Kuhn (1962) later called normal science – are impossible in the absence of conceptual consistency and routine commensurability between researches. Either we must succeed where Parsons failed or we must reconsider our theoretical goals. I shall be arguing for the latter.

It must be emphasized that Parsons's failure has to do with his conception of scientific sociology, not the scale of his theorizing. Merton may have eschewed grand theory in favour of theories of the middle range, but that theorizing is still located on the third and fourth of Parsons's levels. It presumes the establishability, if not the establishment, of a categorial system, albeit bit by bit. 'No study can become scientific...', we are told, 'until it provides itself with a suitable technical nomenclature, whose every term has a single definite meaning universally accepted' (Merton and Lazarsfeld, 1954, p. 24). Unlike Parsons, Merton did not believe generation of such a nomenclature was a task for any single theorist and his (or her) associates. Instead it would develop from the contributions of numerous sociologists who took care, as Merton did, to consider past and present uses of a term before engaging in concept formation. In chapter 2 I shall examine at length the general issue of concept formation and its connection to workable and unworkable conceptions of sociology. For the moment, I will just say that the labours of numerous sociologists, whether careful or careless about concept formation, have not in practice generated the categorial system or universal nomenclature sought by those who would model sociology on natural science.

The linguistic turn

The initial challenge to social science as Merton conceived it came from proponents of the linguistic turn, and, among other things, it indicates why a single categorial system for all social science, or even all sociology, is bound always to elude us. The expression 'the linguistic turn' originated in Bergman's *Logic and Reality* (1964): 'All linguistic philosophers talk about the world by means of talking about a suitable language. This is the linguistic turn, the fundamental gambit as to method, on which ordinary and ideal language philosophers . . . agree' (p. 177). Rorty's use of it for the title of his 1967 volume on philosophical method made it more generally known. In sociology it has prompted what has sometimes been called 'the hermeneutic turn' (cf. Phillips, 1986, p. 2). Social scientists who make the turn acknowledge the language and understandings of the (types of) person whose action they seek to account for and about whom they seek to generalize. 'Language use', as Giddens says, 'is embedded in the concrete activities of everyday life and is in some sense partly constitutive of those activities' (Giddens, 1984, p. xvi). That this has important consequences for the kinds of laws and generalizations which sociologists are able to formulate is generally agreed, even if not everyone would subscribe to Giddens's version of what they are.

> Generalizations tend towards two poles, with a range and variety of possible shadings between them. Some hold because actors themselves know them – in some guise – and apply them in the enactment of what they do. The social scientific observer does not in fact have to 'discover' these generalizations, although that observer may give a new discursive form to them. Other generalizations refer to circumstances, or aspects of circumstances, of which agents are ignorant and which effectively 'act' on them, independently of whatever the agents may believe they

are up to . . . and each form of generalization is unstable in respect of
the other. The circumstances in which generalizations about what
'happens' to agents hold are mutable in respect of what those agents
can learn knowledgeably to 'make happen'. (1984, p. xix)

The two-way tie between ordinary members' and sociologists'
language and knowledge (Giddens's double-hermeneutic) is inimical
to Merton's conception of theory proper not only because it connects
what he would separate – social science and common sense – but also
because it precludes cumulation of the kind he sought.

For theory proper to be possible, societies would have to be constituted differently from the way they are. How societies are constituted
– the ontology of the social – has been the subject of the micro–macro
and agency–structure debates which have enjoyed a renewed intensity
in the last twenty years. They are discussed at length in chapter 3 in
relation to the formulations of Elias, Bourdieu, Habermas, Bhaskar,
Giddens and others. However recondite they may first seem,
ontologies of the social are of great practical consequence. Miscon-
ceive the constitution of society and strategies for the application of
sociology are highly likely to go wrong. Accordingly, models of
applied sociology are discussed in chapter 5.

The notion of social science as moral inquiry (Haan et al., 1983),
or what Alexander refers to as 'the distinctively evaluative nature of
social science' (1988, p. 80), follows from that of the linguistic turn.
In the 1950s and 1960s sociologists sought an objectivity and value
neutrality which required that social science and moral inquiry be
quite separate. Once the double-hermeneutic is recognized, however,
this dissociation loses all plausibility. The language sociologists use in
constituting their objects of inquiry can never be purged of all normative content, and what they say and write can, and often does, enter
extra-sociological discourses, either directly or as mediated by others
from politicians to social workers. The rational justification of values
is thus back on the social science agenda, and this most difficult of
issues is explored at some length in chapter 4.

Anti-foundationalism

Anti-foundationalism poses a further challenge to the ideas of theory
proper and cumulative science. The metaphor of a sure foundation
for our knowledge originates in Descartes. Strictly speaking it belongs
to epistemology but, like many notions in epistemology, it also shades

into ontology in so far as ideas about how we can know are connected to ideas about what there is to be known. It refers to knowledge as a mirror of nature, to knowledge as a faithful representation of how the world is. This is how Rorty characterizes it:

> we may think of both knowledge and justification as privileged relations to the objects those propositions are about. . . . If we think of knowledge in [this] way we will want to get behind reasons to causes, beyond argument to compulsion from the object known, to a situation in which argument would not be just silly but impossible, for anyone gripped by the object in the required way will be unable to doubt or to see an alternative. To reach that point is to reach the foundations of knowledge. (1980, p. 159)

This is, of course, precisely the version of knowledge which Rorty demolishes so compellingly in his celebrated *Philosophy and the Mirror of Nature* (1980).

Anti-foundationalism goes against the historical grain of sociology as well as of philosophy. The whole point of Comte's positive philosophy and sociology was to abandon the 'intellectual anarchy' which was responsible for the 'great political and moral crisis' of the time (Martineau, 1853, vol. 1, p. 22), in favour of sure (but circumscribed) knowledge. The same can be said of Durkheim on the *sui generis* character of society and the rules of sociological method. In the 1920s and early 1930s the Vienna Circle made its own bid to end the 'anarchy of philosophical opinions' (Schlick, 1930, p. 54) by combining logic and empiricism – and there are filiations, albeit complicated ones, from logical positivism through particular methodologies of social research to the American tradition of empirical sociology. The quest for certainty also figures in the Marxist and hermeneutic traditions. There are elements of it, for example, in the privileged status Marx gives to the mode of production and the dialectical method, and these elements feature prominently both in readings of Marx coloured by Engels's conception of science or Lenin's materialism and empirio-criticism and in derivations from Lukács's notion of the proletariat's privileged access to truth. It is also instructive that Kolakowski (1975) related his lectures on Husserl to the quest for certitude and in recent times a number of interpretivist sociologists have made plain their foundationalism (cf. Williams, 1990). Cicourel, for example, opens his *Method and Measurement in Sociology* (1964) by expressing his critical concern for the foundations of social science research. Sure foundations for knowledge were also integral to the dominant conceptions of sociology in the mid-twentieth century, those of Parsons and Merton.

Securing the foundations for social knowledge was not just a matter of intellectual interest; it was also of great practical value and political importance. Marx sought not just to interpret the world but to change it. Comte and Durkheim in their different ways each sought to move from positive philosophy to a positive polity. And Parsons and Merton in their different ways each sought to provide for usable knowledge. Anti-foundationalism thus calls in question, as Crook (1991) notes, the whole project of 'modernist radicalism'.

What marks much contemporary sociology off from both the structural–functional orthodoxy of the 1950s and the alternative paradigms in the subsequent war of the schools is widespread doubt about the availability of any such foundation. There are a number of reasons for this. They include the impossibility of sealing off socio-logical discourse from natural discourse and the consequent elusive-ness of a universal categorial system for all sociology, the impossibility of effecting any closure on the constitution of society, the limitations of all known research methods and the contested character of objectivity.

Once foundationalism is discarded, objectivist claims become highly problematic. By 'objectivism' I mean the idea that 'there must be some permanent, ahistorical matrix or framework to which we can ultimately appeal in determining the nature of rationality, knowledge, truth, reality, goodness, or rightness' (Bernstein, 1983, p. 8); and by realism I mean Francis Bacon's thesis that science reveals the true and hidden nature of the world. Even so, I shall not subscribe to Lyotard's identification of 'incredulity toward metanarratives' with the postmodern (1979, p. xxiv) for three reasons. First, the postmodern is associated with postmodernism in the arts as well as postmodernity in social organization and comment on the former exceeds my com-petence as a sociologist. Second, postmodern incredulity towards metanarratives – the metadiscourses in which sciences pronounce their self-legitimation by appealing 'to some grand narrative, such as the dialectics of Spirit, the hermeneutics of meaning, the emanci-pation of the rational or working subject, or the creation of wealth' (p. xxiii) – often takes a post-structuralist form and I do not want to be diverted by the convoluted debates about post-structuralism. Suffice it to say that anti-foundationalism does not have to be post-structuralist. Third, postmodern responses to the absence of foundations have embraced radical relativism and playfully self-indulgent eclecticism; mine will not.[3]

Anti-foundationalism is more disputed than the linguistic turn. In later chapters I shall reject two responses to it, reframe a third and endorse a fourth. The first response I shall reject is that of Bhaskar (1975, 1979), Pawson (1989) and other scientific realists who have been very influential in Britain but less so elsewhere. In chapter 3 I shall argue that the underlying realities they posit do not have the privileged ontological status they think they do. In addition, their empirical confirmation presents difficulties which are no different in principle from those which accompany attempts to establish the utility of any ideal-type, logical construction or deductive system in the explanation of the actual social world or the real economy in the economist's sense of real. In short, scientific realists fall foul of Ockham's razor; they make additional ontological assumptions for no additional explanatory benefit.

The second response, which I shall reframe in chapter 4, is that of Habermas. I reject the attempt made by Habermas (1970), who otherwise accepts much of the anti-foundationalist case, to vest the ideal-speech situation with a transcendental character which privileges it over other idealizations, such as Weberian ideal-types, by claiming that it is anticipated in all discourse. I shall argue that the ideal-speech situation is better regarded as a normative counterfactual (and that the undistorted communication of the ideal-speech situation need not eventuate in rational consensus).

Alexander (1988) has readily conceded Rorty's basic point that we must 'give up the utopian hope that a single ahistorical standard of truth can ever be established' (p. 94), but fears that in Rorty, or perhaps in Rorty's more misguided followers, this opens the way to irrationalism. This third response to anti-foundationalism is another I reject. I suggest that Rorty is better understood as playing with the interminable dialectic between 'systematic' and 'edifying' philosophy, normal and abnormal discourse. Rorty's complaint about systematic philosophy concerns its historic, but false, quest for apodictic truth. The alternative he proffers is inquiry within a framework of justification, and 'conversations' between different frameworks. The rules which guide the first, and the devices which make possible the second, are reasonable, learnable, discussable, justifiable. By application, then, sociology prosecuted within a particular framework of (non-apodictic) justification, and sociology dedicated to the construction of 'conversations' between different claims to knowledge (whether social scientific or not), are both reasonable, learnable, followable, discussable, justifiable. It is only those who will not, or cannot, engage others in conversation who succumb to solipsism. Contrary to

Alexander, there would thus seem no warrant for irrationalism in Rorty.

What Rorty does warrant is a pragmatic response to post-foundationalism. This fourth response is the one I shall support throughout this book. It does not deny the non-availability of a single metalanguage or metric but refuses to draw from this the conclusion of radical incommensurability. Instead it treats comparisons between paradigms and conceptual vocabularies, cultures and epochs, as exercises in translation in which there may be some direct equivalences but there will also have to be many discursive glosses. The object of these pragmatic exercises is to construct a 'conversation' between one's own culture, age, position, etc., and some other(s). For distinguished examples of this kind or work, one can turn to Geertz (1973); for more of its rationale, to Rorty (1980, 1982) in philosophy and Bernstein (1971, 1983) in social theory. It is a pragmatic approach in that it is guided by the notion that knowledge is better regarded not as a representation of reality but, rather, as an engagement with it. This response to the anti-foundationalist challenge is still being worked out, but it is already possible to discern something of its sources and its uses. The former include Rickert and Weber on theoretical and practical value-relations, and Peirce and other American pragmatists. The latter include the interactive and dialogical models of applied social research, discussed in chapter 5, which capitalize on the double-hermeneutic.

Post-empiricism

The linguistic turn and anti-foundationalism have led to what Alexander calls post-positivism but what I, in deference to Hesse (1980), who did so much to formulate it, prefer to call post-empiricism (though Hesse, herself, also refers to post-deductivism). Put at its simplest, post-empiricist social science is social science after the linguistic turn.

Empiricism, for Hesse, is a philosophy of natural science, developed by Carnap, Hempel, Nagel, Braithwaite and Popper, which rests on the assumptions of a naive realism, a universal scientific language and a correspondence theory of truth. For empiricists:

> there is an external world which can in principle be exhaustively described in scientific language. The scientist, as both observer and language-user, can capture the external facts of the world in propo-

sitions that are true if they correspond to the facts and false if they do not. Science is ideally a linguistic system in which true propositions are in one-to-one relation to the facts, including facts that are not directly observed because they involve hidden entities or properties, or past events or far distant events. These hidden events are described in theories, and theories can be inferred from observation. Man as scientist is regarded as standing apart from the world and able to experiment and theorize about it objectively and dispassionately. (1980, p. vii)

By the 1970s all three basic assumptions had been undermined by more historically oriented philosophers of science – such as Kuhn, Feyerabend and Toulmin; by the epistemology of Quine, which was itself derived partly from that of the historian of science, Duhem; and by the linguistic philosophy of Wittgenstein.

Hesse called the position which emerged from the onslaught on the old orthodoxy 'post-empiricism' and agreed that it had been sufficiently demonstrated

that data are not detachable from theory, and that their expression is permeated by theoretical categories; that the language of theoretical science is irreducibly metaphorical and unformalizable; and that the logic of science is circular interpretation, reinterpretation, and self-correction of data in terms of theory, theory in terms of data. (p. 173)

What she says here applies to natural and social science.

This new philosophy of science has had a major impact on sociology, prompting Giddens and Turner (1987) to give their own succinct version of it:

the idea that there can be theory-neutral observation is repudiated, while systems of deductively-linked laws are no longer canonized as the highest ideal of explanation. Most importantly, science is presumed to be an interpretative endeavour, such that problems of meaning, communication and translation are immediately relevant to scientific theorizing. (1987, p. 2)

In its emphases on metaphor, models, imaginary constructions and networks of propositions, its combination of elements of both the correspondence and coherence theories of truth, and its refusal to dichotomize either the pre-theoretical and the theoretical, or the theoretical and the empirical, post-empiricism clearly no longer allows a stark contrast between natural science and social science, let alone between the analytical and hermeneutic traditions within the social sciences.

This is not to proclaim some new version of a unified science, however, for two reasons. First, the double-hermeneutic applies only to social science. Second, the underdetermination of theory by data has a different import in the social sciences in so far as the values and images which inform and complement data should not be regarded as unfortunate intrusions but, rather, as contributants to be argued for and justified in their own right – as assets rather than liabilities. '[T]he proposal of a social theory is more like the arguing of a political case,' Hesse contends, 'than like a natural science explanation' (1978, p. 16) – except that there are parallels in the way claims for each are constructed and accepted in Hesse's own network theory (and in Habermas and others) to which I shall return in chapters 2 and 4. One way or another, then, the philosophical grounds for the mutual respect of adherents to the analytical and interpretivist traditions in sociology are stronger than the partisans of each have often cared to suppose.

The anguish of proper theorists

I have argued that theory in sociology is undergoing a post-empiricist reconstruction. This reconstruction disallows the Mertonian notion of theory proper and the conception of science which goes with it. Not everybody, however, is happy about this; from some, such as Jonathan Turner in America and Peter Abell in Britain, there are increasingly anguished cries of protest.

Also starting from Merton, Boudon (1970) distinguished (in his 'Theories, theory and Theory') between theory in the narrow sense which 'corresponds to the notion of the hypothetico-deductive systems of proposition' and theory in the broad sense which includes 'at least three distinct categories of paradigms, namely theoretical or analogical paradigms, formal paradigms and conceptual paradigms' (p. 165). The theory of migration is an example of a theoretical paradigm in so far as it involves 'the application by analogy of Newtonian mechanics' (p. 165). Merton's paradigm for functional analysis is an example of a formal paradigm in that the propositions it contains 'do not have reference to any specific content' (p. 165). Parsons's pattern variables provide an example of a conceptual paradigm. Boudon argues that theories in the narrow sense, the sociological theories which Merton sought, are governed by the epistemology of the natural sciences, an epistemology which is relevant only where the social sciences try to explain universal or quasi-universal phenomena. This 'logical situation' is the exception, not the rule, in the social sciences – so it is hardly surprising that theoretical activity should have taken different forms according to context. For good measure, Boudon adds that 'It is by no means certain that the notion of theory in the natural sciences is as monolithic as philosophers of science and sociologists tend to assume' (p. 167).

Boudon does not systematically address the concerns of the hermeneutic tradition in sociology, but he does depart from Merton very significantly in his legitimation of theory in the broad sense. In his entry on 'Theory' for *A Critical Dictionary of Sociology* (1982), written with Bourricaud, Boudon argues, for example, that paradigms can and do progress. New paradigms are often more powerful than old ones in that they help us to explain phenomena less clearly understood before: 'The structural analysis of kinship in archaic societies', for example, 'helps us to understand the apparently anarchical rules of incest prohibition' (1982, p. 414). In a later discussion of social systems which by virtue of their openness display considerable disorder, Boudon (1984) concedes that the scope for universal theories in the strict sense is smaller than ever. The possibility of partial or local theories in the strict sense remains, however, where there are partial or local degrees of closure (cf. Henk A. Becker, 1990, pp. 10–11). In sum, Boudon's conception of sociological theory is more complex, less beholden to the natural science model and less censorious than Merton's.

Turner and Abell are each less tolerant than Boudon of versions of theory other than their own. Turner has recently complained that what passes as theory is often metatheory, and that metatheory can 'often suffocate theoretical activity' – 'the goal of all theory [being] to explain how the social universe works' (1987, p. 162). In similar vein, Abell complains that 'as a discipline we are ill-served by our theoreticians', that theory usually turns out to be metatheory, and that ' "theoreticians" still operate in a largely quasi-philosophical, non-propositional framework' (1990, p. 110). Their notions of theory are, however, more complex than either sometimes cares to admit.

Turner concedes that the ascendancy of logical empiricism in the philosophy of science has been shattered by the assaults of writers like Kuhn, Toulmin, Lakatos and Hesse (Giddens and Turner, 1987). But their assaults cannot be entirely welcome to him in so far as they may be presumed to have contributed to that suffocation of theory by metatheory which he so much deplores. After all, Turner also insists that 'there are generic, timeless and universal properties of social organization', that it is the job of theory to isolate and develop abstract models about their operation and that Comte and Radcliffe-Brown were right to prescribe a natural science of society (Turner, 1987, p. 191). In an attempt to have it both ways, Turner describes an ideal relationship in the building of theory in which there are reciprocal links between each of the eight theoretical approaches in the following sequence: metatheory, naturalistic analytical schemes, sensitizing analytical schemes, formal propositions, analytical models, middle-range propositions, causal–empirical models and empirical generalizations. It is the synergy between sensitizing analytical schemes, formal propositions and analytical models which is deemed most likely to generate testable theory. By contrast, Merton's theories of the middle range are, he contends, not really theories at all but, rather, 'empirical generalizations whose regularities require a more abstract formulation to explain them' (p. 164) – for admirers of Merton a wounding accusation.

Turner offers his own 'sensitizing scheme for the analysis of human organization' (p. 168). It seems to me no less an exercise in the ontology of the social than Giddens's *The Constitution of Society* (1984), even if Turner's constitution of society is insensitive to the double-hermeneutic and includes laws of a kind Giddens considers misconceived. Turner's real objection is, it would seem, to theorists who do not view their work as contributing, however indirectly, to theory-building as he conceives it. For the metatheory which he condemns in others has its justification when he himself practises it.

There is a similar contradiction in Abell. He abhors work in metatheory and philosophy of social science because those who do it typically do not go on to generate the rigorous propositional and explanatory theories he craves. But there are no propositions, only metatheory, philosophy of social science and methodology in his own extraordinary book *The Syntax of Social Life* (1987). In his way, Abell bears the most remarkable testimony to the linguistic turn. The holy grail of variable-centred sociologists, such as his former self, has, he concedes, eluded them.

A couple of decades or so ago, the faith was widespread amongst variable-centred methodologists that, with time and patience, more complex and refined statistical techniques would lead to better and better explanatory – even predictive – models. One could then envisage a giant multiple-equation model containing many variables – rather like econometric models of the economy – describing the workings of the 'social system'. Non-linear and interactive effects would abound, furthermore, many variables would be categorical in nature, but the intellectual horizon was clear – more, and more accurately measured, variables were what constituted progress. Great ingenuity was and would be exerted not only in plotting complex patterns of covariation but also in measuring multidimensional variables in both metric and non-metric spaces ... few if any, have this faith in statistical procedures nowadays. (1987, p. 103)

Abell's response to this is that 'Sociologists must, in the first instance, return to natural language descriptions of systems of interconnected actions and there seek for general patterns' (p. 104). In his own case, this has led him to propose the logical foundations of a new method in the social sciences which he calls 'comparative narratives'. By narratives he means sequences of action descriptions. The syntax of social life has then to do with the connectivity of narratives and is here expressed in formal (algebraic) terms. A promised subsequent volume will 'formulate a semantics of action which will enable the social analyst readily to translate descriptions of what goes on in the social world from natural language into a computer-readable language appropriate to narrative analysis' (p. 2). This should facilitate the ultimate combination of variable-centred and account-centred methods. Time will tell whether this heroic project, announced in 1987, can be completed. I have to say I fear a tragic outcome. Abell cherishes rigour, identifies it with formalism, and laments its absence from the work of most so-called theorists, but I suspect that the very formalism he embraces will so encumber him as to render impossible that which he knows to be necessary – negotiation of the linguistic turn.

I have stressed that post-empiricism justifies a broader range of theoretical activities than Merton allowed, and that, in particular, it treats the interpretive dimensions of theorizing as indispensable. If one takes Boudon, Turner and Abell as examples of writers since Merton who have continued to subscribe to some notion or other of theory proper, one can detect both common qualities and a basic split in their responses to such claims. The common qualities are, first, an acknowledgement that there is more to the generation of theory proper than the likes of Merton allow and, second, an inability to come adequately to terms with the intepretive dimensions in theorizing. The basic split is that Turner and Abell feel beleaguered and use 'metatheory' as a term of abuse for the work of theorists who do not share their ultimate objectives, whilst Boudon acknowledges the retreat from Merton with great good grace.

Discourse and the new theoretical movement

Smelser's *Handbook of Sociology* (1988) opens with two overviews which represent incompatible approaches to sociology. The first, by Wallace (1988), which I mentioned above, maintains a natural-science-inspired notion of theory proper. The second, by Alexander (1988) on 'The new theoretical movement', welcomes the developments which flow from the linguistic turn and post-empiricism. It is a movement which I support and whose prospects I shall consider in the Conclusion.

I have argued that the dichotomization of theory and metatheory is distortive. Even works sympathetic to metatheory, such as the collection edited by Ritzer (1992a), can sometimes mislead by treating consideration of all matters other than substantive theory-building within the analytical tradition as metatheory, instead of recognizing that many of them are integral to modes of theorizing themselves.[4] Alexander's essay proposes a way round the division which, suitably modified, I wish to endorse. Like Alexander, I believe that the term 'discourse' has merit because it combines characteristics separately attributed to theory and metatheory by the friends and foes of each.

'Discourse' in ordinary English refers (among other things) to conversations and exchanges about something, to continuous processes of formulation in which various parties participate. In the social sciences 'discourse' derives its significance from the linguistic turn and provides 'a term with which to grasp the way in which language and other forms of social semiotics not merely convey social experience, but play some major part in constituting social subjects . . . their relations, and the fields in which they exist' (Purvis and Hunt, 1993, p. 474). And as Foucault reminded us, there are no extra-discursive phenomena; all things are constructed within discourses.[5] In addition to all of these, Alexander (1988) contrasts the qualities of sociology as discourse with those of sociology as explanation. By 'discourse', he refers to

> modes of argument that are more consistently generalized and speculative than normal scientific discussion. The latter are directed in a more disciplined manner to specific pieces of empirical evidence, to inductive and deductive logics, to explanation through covering laws, and to the methods by which these laws can be verified or falsified. Discourse, by contrast, is ratiocinative. It focuses on the process of reasoning rather than the results of immediate experience, and it becomes significant where there is no plain and evident truth. Discourse

seeks persuasion through argument rather than prediction. Its persuasiveness is based on such qualities as logical coherence, expansiveness
of scope, interpretive insight, value relevance, rhetorical force, beauty,
and texture of argument. (p. 80)

Alexander's characterization of discourse needs two modifications.
First, persuasive qualities, I would insist, additionally include respect
for evidence – there being no need to make the qualities of sociology
as discourse and as explanation mutually exclusive – provided always
that regard be given to the constitution of evidence. Second, as
'normal scientific discussion' is itself a discourse – there being in the
social sciences, as Alexander himself says, not discourse but discourses – it would be better to distinguish between the post-empiricist
or post-deductivist discourse of the new theoretical movement, which
Alexander supports, and the deductive–nomological discourse of the
theory-builders, which he rejects. In other words, sociology is a set of
discourses, and sociology as discourse is shorthand for a particular
discourse, viz. post-empiricist discourse.

The relatively simple conception of (post-empiricist) discourse,
here derived from the linguistic turn via Alexander, incorporates all
the elements internal to knowledge claims made and accepted among
sociologists, but does not require attachment to either the theory of
communicative action of Habermas or the post-structuralism of
Foucault. For Alexander this is quite deliberate: 'Between the ration-
alizing discourse of Habermas and the arbitrary discourse of
Foucault, this is where the actual field of social science uneasily lies'
(1988, p. 80). In this I suspect he is right, and if I were to help
sociology lie there a shade more easily I would be well pleased.

2

Concept Formation:
Contest and Reconstruction

We all know that words are multimeaning, that our concepts are conceived very differently, and that our arguments are plagued by ambiguities and inconsistencies. The point is what to do about all of this.

Sartori, 'Guidelines for concept analysis' (1984a)

Science and concepts: Hempel and the empiricists

Concern about conceptual variation in social science is nothing new. In the early decades of the American Sociological Society both leading members and the Committee on Introductory Sociology tried to publish lists of suitably defined concepts for all members to use; another attempt was made in the early 1940s by the Committee on Conceptual Integration. All their considerable efforts, and the hopes they came to place in the elaboration of operational definitions of supposedly transparent appositeness, came to nothing (Lundberg, 1929, pp. 54–9, 1936a, 1936b, 1939, pp. 62ff, 1942; Eubank, 1931; Alpert, 1938; Dodd, 1939, 1942; Hornell Hart, 1943). Later, in rather different vein, Parsons tried to establish a categorial system for all the social sciences – but he too failed. In these two cases and others the quest for conceptual consistency is associated with a particular conception of social *science*. The reasoning behind the quest has been classically stated by Hempel. Scientific concepts have two basic functions:

first, to permit an adequate description of the things and events that are the objects of scientific investigation; second, to permit the establishment of general laws or theories by means of which particular events may be explained and predicted and thus scientifically understood; for to understand a phenomenon scientifically is to show that it occurs in accordance with general laws or theoretical principles. (1965, p. 139)

To fulfil these functions, concepts have to be consistent.

Science aims at knowledge that is objective in the sense of being intersubjectively certifiable, independent of individual opinion or preference, on the basis of data obtainable by suitable experiments or observations. This requires that the terms used in formulating scientific statements have clearly specified meanings and be understood in the same sense by all those who use them. (p. 141)

In chapter 1 I mentioned that Merton had a similar desire for a universal technical nomenclature. In effect, he never made the linguistic turn. As late as 1984, he was still writing about how to get from proto-concepts infected by ordinary usages to precise scientific concepts and their standardized operationalization and quantification in measurable variables (Merton, 1984). And in 1990 history repeated itself when Wallace urged the American Sociological Association to address the standardization of concepts.

Today, of course, many social scientists would question whether specification of laws understood as natural laws of society is an appropriate goal for the social sciences, and after the linguistic turn they would reject any suggestion that the social world is external to them in Hempel's sense – interpenetration of social scientific and natural discourses simply does not allow it. Even so none can remain indifferent to the abundant conceptual variation of contemporary social science because it obstructs routine, but systematic, comparison and cumulation of social science findings, and it makes it difficult to arrive at any kind of empirical generalization.

In this chapter I shall work through some important discussions of concept formation and categorial system elaboration with a view to formation of a proposal of my own for accommodating conceptual inconsistency. I shall discuss Weber on basic concepts and value relevance; Parsons on categorial systems; Schutz on first-order and second-order constructs; symbolic interactionists on concept, theory and world; Kuhn on concepts and incommensurability between paradigms; Gallie and others on the essential contestability of concepts (including Connolly's use of Foucault on the deconstruction of concepts); Oppenheim, Sartori and the Committee on Conceptual and Terminological Analysis (COCTA) on the definitive reconstruction of concepts; Barnes on finitism; and Pawson on realism and conceptual certitude. Two motifs recur throughout: the relation between social scientific and natural discourses; and the alternative claims of contestabilists (who acknowledge conceptual variation as inevitable and/or desirable) and reconstructionists (who associate conceptual standardization with being scientific). The two latter camps might be called the shakers and the shapers.[1] My own proposal will recognize the part played by concepts in the constitution of society. It will also welcome those conceptual inconsistencies which are a product of the openness of all social systems to reconstitution.

It might help if I were to offer a few preliminary remarks on the difference between 'concept' and 'term'. By 'concept' I do not mean 'idea' or 'theory' (as Jarvie does in his *Concepts and Society*, 1972). I would just say that 'concepts' are things conceived and 'terms' are the names given to them. Concepts and terms do not always have a one-to-one relationship. On the contrary, part of the conceptual and terminological confusion in the social sciences stems from use of the same term for different concepts and different terms for the same concept. I refer to some concepts as 'categories' only because the writers discussed – notably Weber and Parsons – do. I shall not attempt to show how their categories compare with those of Aristotle, Kant or Hegel. I merely note that categories, like classes, often come in systems, and that they tend to be analytic, either in that they refer to the elements of which real historical objects or events are composed, or in so far as they provide a framework or schema within which real historical objects or events can be placed and their properties defined. The components of Parsons's action frame of reference, for example, were presented as categories.

Weber on concepts and value relevance

In his famous essay on ' "Objectivity" ', Weber affirmed that

> the choice of the object of investigation and the extent or depth to which this investigation attempts to penetrate into the infinite causal web, are determined by the evaluative ideas [*Wertideen*] which dominate the investigator and his age. In the *method* of investigation, the guiding 'point of view' is of great importance for the *construction* of the conceptual scheme which will be used in the investigation. (1904, p. 84)

In this passage, Weber refers to value-ideas which dominate the investigator and his (*sic*) age. It is clear from other passages, however, that Weber neither expected nor desired every investigator to be so dominated. In a note to his essay on Knies, for example, he declares the historian to be 'free' to constitute objects of inquiry according to whatever guiding values he or she chooses (1903–6, p. 273, n. 89).

Both Rickert and Weber argued that the 'objectivity' of a historical account is limited by the empirical currency of the value to which it is related in the community of which the investigator is a member (Rickert, 1902). Both, too, acknowledged not only that different communities could thereby give rise to different accounts of the 'same' historical objects, but also that different fractions of groups within a community, or even more or less dissenting individuals, could do so. Rickert viewed different national accounts with equanimity but chose not to dwell upon the possibilities of different sectional or individual accounts. Instead he preferred to look forward to the eventual establishment of a world community capable of guaranteeing universally valid values. Weber, by contrast, deferred less to the value of the well-ordered, harmonious and integrated national community favoured in leading circles in Germany, and seems positively to have relished the prospect of competing accounts and the consequent interminable rewriting of history. No 'Chinese ossification of intellectual life' for him (Weber, 1904, p. 84).

Values enter into the formation of all concepts, but all concepts are not of the same kind. Weber distinguished four different types – genetic, individual, generic and ideal-typical. A *genetic* concept links a subjective intention, or other mental state, with a course of action and its consequences; 'shopper' is thus a genetic concept, whereas 'ancestor' is not. Alternatively, a genetic concept links an idea which has some cultural currency, and thus objective validity, with courses of action and their consequences; Weber gave the example 'sect' in relation 'to certain important cultural significances which the "sectarian spirit" has for modern culture' (1904, p. 93).

Individual concepts refer not to phenomena of which there is only one instance but, rather, to 'historical individuals', to singular configurations. Weber offered the example of 'city economy', a mode of economic organization peculiar to a particular period in the history of the West – but one of which there was a number of cases (1904, p. 95). The elements which make up the configurations are themselves frequently transhistorical or transcultural. Weber called them *Gattungsbegriffe*, which is variously translated as *generic*, general or class concepts, and he commented about them that the nearer they came to universal application the less content they possess. The concept 'exchange', for example, has wider application but less content than the concept 'market'. It was in recognition of this that von Schelting (1934) referred to the 'double-face' of individual concepts. The external face expresses their individuality *vis-à-vis* other historical configurations; the internal face records the generality of the elements of which they are composed.

The *ideal-type* is the kind of concept most often associated with Weber, but he did not himself consider it anything new. At the most he believed himself to be refining something which had long proved its value in classical and neo-classical economics. Weber argued that abstract economic theory 'offers us an ideal picture of events on the commodity-market under conditions of a society organized on the principles of an exchange economy, free competition and rigorously rational conduct' (1904, pp. 89–90). It is 'ideal' in that it is an ideal-type, which he defined as follows.

> An ideal-type is formed by the one-sided *accentuation* of one or more points of view and by the synthesis of a great many diffuse, discrete, more or less present and occasionally absent *concrete individual* phenomena, which are arranged according to those one-sidedly emphasized viewpoints into a unified *analytical* construct (*Gedankenbild*). In its conceptual purity, this mental construct (*Gedankenbild*) cannot be found empirically anywhere in reality. It is a *utopia*. (1904, p. 90)

Weber continued with examples from economics including 'the delineation of an "*idea*" of *capitalistic culture*' (p. 91). He said of this 'that numerous . . . utopias of this sort can be worked out of which *none* is like another', but each of which represents the idea of capitalistic culture according to a particular point of view and the selection criterion appropriate to it (p. 91). The influence of Rickert is evident.

Weber always insisted that the historical sciences, to which he owed primary allegiance, are concerned with the real concrete world of individual phenomena. For such sciences, the formation of ideal-types should never be an end in itself, merely a means to understanding and explanation. Weber repeated the point when he declared ideal-types not to be hypotheses but guides to the construction of hypotheses. Ideal-types cannot be hypotheses because hypotheses pertain to the real world; ideal-types, by contrast, are utopian and cannot be empirically disconfirmed. What is testable about Gresham's Law that bad money drives out good, for example, is the hypothesis that what one is confronted with is an example of its operation; the law itself is part of a utopian construction and as such is beyond empirical test. For the most part, then, evaluation of an ideal-type is a matter of utility; it proves useful or it does not. The exception is where something is remiss in its construction: either the process of one-sided accentuation has not been completed with sufficient rigour; or the elements combined in the type are not the most appropriate ones in that the 'rules of experience' (empirical generalizations) upon which the constructor drew in its construction are in some way deficient. Values and experience, then, are the two factors which govern what goes into an ideal-type in the first place; both are subject to variation and both present problems of justification which Weber largely ignored.

Weber's ideal-typical presentation of basic categories in *Economy and Society* (1922) makes use of two distinctions of interest here. The first is between direct observational understanding, in which the observer grasps immediately what the actor is doing, and explanatory understanding, in which the observer imputes a motive for what the actor is doing. It is hard to make these categories work because, with regard to the former, action descriptions unnuanced by language and culture are rare, and with regard to the latter, action descriptions often imply motives. The action description 'he is driving a train', for example, implies that the actor is a train driver doing his or her job. Of course he or she might be a bank clerk driving for a railway preservation society at the weekend, but the casual observer who knows nothing of the railway's ownership is likely to fit the abbreviated description which implies the customary motive. Weber's difficulties stem from a failure to ask closely how individuals understand one another, a question to which Simmel, and especially Schutz, devote more attention. The second is between subjectively intended and objectively valid meanings, a distinction Simmel is accused of blurring. For the English couple, purchase of the weekend cottage means an escape from city stress and an investment; for the Welsh-speaking villagers, it represents an erosion of their language and way of life. This distinction does work and is important.

For those like Hempel who laud conceptual consistency, Weber is the *enfant terrible*. His version of the theory of value relevance and his singular conception of objectivity invite conceptual inconsistency and the multiplication of historical accounts. His basic categories are meant to have a transhistorical and transcultural reference but they have still been formed in relation to values; they do not represent a comprehensive and exclusive categorial system and they are not put forward with a view to their adoption by all other historians and social scientists. On the contrary, they are, to anticipate a subsequent section, 'essentially contestable'. Weber's approach to concept formation is, in effect, radically subversive. It is hard to imagine a position more opposed to it than that of Parsons, to which I now turn.

Parsons on categorial systems

In the closing pages of *The Structure of Social Action* Parsons lamented the common view that 'there are as many systems of sociological theory as there are sociologists, that there is no common basis, that all is arbitrary and subjective' (1937, p. 774). But deliverance was at hand; his own voluntaristic theory of action would put an end to this unhappy state. Subsequently Parsons's theoretical development went through a number of stages but throughout it all there persisted this preoccupation with the common basis. It took the form of an elaboration, in every sense of the word, of a common categorial system, not just for sociology, but for all the social sciences which contribute to what he came to call the general theory of action. He took a categorial system to be a system of classes in which

> The elements are so defined as to constitute an interdependent system. And the system has sufficient complexity and articulation to duplicate, in some sense, the interdependence of the empirical systems which are the subject matter. A categorial system, thus, is constituted by the definition of a set of interrelated elements, their interrelatedness being intrinsic to their definition. (Parsons and Shils, 1951, p. 50)

Mechanics had its interrelated concepts of space, time, particle, mass, motion, location, velocity and acceleration. It was imperative that the social sciences establish an analogous system as a necessary step on the way to the ultimate objective – a general theory which would afford precise predictions under real conditions (see above, p. 4).

Parsons's whole theoretical edifice rests upon a quite extraordinary claim about the relationship between concepts and object-world. Chapter XVIII of *The Structure of Social Action* is devoted to 'empirically verified conclusions'; the claim is made that the convergence of Marshall, Pareto, Durkheim and Weber, unbeknown to themselves, upon the elements of a common theory, the voluntaristic theory of action, confirmed their 'correct observation of the empirical facts of social life' (1937, p. 721). Their convergence of thought could only be attributed to a degree of empirical verification, to an emergent common understanding of how the world is. Not only then did it constitute notable scientific progress in itself, but also it promised further progress to those able and willing to build upon it. Foremost among these was, of course, Parsons himself. This foundation supported his labours on the general theory of action, the social system, sub-system changes (the AGIL scheme) and the cybernetic hierarchy (the LIGA scheme).

However imposing the edifice constructed upon it, Parsons's founding claim is untenable. Convergence could never in itself confirm correct observation of the empirical facts of social life; errors are frequently shared. In any case, the convergence upon a voluntaristic theory of action which Parsons announced depended upon selective and contestable readings of the famous four and the omission of other figures of comparable stature who might have disturbed it – notably Marx. For example, Parsons grossly underestimated Weber's radical scepticism (cf. Lassman, 1980). As Mulkay has argued, 'It is . . . relatively easy to show some kind of "theoretical convergence" among virtually any group of theorists simply because their theoretical notions are open to a variety of interpretations. This is particularly true when the supposed convergence operates at a high level of abstraction' (1971, p. 69). In addition, it was a convergence, as Parsons acknowledged, of writers much preoccupied with interpreting 'the main features of the modern economic order, of "capitalism", "free enterprise", "economic individualism", as it has been variously called' (Parsons, 1937, p. vi). Even if they had correctly observed the empirical facts of this historical individual, to use Weber's term, it would not follow that they had provided the rudiments of a categorial system of universal application.

For all his reliance upon his predecessors' 'correct observation of the empirical facts of social life', Parsons rejected as empiricism the view that concepts are reflections of reality. He also rejected the opposite view, attributed to Weber, that concepts are no more than useful fictions, utopian constructions of heuristic value in so far as the real world can be compared with them. In opposition to both, Parsons advocated 'analytical realism':

> As opposed to the fiction view it is maintained that at least some of the general concepts of science are not fictional but adequately 'grasp' aspects of the objective external world. This is true of the concepts here called analytical elements. Hence the position here taken is, in an epistemological sense, realistic. At the same time it avoids the objectionable implications of an empiricist realism. These concepts correspond, not to concrete phenomena, but to elements in them which are analytically separable from other elements. There is no implication that the value of any one such element, or even of all of those included in

one logically coherent system, is completely descriptive of any particular concrete thing or event. (1937, p. 730)

It transpires, then, that the correct observation of Marshall, Pareto, Durkheim and Weber issued not in a system of categories for the description of historical particulars but in the beginnings of a system of categories for the specification of the elements of which they are composed. This latter system is supposedly both analytical in so far as it involves abstraction, and realist in so far as it makes possible reference to objects in the real world (cf. Adriaansens, 1980, pp. 20–7). Weber's offence was not his characterization of ideal-types as utopian, but his refusal to grant any of them transcendental status. By contrast, Parsons claimed that the action frame of reference, and its means-ends schema is both analogous to the space–time framework in physics and 'phenomenological' in Husserl's sense, i.e. grounded in universal human experience. Even so, the difficulties outlined in the last but one paragraph remain. It is still assumed that there has been convergence, that the analytical elements of the phenomena of the modern 'economic' world are refinable into a coherent system of categories and concepts for all social scientists to use without limitation of time and place, and that the concepts so obtained are not so abstract as to preclude unambiguous application.

In his subsequent work, Parsons elaborated the most complex categorial system in all the social sciences. He welcomed collaborators but not the architects of alternative structures which potentially threatened his own exclusive claims, as Schutz discovered to his dismay (Grathoff, 1978). This elaboration involved very important developments after *The Social System* (1951) which defenders of Parsons claim his critics have usually ignored – notably the AGIL/LIGA scheme and the cybernetic hierarchy (Bourricaud, 1977; Adriaansens, 1980). But if they removed some of the inconsistencies of the old, the new versions are even more complex and no less abstract. It is hardly surprising, therefore, that they too did not find general favour among social scientists. Occasional *dévotés* still await the Parsonian new dawn but there can be very few others who share Johnson's view that 'the future of sociology . . . depends, now, mainly on the correction, development, and further integration of Parsons's theory of action' (1981, p. xiv). In particular, the neo-functionalists of the 1980s are 'post-Parsonian' in their selective reconstruction and outright revision of the master's work, their interest in syntheses with work derived from other traditions, and their 'post-positivist' model of knowledge cumulation and decline (which is discussed in chapter

6) (Colomy, 1990b). Certainly none shows any inclination to proffer a new categorial system for all the social sciences.

Parsons failed in his self-appointed mission to establish an exclusive categorial system for all the social sciences. I suggest that this failure is final, that it is idle to suppose that someone else may yet achieve what Parsons himself could not. It is not just that any such general system is always likely to be too complex to remember and utilize consistently. Nor is it simply that an analytical system, purged of all historical individualism, is always likely to prove too abstract to apply incontestably. It is also that all such conceptual systems aim at closure when actual social systems are inherently open.

There are three inexhaustible sources of conceptual variation in social science. The first is the ambiguous or multifaceted character of human acts and social relations which enables both those whom social scientists study, and social scientists themselves, to conceive, constitute and interpret the 'same' act or relation differently. This issue is discussed in the next section on Schutz. The second, closely connected to the first, has to do with the possibilities of innovation and invention inherent in all natural languages. The third is the unending variation in the forms of social life. Each new form does not just provide sociology with a new object of inquiry, it also presents it with a new opportunity for theorizing (cf. Peel, 1971, p. 264). My favourite recent example is Solidarity in Poland in 1980–1. Was it a trade union, a political party, a national liberation movement, a new type of social movement or what? In reaching an answer, I see no reason why one must assume that all the elements of which it was composed were preconceivable in any categorial system of the kind Parsons envisaged. Parsons was right to reject idealism but his analytical realism does not provide a satisfactory way of coming to terms with the part played by concepts in the very constitution and reconstitution of society.

Schutz on first-order and second-order constructs

Like Parsons, but unlike Weber, Schutz sought conceptual consistency. Unlike Parsons, he did not seek a single categorial system for all the social sciences, or conceptual closure in the face of the openness of social systems. 'All our knowledge of the world, in commonsense as well as scientific thinking', according to Schutz, 'involves constructs, i.e., a set of abstractions, generalizations, formalizations, idealizations specific to the respective level of thought organization' (1953a, p. 5). Constructs of the first order are those used by ordinary members in the course of their everyday lives; they are relevant to the daily life-world. The social scientist is able to grasp them because the everyday world is intersubjective, or 'socialized', and he or she can employ variations on the same devices that ordinary members use to understand one another, of which typifications are the most obvious. Constructs of the second order are formed by social scientists in connection with the relevances given them by their different disciplines. They must also respect the postulates of logical consistency, subjective interpretation and adequacy. Logical consistency is about the avoidance of non-sequiturs and contradictions. 'The postulate of subjective interpretation has to be understood', Schutz tells us, 'in the sense that all scientific explanations of the social world *can*, and for certain purposes *must*, refer to the subjective meaning of the actions of human beings from which reality originates' (1953b, p. 62). The postulate of adequacy requires that an act attributed to an actor in the real world in consequence of the application of an ideal-type or model be understandable to that actor and to his or her fellows 'in terms of commonsense interpretation' (p. 64).

'The thought objects constructed by the social sciences', Schutz writes, 'do not refer to unique acts or unique individuals occurring within a unique situation' (1953a, p. 36). Social sciences are not so much generalizing as typifying disciplines which proceed by constructing models of the sectors of the social world within which the matters which interest them occur. The social scientist's definition of a problem owes something to the structure and content of his or her relevant discipline, and must respect the three postulates mentioned above, but is not otherwise formally limited. The resultant models are, to use Weber's word, utopian. The actors who populate them are creations of the social scientist – puppets or homunculi as Schutz calls them – and have only such characteristics as their creators give them. Unlike real men and women, the homunculus 'placed into a social relationship is involved therein in his totality' (p. 41). Such an approach particularly lends itself to the modelling of rational action, but is by no means confined to it.

Schutz cites with approval James's view that reality consists of whatever excites our interest (Schutz, 1945, p. 207). There is, it is argued, a multiplicity of orders of reality. James called them subuniverses and gave as examples the worlds of physical things, of science, of ideal relations, of 'idols of the tribe', of mythology and religion, of individual opinion, and of madness and vaguery. Every object we think of is referred to one such world. Moreover, 'Each world whilst it is attended to is real after its own fashion; only the reality lapses with the attention' (James, 1890, vol. 1, p. 293). Schutz prefers 'to speak of provinces of meaning, and not of subuniverses, because it is the meaning of our experiences and not the ontological structure of the objects which constitutes reality' (1945, p. 230). The upshot is a more variegated and open-ended reality than Parsons would allow, but Parsons does have one legitimate complaint (Parsons, 1974, pp. 123–4). Schutz tends to treat each world as discrete. In particular, he rigidly separates the everyday life-world in which the actor has a practical interest and the non-interacting, and therefore disinterested, observer of action has a cognitive interest, from the world of science in which the social scientist has only the special cognitive interest appropriate to his or her discipline. Interpenetration of everyday life-world and science is ruled out. In particular no allowance is made for the part scientific concepts may play in the constitution of society; there is no room for sociology in action (cf. Bryant, 1976). Marx was wrong, it seems, to have complained that 'The philosophers have only *interpreted* the world in various ways; the point, however, is to *change* it'; and Durkheim asked idly, 'what good is it to strive after knowledge of reality if the knowledge we acquire cannot serve us in our lives?' (Marx, 1845, p. 8; Durkheim, 1895, p. 85). But this is folly; it makes no sense to deny the social scientist, *qua* scientist, a practical interest. Put another way, the traffic between lay concepts and social scientific concepts is not one-way from lay to social scientific concepts, but two-way; indeed it was reflection on the inadequacy of Schutz which prompted Giddens (1976) to formulate his notion of the double-hermeneutic.

Zijderveld has argued that the postulate of adequacy spared Schutz the solipsism which overtook Weber. Whereas Weber endorsed ideal-types without limit, Schutz 'posed the taken-for-granted daily lifeworld and its commonsense as the objective (i.e. intersubjective) ground of all theoretical statements about the socio-temporal world' (Zijderveld, 1972, p. 182). Certainly in temper Schutz seems closer to Parsons than to Weber, though the conceptual consistency he sought very definitely did not extend to a common categorial system for all the social sciences. On the other hand, I doubt whether the postulate of adequacy serves in practice to distinguish Weber and Schutz as clearly as Zijderveld supposes. With regard to the past, evidence of the daily lifeworld is frequently incomplete, ambiguous or contradictory; the postulate of adequacy is then no bar to competing accounts. With regard to the present, the daily lifeworld of modern societies is

highly complex, differentiated, even contested; what respect for the
postulate of adequacy would consist of is often far from obvious.
With regard to the future, the everyday world has yet to be made, that
is what the argument is about, and social science, as Weber and
Parsons recognized, but Schutz did not, is part of that argument.
There is sometimes nothing so elusive, differentiated and contradictory as common sense. And, in any case, who is to say when the
postulate of adequacy has been met? Schutz assumes social scientists
can decide for themselves, but Carroll (1982) argues that this should,
in principle, be a matter of negotiation between investigator and
investigated – though he accepts this will frequently be impossible in
practice. In short, the postulate of adequacy is easier to invoke in
principle than justify in practice.

Symbolic interactionists on concept, theory and world

It is possible to treat contributions to the interpretive tradition from
Blumer, Glaser and Strauss, and Goffman as variations on the postulate of adequacy.

Blumer indicated his misgivings about operational definitions as
early as 1942. Then, in a seminal essay in 1954, he introduced the
distinction between the 'definitive concepts' integral to an empirical
science dedicated to the formulation and testing of laws (the object of
both Parsons's and Merton's desires), and the 'sensitizing concepts'
integral to a science dedicated to development of meaningful interpretations which better enable people to understand their world and its
possibilities. The latter are sensitizing because 'They lack precise
reference and have no bench marks which allow a clean-cut identification of a specific instance, and of its content. Instead, they rest on
a general sense of what is relevant' (Blumer, 1954, p. 149). Such
concepts are not fixed – indeed they shape up differently from instance to instance – but they are definable in relation to apt illustrations and they are entrenchable 'through the sheer experience of
sharing in a common world of discourse' (p. 144). What Blumer does
not address is the possibility of multiple worlds of discourse beyond
the academy and also, on occasions, within it.

Blumer's intention is not to divide the stock of concepts between
two types, the definitive and the sensitizing, but, rather, to promote
an alternative view of what concepts can be and can do. 'Working-

class', 'status passage', 'rational choice' and 'ideal-speech situation', to take a mixed bag, may all be regarded as sensitizing concepts. In their openness to more or less subtle, but chronic, revision in actual use, sensitizing concepts are, to anticipate the approach to concepts developed by Barnes some two decades after Blumer and discussed below, 'finitist'.

Blumer's position is much more coherent than Glaser and Strauss's (1967) in their celebrated advocacy of grounded theory – theory discovered from data. Glaser and Strauss have much to say about why it is more profitable to generate a theory from evidence inductively, in the manner of their own research on the social loss of dying patients (1965), than find evidence to verify a logico-deductive theory, in the manner then favoured by Stouffer, Lazarsfeld and other would-be theory-builders (cf. Blaikie, 1993, pp. 191–3). Writing before the linguistic turn, however, they unselfconsciously regard data as preconceptual and precategorial givens. They then recommend that sociologists generate from their data concepts that are both *analytic* – sufficiently generalized to designate characteristics of concrete entities, not the entities themselves . . . [and] *sensitizing* – yield a "meaningful" picture, abetted by apt illustrations that enable one to grasp the reference in terms of one's own experience' (1967, pp. 38–9). This seems to be an attempt to combine Parsons and Blumer – analytical interactionism, perhaps – except that it omits any reference to common worlds of discourse. Here, as elsewhere, Glaser and Strauss do not bear close scrutiny.

In setting out his frame analysis, Goffman reveals a sophistication about language which Glaser and Strauss lack, and a nice irony – 'I coin a series of terms – some "basic"; but writers have been doing that to not much avail for years' (1974, p. 13). (Examples include 'frame', 'keys and keyings' and 'designs and fabrications'.) One of Goffman's main concerns is to contest Schutz's overly discrete treatment of provinces of meaning. In the organization of experience, elements of one realm – everyday life, the theatre, science, dreams, etc. – often pass into another. In particular, 'everyday life, real enough in itself, often seems to be a laminated adumbration of a pattern or model that is itself a typification of quite uncertain realm status' (p. 652). What we get from Goffman on concept formation and use turns out to be a multidirectional traffic in concepts whose form and content chronically shift in more or less nuanced ways over time and between realms. It is not practical to illustrate it with a brief example, however, because, as ever in Goffman, the art is in the telling.

Kuhn on concepts and incommensurability between paradigms

The issue of conceptual variation has both an intended and an unintended place in the work of Kuhn. With regard to the latter, Kuhn is notorious for having used the term 'paradigm' in a multiplicity of ways in *The Structure of Scientific Revolutions* (1962; Masterman, 1970). Acknowledging this in a postscript to the second edition, he introduced a distinction between paradigm as disciplinary matrix and paradigm as exemplar. Disciplinary matrix 'stands for the entire constellation of beliefs, values, techniques and so on shared by members of a given community'; exemplar 'denotes one sort of element in that constellation, the concrete puzzle-solutions which, employed as models or examples, can replace explicit rules as a basis for the solution of the remaining puzzles of normal science' (1970a, p. 175). Kuhn has never offered more than passing remarks on the social sciences, but many social scientists have themselves found it instructive to consider the development of their disciplines in Kuhnian terms (Harvey, 1982). Eckberg and Hill (1979) are right that sociologists have mostly applied the idea of paradigm as disciplinary matrix to their discipline whereas Kuhn stresses the centrality of paradigm as exemplar in his accounts of natural science, but unlike them I see nothing wrong in this if it is the former concept which has the more obvious application. Similarly, Martins (1972) has noted that Kuhn's paradigms are not discipline-wide but, rather, have to do with specialties, whereas the paradigms of which sociologists speak are often attributed to the whole discipline, or even, as in the case of historical materialism, many disciplines. Again, I see no objection in principle to what is also Kuhn's own practice when he does refer to social sciences.

I suggest that sociology is a multi-paradigmatic science, in the disciplinary matrix sense, with few, if any, exemplars of the authority Kuhn demands – though Durkheim's *Suicide*, or Malinowski's analysis of the kula ring, or Becker's account of becoming a marihuana user, are like exemplars in so far as they play a part in the induction of entrants to the discipline. In any case other elements in disciplinary matrices besides exemplars – notably concepts – involve ways of seeing. But learning to use concepts is a question not only of learning to follow rules, but also of attending to examples of their use. Kuhn calles this learning by ostension.

Conceptual variation also has an intended place in Kuhn in his argument that the non-availability of a theory-neutral language presents science with a problem which some philosophers of science, such as Popper, have ignored.

> The point-by-point comparison of two successive theories demands a language into which at least the empirical consequences of both can be translated without loss or change. That such a language lies ready to hand has been widely assumed since at least the seventeenth century when philosophers took the neutrality of pure sensation-reports for granted and sought a 'universal language' ... Ideally the primitive vocabulary of such a language would consist of pure sense-datum terms plus syntactical connectives. Philosophers have now abandoned hope of achieving any such ideal, but many continue to assume that theories can be compared by recourse to a basic vocabulary consisting entirely of words which are attached to nature in ways that are unproblematic and, to the extent necessary, independent of theory. That is the vocabulary in which Sir Karl's basic statements are framed. (Kuhn, 1970b, p. 266)

Kuhn continues that 'In the transition from one theory to the next words change their meanings or conditions of applicability in subtle ways' (p. 266). He gives as examples force, mass, element, compound and cell, and concludes that successive theories are 'incommensurable'.

Incommensurability does not mean non-comparability, but it does lead to difficulties similar to those associated with translation between languages. Translation always involves distortion, or at least loss of nuance – different languages make different discriminations – but coping with this is not impossible. As Kuhn notes:

> a good translation manual, particularly for the language of another region or culture, should include or be accompanied by discursive paragraphs explaining how native speakers view the world, what sort of ontological categories they deploy. Part of learning to translate a theory or a language is learning to describe the world with which the language or theory functions. (1970b, p. 270)

Those who move from paradigm to paradigm – whether they are historians of science, scientists making comparisons, or scientists attached to one paradigm trying to communicate with scientists attached to another – have always to respect the hypothetical manual for the translation they are engaged in.

Kuhn returns to the issue of incommensurability in his 'Second thoughts on paradigms'. There he concludes 'that, though data are the minimal elements of our individual experience, they need be shared responses to a given stimulus only within the membership of a relatively homogeneous community, educational, scientific, or linguistic' (1974, p. 473). He adds in a footnote that he still considers that 'members of different scientific communities live in different worlds and that scientific revolutions change the world in which a scientist works', but he 'would now want to say that members of different communities are presented with different data by the same stimuli' (p. 473, n. 18). These stimuli seem to be like Kant's noumena, and data like Kant's phenomena, in that stimuli and noumena are unknowable in themselves.

In the text of the essay Kuhn describes how a child learns to discriminate between swans, geese and ducks by having examples of each pointed out on a visit to a zoo. A Parsonian might here object that Kuhn is dealing not with analytical categories like force, mass, element, compound and cell but, rather, with the names of natural species. A Kuhnian would presumably reply that this makes no difference; all concepts, in part at least, are learned ostensively ('we have here . . .').

Reflecting on the same text, Barnes has related ostensive learning to the conventional character of knowledge:

> Nothing can be learned *ab initio* by verbal means. The child may learn 'swan' directly, or (for example) via 'all swans are white', which connects with previous processes of ostension involving 'white'. It follows that all systems of empirical knowledge must rely upon learned similarity relations transmitted by ostension or practical demonstration, and that what any given term in such a system refers to can never be characterised without reference to learned similarity relations, i.e. to finite clusters of accepted instances of terms. Knowledge is conventional *through and through*. (1982b, p. 27)

But why, in any given case, should particular conventions be adopted and not others? Kuhn does not address this question, but Hesse and Barnes do and I shall return to it in the concluding section of this chapter.

Gallie, Connolly, etc., on the essential contestability of concepts

The literature on the essential contestability of social and political concepts is about what makes closure in the use of such concepts impossible to obtain – impossible because we are confronted with an essential, and not a contingent, characteristic of such concepts. It began with an essay by Gallie in 1956, revised in 1964, in which he argued that 'there are disputes, centred on . . . [certain] concepts . . . which, although not resolvable by argument of any kind are nevertheless sustained by perfectly respectable arguments and evidence' (1956, p. 169). Gallie did not claim that all concepts are essentially contested and endlessly disputed in this way. On the contrary, he limited essential contestedness to the concept which (I) is '*appraisive* in the sense that it signifies or accredits some kind of achievement' (p. 171), where (II) this achievement is internally complex, (III) different explanations of its worth emphasize different constituent elements of it, and (IV) it is open to modification in the light of future circumstances which cannot be prescribed or predicted. By definition, the essentially *contested* concept is used offensively and defensively.

As all these characteristics might also be attributed to concepts which are merely radically confused, Gallie, in his revised version, adds two more:

These are . . . (V) the derivation of any such concept from an original exemplar whose authority is acknowledged by all the contestant users of the concept, and . . . (VI) the probability or plausibility, in appropriate senses of these terms, of the claim that the continuous competition for acknowledgement as between the contestant users of the concept enables the original exemplar's achievement to be sustained or developed in optimum fashion. (1956, as revised 1964, p. 168)

The exemplar ensures that the contestants are, in one sense at least, all talking about the same thing; it also promotes the quest for its ideal realization. Gallie gives as examples of essentially contested concepts, religion, art, science, democracy and social justice. Given that such concepts have a normative dimension, it is not surprising that further contributions to their clarification by MacIntyre (1973), Care (1973) and Swanton (1985) should have been published in the Chicago journal *Ethics*, or that discussion should particularly have centred on political concepts. Perhaps the most important contribution of all is Connolly's *The Terms of Political Discourse* (1974).

MacIntyre begins by distinguishing essential contestedness from Waismann's earlier idea of the open texture of concepts (Waismann, 1945). Open texture has to do with the incompleteness of all empirical descriptions and the need to be alive to the possibility of some future object displaying a characteristic hitherto not associated with the class to which it belongs. Essential contestedness goes further than this because it has to do with the constitution of society; it extends, too, to debate about how things should be. It is easier for natural scientists to effect conceptual closure, to agree on the use of terms (at least in Kuhnian normal science), because they are not involved in a debate about what the natural world should be like and the concepts they use play no part in its constitution. Social scientists, by contrast, have to accept that agreement on concepts is contingent upon agreement on how the world should be. Beliefs that enter into the constitution of the object world may form a relatively homogeneous and consistent set, as, for example, with a modern monetary system, or a relatively diverse and conflicting set, as, for example, with political parties. In other words, it is clearer what a monetary system consists of than a political party, it is easier to decide whether something falls within the class 'monetary system' than the class 'political party', and in consequence it is also easier to generalize about monetary systems than about political parties. Again, not all concepts are essentially contestable.

> A legal-cum-economic system, for example, cannot function unless there is a kind of agreement in definitions which precludes essential contestability. What counts as a contract, what counts as a bill of exchange between currencies must be fixed in a way that such concepts as those of political party or tragic drama or education are not. It follows that the generalizations embodied in demand curves or in theories of monetary flow do achieve a noncontestable character. Hence one crucial difference between economics on the one hand and sociology and political science on the other. (MacIntyre, 1973, p. 9)

It is also of the nature of contest, of argument, that innovatory moves may occur. Outcomes are therefore, in some degree, unpredictable. Complete conceptual agreement on concepts is also a bid to bring history to a close. 'Chinese ossification' is no more attractive to MacIntyre than it was to Weber. It is also questionable whether the difference between economics and other social sciences would seem so great to MacIntyre today in the light of the disputes of the 1980s over monetarist economics, which included argument about what is to be counted as money.

MacIntyre's position can usefully be compared with Kuhn's. Kuhn argues that all concepts are conventional but that normal science makes progress by taking its concepts for granted and treating them as natural. He does not explain why natural scientists are able to do this but social scientists are not. MacIntyre does not consider whether all concepts are conventional but he does argue that normal practice in some areas of life depends upon conceptual consistency and that the social sciences that account for them take advantage of it in the production of generalizations which elude colleagues who study other areas. By contrast, normal practices in other areas of social life depend upon conceptual contestedness and the social sciences which account for them are part of the contest. Put in Schutz's terms, MacIntyre argues that stable constructs of the second order are contingent upon stable constructs of the first order, but, contrary to Schutz, MacIntyre insists that social scientists have a practical as well as a cognitive interest in what they study. Care (1973) has pushed this point further by suggesting that social scientists may contest concepts not contested by those who are the object of their inquiries, that they may, in effect, have a critical role.

Gallie alluded to a difference between contestedness and contestability without fully making it clear. Clarke (1979) has formally distinguished the two – and has associated each with a distinctive philosophical position. To say a concept is contested is to make an empirical claim about it; to say it is essentially contested is to invoke some mechanism, outside of the concept itself, which guarantees that there is, or will be, a contest. Clarke associates *essential* contestedness with structural determinism. To say a concept is (essentially) contestable is to claim that there is something about it which could be contested whether or not it currently is or looks likely to be. What follows from this, Clarke insists, is radical relativism – an inability to specify how, in the absence of any incontestable principle, one conceptual variant is superior to any other. Clarke rejects both structural determinism and radical relativism.

I think it is useful to distinguish empirical contestedness and theoretical contestability but I believe it is wrong to link essential contestability to a radical relativism which precludes all evaluation. Clarke makes this connection in the course of criticizing Lukes's twin claims in his book on power that his own radical view is *both* 'ineradicably evaluative and "essentially contested"' *and* 'superior to alternative views' (Lukes, 1974a, p. 9). Even if 'contestable' is substituted for 'contested', Lukes's argument is still deemed incoherent because the radical relativism which supports the first claim undermines the second.

Swanton (1985) offers a way of countering this line of attack.[2] Lukes argues that moral concepts like justice and power are essentially contestable because they are always embedded in moral theories which are incommensurable in that 'adjudications in favour of one rather than another are always made from within a particular point of view' (Lukes, 1974b, p. 177). No best conception of justice or power can therefore be established; there is no transcendental *moral* truth to which any such conception could be attached. Notwithstanding this, it is still possible, Swanton argues, for Lukes 'to favor one conception of power because it is superior to certain other salient conceptions' in the way it treats matters for whose priority he is prepared to argue (1985, p. 815). That the principle that affords the comparison may itself be contested is irrelevant; Lukes's twin claims are at least coherent.

Swanton levels a different objection at Lukes. She complains that he cannot consistently subscribe simultaneously to the theses of essential contestability and incommensurability, because properties ascribed to an object by different theories may be judged 'incompatible', and therefore contestable, only if statements about the object and its properties are comparable, i.e. 'intertranslatable' – and this, she claims, is what the incommensurability thesis disallows (1985, p. 823). Her claim is, however, an instance of a common misreading of Kuhn, who has taken pains to re-emphasize that 'incommensurable' does not mean 'non-comparable' (Kuhn, 1977, ch. 13). Translation from one theory to another is always possible though never perfect; it always involves some change in the way the world is seen.[3]

Compared with Gallie, Lukes has retained the notion that essentially contestable concepts are appraisive but has dispensed with original exemplars whose authority is acknowledged by all contestant users (Lukes, 1974a, pp. 26–7; cf. Macdonald, 1976, p. 381). How, then, does he ensure that X^1, X^2, X^3 are indeed different conceptions of X and not conceptions of X, Y and Z? His method is, it transpires, similar to that of the reconstructionists discussed in the next section. After inspecting the literature on power, he concludes that different concepts of power represent so many variations on the single theme that 'A exercises power over B when A affects B in a manner contrary to B's interests' (1974a, p. 34). The problem is to decide what counts as agency, exercise, affect and interest and how power is related to other concepts in its field such as force, authority, influence and persuasion. Put another way, the justification for speaking of different concepts of power is that translation between them is possible if imperfect. Indeed it could be argued that what is involved in substantiating Lukes's claim that his concept of power is superior to the alternatives is a discursive exercise in which it is shown that the alternative concepts can be translated into his with less loss or distortion than his can be translated into the alternatives. Even then, however, it would have to be assumed that that which is lost or distorted in translation is less important than that which survives.

Connolly arrives at the notion that political concepts in part constitute the object world, not through Rickert and Weber, but through Wittgenstein (1930), Winch (1958) and MacIntyre (1973). He flatly rejects Brodbeck's stricture that 'our concepts may be open textured, but the world is not. If language is to be descriptive, it must indicate what there is in the world, no matter how variably we talk about it' (Brodbeck, 1968, p. 396). On the contrary, he replies, 'Actions and practices are constituted in part by the concepts and beliefs the participants themselves have' (1974, p. 36). Furthermore, political scientists are themselves participants in the political process; it is always possible that their new concepts, more or less modified, will acquire a currency outside the academy and their glosses on old concepts will colour usages elsewhere. 'Institutional racism' provides him with an example.

When probing 'the settled usage and practices of a quiescent community', the political scientist may try to embrace its prevailing concepts – what Kariel (1973) calls the indicative mode – or he or she may aim to challenge them – what Kariel calls the transactional mode (Connolly, 1974, p. 180). Even here, though, the real choice and the actual outcome may not be so clear cut. Much more frequently the political scientist 'confronts a complex political practice in which many of the concepts that help to form political practice are themelves contested by the participants' (p. 181). Connolly's own affinity is with Wright Mills; he desires a society in which ordinary men and women can take effective responsibility for their own lives. Indeed he goes so far as to claim that 'the social scientist has an obligation to endorse those ideas that he [*sic*] thinks would help to nourish a politics of responsibility were they to be incorporated into the practices of our polity' (p. 204).

Contest and deconstruction

In a new final chapter for the second edition of *The Terms of Political Discourse* (1983), Connolly enlists Foucault in support of the essential contestability thesis (despite misgivings about his intentions).

> Deconstructionists show how every social construction of the self, truth, reason, or morality, endowed by philosophy with a coherent unity and invested with a privileged epistemic status, is actually composed of an arbitrary constellation of elements held together by powers and metaphors which are not inherently rational. To deconstruct these established unities is to reveal their constructed character and to divest them of epistemic privilege. Genealogy is a mode designed to expose

the motives, institutional pressures, and human anxieties which co-
alesce to give these unities the appearance of rationality or necessity.
(2nd edn (1983) of 1974, p. 231; cf. Foucault, 1966, 1969)

Social practices in which concepts play a constitutive part are treated
by Foucault as 'discursive practices'. In each, 'heterogenous elements
such as architectural design, available instruments, concepts, and
rules of evidence congeal into a particular structure of mutual
determinations' (2nd edn (1983) of Connolly, 1974, p. 233).
Foucault's own work has centred on the history of claims to knowledge ('epistemes'), sickness, madness, punishment and sexuality, but
deconstruction can be applied to any discursive formation.

Connolly does not make clear that the term 'deconstruction' is
Derrida's, not Foucault's (Derrida, 1972). This does not matter as
long as deconstruction is associated, as in Connolly, with exposure of
the non-naturalness of constructions and denial of epistemic privilege. It would matter, however, if it also evoked Derrida's notion of
intertextuality. According to deconstructionists, once we abandon the
notion of representation of objects unmediated by language we have
to accept that texts, written accounts, can ultimately refer only to
other texts and what Hoy calls 'an intersecting and indefinitely
expandable web' of intertextuality (Hoy, 1985, p. 53). Of course a lot
can happen before the ultimate, but there remains a fundamental
sense in which for Derrida there can be nothing outside the text
except other texts. Foucault's position is different and is nearer to
Connolly's. Foucault would agree that there is nothing outside discourse in that nothing can be grasped independently of the (specialist)
language in which it is constituted, but he also connects discursive
formations to social practices (say medicine, or factory work or child
rearing). Within discursive formations knowledge is knowledge-
power, where power refers to the capacity of one agent to affect the
actions of another (Gordon, 1980; Foucault, 1982). Discourse
structures the field of possibilities in practice; medical discourse, for
example, informs medical practice and practitioners define and classify the sick and the well and the field of possibilities open to each.
Without this reference to social practices there is no convergence with
Connolly. Concepts are contestable, and indeed contested, because
knowledge-power matters.

Total deconstruction can serve nihilism, which Connolly deplores,
or it can promote reflection, evaluation and action, which he endorses. Shortly before his death in 1984, Foucault said his objective
was to erode 'certain self-evidentnesses and commonplaces' about

madness, normality, etc., in order to promote reflection, encourage change and displace 'forms of sensibility and thresholds of tolerance' (1981, p. 80). Presumably Connolly would find some reassurance in this. In the end, however, Foucault can only disturb Connolly because he decentres the subject, the agent, and treats the self as a product of modernity with a circumscribed view of the possible. Instead of exercising power, the agent is an artefact of power. Connolly, by contrast, has to give a privileged status to the subject and to agency because without them the essential contestability thesis falls; concepts cannot be essentially contestable if subjects are incapable of contesting them. But if reason is to be brought to bear in that contest, there must be a position between belief that social constructions are inherently rational or rest on sure foundations and belief that they are arbitrary and irrational. This is an issue which will recur throughout the book and to which I shall return in chapter 6.

Oppenheim, Sartori, COCTA and the definitive reconstruction of concepts

The essential contestabilists, the deconstructionists and the reconstructionists all address the historical formation of concepts, but whereas Connolly is ready to discuss Foucault, Oppenheim and Sartori ignore him. The explanation for this is simple: whilst a weak deconstructionism is compatible with the essential contestability of concepts, all versions are incompatible with the definitive reconstruction of concepts. Definitive reconstructionists review the historical formation of concepts in order to escape it. Their aim is similar to that of the early American Sociological Society and Parsons. Prompted by their pre-Kuhnian understanding of natural science, they want to arrive at standard concepts which all social scientists will use. Their aim is not just to fix a theme around which there are variations, but to do away with variations altogether (cf. Care, 1973, on H.L.A. Hart, 1961, pp. 189–95). As not everyone who engages in conceptual reconstruction shares these objectives, I have called those that do *definitive* reconstructionists.

There are two main ways in which definitive reconstructionists can go about achieving their ambition. The first, the lone hero, represented by Oppenheim, sets out to offer a principled reconstruction of concepts which yields results of such transparent appositeness that the rest of us, being reasonable, will feel compelled to adopt them. The second, the committee of conceptual thought police, as led by

Sartori, propagates rules for concept reconstruction, applies the rules concept by concept, and looks to the associations to which social scientists belong to endorse them and, hopefully, enforce them.

According to Oppenheim, a colleague of Connolly's at the University of Massachusetts, reconstructed concepts are neither reportative nor stipulative but explicative. Ordinary language philosophers, basing themselves on Wittgenstein's *Philosophical Investigations* (1930), urge social scientists to remain faithful to ordinary language usages wherever possible. The resultant definitions are reportative in that they report how particular groups use the words concerned, and empirically verifiable in that misreporting is possible. Sometimes, however, the social scientist will have cause to introduce new concepts. These concepts are stipulative; the *definiendum* is synonymous with the *definiens*, whose meaning is already clear. Dahl's 'polyarchy', for example, refers to 'political systems with widespread suffrage and relatively effective protection of [certain] freedoms and opportunities' (Oppenheim, 1981, p. 179; Dahl, 1976, p. 81). Stipulative definitions are analytical and not empirically verifiable. Basing himself on Wittgenstein's *Tractatus* (1921), Oppenheim proposes a third, 'explicative', type of definition which is neither wholly reportative nor merely stipulative. 'Like stipulative definitions, explications are not verifiable as either true or false; but unlike the former, they can be appraised as good or bad in terms of their suitability for scientific communication' (1981, p. 179). Reconstructed concepts are explicative in character.

Oppenheim reconstructs ordinary language usages where they are ambiguous or inconsistent. He concedes that others attempting the same exercise may generate different concepts but he hopes to establish certain principles of reconstruction, common respect for which will keep conceptual variation within manageable bounds. These principles are not formally elaborated but include clarity, internal consistency, external systematicity, avoidance of redundancy and empirical sensitivity. Oppenheim's reconstructions of power, social freedom, egalitarianism and self-interest and public interest are certainly carefully done but they take no account of Kariel's transactional mode. Like Schutz, Oppenheim supposes that social scientific concepts are for scientists only and have no bearing on ordinary life. Ordinary language concepts may play their part in the constitution of the social world, and for that very reason be contestable, but scientific concepts do not.

The most that Oppenheim will allow is that some social scientific concepts are open-ended or open-textured in that it is not possible to define them by some set of necessary and sufficient conditions of their application: 'One may define "democracy" by a combination of criteria such as periodic elections, competitive parties, representation, freedom of expression, diffusion of political power, implementation of collective preferences; but the presence of all these traits is neither necessary nor sufficient to characterize a given political system as democratic' (1981, p. 183). They do not, for example, settle whether Turkey is a democracy. Why is this? It could have to do with difficulties associated with the use of cluster concepts, or it could be that the criteria are contestable. Oppenheim omits to give a reason. As a consequence, he does not so much rebut contestabilism as anathematize it.

Sartori's strategy is less heroic, but hardly more plausible. Having complained about conceptual overstretch in comparative politics (1970), Sartori joined with Riggs in 1970 to found a Committee on Conceptual and Terminological Analysis (COCTA) under the auspices of the International Political Science Association (IPSA); it is now also a committee of the International Sociological Association (ISA) and the International Social Science Council (ISSC). Participants have met at a succession of IPSA and ISA congresses. In addition, COCTA held its own European Symposium on Concept Formation and Measurement in Rome in 1984. In 1975 Sartori, Riggs and Teune published 'Tower of Babel: on the definition and analysis of concepts in the social sciences', but COCTA's main product is the 1984 volume *Social Science Concepts*, edited by Sartori (1984b), which contains its editor's own guidelines for concept analysis. I shall base my comments on the latter.

In contrast to Oppenheim, Sartori formally sets out what is involved in concept analysis – to the point of sequencing an elaborate set of rules. I have not the space here to examine Sartori's guidelines step by step or to assess systematically the use other contributors make of them in their reconstructions of 'consensus', 'development', 'ethnicity', 'integration', 'political culture', 'power' and 'revolution'. Instead, I aim to convey the general character of the exercise and add some comments.

There are two stages in Sartori's concept analysis. The first, concept reconstruction, has to do with recovery of as usable a concept as possible from the literature; the second, reconceptualization, recasts the recovered concept for future use. Sartori deploys a series of figures to help him make his points; my figure 2.1 is a composite of his figures 1.2 to 1.5.

For Sartori, the meaning is the concept; problems about meaning arise from the relations between meaning and term (or the word allocated to the concept) and meaning and referent (or the object it

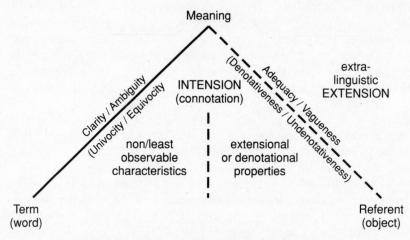

Figure 2.1 Concept intension and extension
Source: Composite of figures 1.2 to 1.5 in Sartori (1984a),
pp. 23, 26 and 27

denotes). The intension, or connotations, of a concept 'consists of all the characteristics or properties of a term, that is, assignable to a term under the constraints of a given linguistic-semantic system' (Sartori, 1984a, p. 24). Those shown to the left of the vertical broken line are the unobservable or least observable; those shown to the right are the observable and denote properties of the referent. The meaning-to-term relation is defective where it is ambiguous and/or equivocal. In natural languages all words are equivocal (have more than one meaning); the ideal for a social scientific language is univocity, but the more achievable remedy for the terminological defect lies in clarification of meaning. The meaning-to-referent relation is defective when it is vague, i.e. when there is doubt about which object (in the real world) the term denotes. The remedy for the denotational defect is not complete specification of the properties of the referent, which is impossible, but specification adequate for consistent use of the term.

The extension of a concept consists of (the properties of) the referent, or object, it denotes. To allow for the possibility that some properties of a referent have not been linguistically apprehended, the meaning-to-referent relation is represented as a broken line and extra-linguistic extension is located outside it. Denotations – properties which have been linguistically apprehended – are a subset of connotations; alternatively put, the extension of a concept is dependent upon the intension. The device of the broken line allows Sartori to

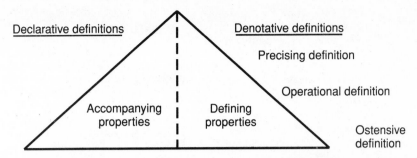

Figure 2.2 Types of definition and defining properties
Source: Composite of figures 1.6 and 1.7 in Sartori (1984a), pp. 29 and 33

sidestep the ontological problem of whether the denotational properties of a referent inhere in it or are imposed on it. This is a very serious evasion because it begs the whole question of the part played by concepts in the constitution and reconstitution of society.

My figure 2.2 is a composite of Sartori's figures 1.6 and 1.7, which map types of definitions and defining properties. Sartori locates a single type of definition, the declarative, on the meaning-to-term line and gives the example 'by "man" I intend males but not females' (1984a, p. 29). On the meaning-to-referent line, he places four types. The first, the denotative, is 'intended to seize the object (by increasing the denotativeness)', i.e. by specifying empirical properties (p. 30). The second, the precising, would seem similar in kind to the denotative; it provides for discretion within a class and gets closer to the individual object. Postgraduate, for example, is more precise than student. Operational definitions are said to get closer still by attending to only those properties of the object which lend themselves to measurement. Ostensive, or see-and-name, definitions are said to get closest of all. Defining properties are so called because they 'identify the referent and establish its boundaries' (p. 32). Accompanying properties are described as 'contingent, accidental or variable' (p. 32) and quite what they are doing on the term side of the figure I am unsure. What I do acknowledge is that the intension of a concept is defective in so far as the properties which comprise it are disorganized or trivial. The remedy for intensional defects is organization and the elimination of trivia.

Sartori sums up his argument so far as follows:

> a concept can be unsatisfactory – either muddled or inadequate – on three grounds:

1 defects in the intension (disorganized or trivial characteristics);
2 defects in the extension (undenotativeness or vagueness);
3 defects in the term (ambiguity).

If so, a complete conceptual and terminological analysis involves three steps. Their logical order is as follows:

1 establishing the connotative definition (by characteristics) of the concept;
2 determining its referents (denotative definition);
3 making sure that the term for it is understood univocally (declarative definition). (1984a, pp. 34–5)

Passage from step 1 to step 3 takes the social scientist from reconstruction to reconceptualization to 'terming the concept'.

Sartori's Rule 4 states that 'In reconstructing a concept, first collect a representative set of definitions; second, extract their characteristics; and third, construct matrixes that organize such characteristics meaningfully' (p. 41). With long-used concepts one must also establish the etymology, follow the '*Geistesgeschichte*' of the word, and analyse the texts of key authors. However one proceeds, the aim must be to extract the characteristics. Though definitions are commonly numerous, characteristics are typically much fewer. There are, for example, more than fifty definitions of 'power', according to Sartori, yet few concepts have, he surmises, even as many as ten characteristics. With regard to vagueness, Sartori's Rule 6 lays down that 'The boundlessness of a concept is remedied by increasing the number of its properties; and its discriminating adequacy is improved as additional properties are entered' (p. 43). Rule 7, dealing with the ladder of abstraction and universal concepts, states that 'The connotation and the denotation of a concept are inversely related' (p. 44).

Figure 2.3 illustrates four different matrixes. A and B are deemed easy to cope with because they have a common core and common

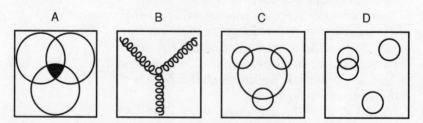

Figure 2.3 Possible configurations of characteristics
Source: Figure 1.8 in Sartori (1984a), p. 47

point of origin respectively. C and D are said to present problems although C seems to me just B at an early stage. Sartori proposes to dispose of cases like C and D by adjusting the populations from which the representative sets of definitions are drawn until they yield acceptable matrixes. One outcome might be two or more concepts which would then have to be termed differently.

When terming the concept, how the term fits into the semantic field is always a prime consideration. For example, the term 'power' is located in a field which includes 'influence', 'authority', 'coercion', 'force', 'sanction' and 'persuasion'. If homonyms, synonyms, redundancy and other sources of confusion are to be avoided, no single concept can be termed without regard for others. Finally, Sartori notes that theorists and empirical researchers often make different demands on a concept; the priority of the former is theoretical fertility, that of the latter empirical usefulness. He does not seem sure what to make of this. (Menzies (1982) has made a similar point in his distinction between theoreticians' theory and researchers' theory, cheerfully commending the creative tension between the two.)

What are we to make of this elaborate exercise? It seems to me to represent the triumph of hope over experience. Sartori wants social science to be more of a Kuhnian normal science:

> A 'real science' does not devote any special attention to concept reconstruction. The need for *reconstruction* results from *destruction*, from the fact that our disciplines have increasingly lost all 'discipline'. Amidst the resulting state of noncumulability, it is imperative to restore or attempt to restore the conceptual foundations of the edifice. This is not to say that an exercise in conceptual reconstruction will restore consensus – we are too far gone for that. However, if the exercise succeeds, it will restore intelligibility, an awareness of the enormous intellectual waste brought about by our present-day indiscipline (and methodological unawareness). This is why I insist on the reconstruction of concepts. (1984a, p. 50)

The language of restoration suggests a golden age that never was. Even so, it is undoubtedly true that varying concepts without due cause is a vice because it inhibits cumulation and comparison as well as making additional demands on the reader's memory. Sartori has no explanation for conceptual extravagance in the social sciences, however, beyond the innuendo that social scientists are a feeble lot whilst natural scientists are made of sterner stuff. Although at the outset he quotes approvingly Taylor's comment that 'language is constitutive of reality, is essential to its being the kind of reality it is', he does not take account of Schutz's problem that social scientists study a pre-interpreted world (Taylor, 1971, p. 24; Sartori, 1984a, p. 17). In other words, one reason for variation in social scientific concepts is the need to ensure consistency with primary concepts. Sartori also overlooks the basic premise of Marx, Durkheim, Weber and the essential contestabilists that social science is not sealed off from ordinary life. On the contrary, its formulations, including its concepts, sometimes inform ordinary life, albeit mostly via various mediations. Conceptual revision can have consequences for political change.

Sartori also misunderstands the premature closure argument. He notes that conceptual constancy is integral to normal natural science and craves something similar for sociology and political science. He asserts that systematic reconceptualization does not risk premature conceptual closure as the innovative combination of concepts can accommodate new phenomena in the real social world. By contrast, I would claim that this is exactly what closed conceptual vocabularies have difficulty in doing and that the smaller the vocabulary the greater the difficulty. Of course, ideal-typification and model-building also involve a fixing of concepts, but both are, to use Weber's term, utopian. This is not to dispute their great value to social science, but it is to insist that there is always a gap between utopian construction and social reality, that the greater the gap the lower the utility of the ideal-type or model, and that the use of ideal-types and models in the analysis of phenomena which were not anticipated when they were formed is particularly likely to reveal large gaps.

Finally, if it be thought that the real test of Sartori's guidelines is whether or not they enable others to effect reconstruction and reconceptualization, then I have to report that even the other contributors to *Social Science Concepts* offer only limited encouragement. None actually follows Sartori's guidelines step by step though all manage some reference to them and all do pronounce some sort of order where formerly there was conceptual variation. One author, Lane, still confesses dissatisfaction; after labouring diligently, he concedes that he knows 'of no method that resolves the semantic puzzle surrounding the concepts of power' (1984, p. 396). Another, Riggs, finds satisfaction only in a utopian strategy. Riggs notes that natural scientists use neologisms in their special languages. By contrast, social scientists favour words derived from ordinary language whose connotations they often cannot shed even where they are inappropriate. It is therefore hardly surprising that even an elaborate reconstruction of 'development', based as it is on past usages, fails to yield the pristine result Riggs wants. His conclusion is more than a little wistful:

> 'You can't make a silk purse out of a sow's ear' . . . I suspect the overloading of 'development' has reached such a high level that we cannot hope to rescue the word to signify any particular concept or variable. If Development Studies are to develop (!) a more promising approach is onomasiological: Let us identify by definition the concepts that we need and then try to find suitable unambiguous terms for each. (Riggs, 1984, p. 184)

In other words, introduce neologisms, get social science associations the world over to persuade/require their members to use them, depoliticize development studies and seal off social science from society so that none of these precious neologisms enters ordinary language and acquires unwanted connotations. Nowhere is the absurdity of the original COCTA agenda more transparent.

COCTA itself has now eased up on its original project and is becoming more a forum for colleagues of different persuasions who share a serious interest in concept formation. It has also now declared its position to be post-positivist (COCTA, 1992).[4] But the mirage of definitive reconstruction by committee continues to claim the odd lost soul. The latest is Wallace (1990), who 'proposes that the American Sociological Association appoint a Committee on Basic Sociological Concepts to investigate and recommend the official adoption of a basic conceptual language in American sociology' (p. 352, abstract).

Barnes on finitism

Building on ideas formulated by Hesse in the course of her challenge to the rejection of induction by Popper and others, Barnes has developed an important alternative to the extensional semantics of the COCTArians which he calls finitism (Hesse, 1974, chs 4 and 8; Barnes, 1982b, 1992).

> Its core assertion is that proper usage [of a concept] is developed step by step, in processes involving successions of on-the-spot judgements. Every instance of use, or of proper use, of a concept must in the last analysis be accounted for separately, by reference to specific, local, contingent determinants. Finitism denies that inherent properties or meanings attach to concepts and determine their future correct appli-

cations; and consequently it denies that truth or falsity are inherent properties of a statement. (Barnes, 1982b, pp. 30–31)

These step-by-step judgements lead Barnes to reject the notion of the extension of a concept because it imposes closure on its legitimate applications. Instead he refers to the (open) tension of a concept (1982a); applications to new instances always involve a judgement that the similarities outweigh the differences. Is the concept 'bird' applicable to the cassowary? Barnes (1981) discusses how Western and Karam judgements differ. One factor that enters into the different judgements is that of flight. But that too is problematic. Do flying foxes fly? Answers to such questions yield what Hesse calls a conceptual net – a structure of conventional judgements that is never finished and is always remakable. Because his concern is (mainly) with natural science, Barnes (1981) can write that ' "Reality" does not mind how we cluster it' (p. 315). Social reality, by contrast, frequently does mind very much; both Schutz's first- and his second-order constructs are involved, and the teaching and learning of similarity relations often acquire a contested, even political, character.

One reason Barnes is so interesting is that he knows his linguistics as well as Sartori but never suggests that it can justify guidelines for the definitive reconstruction of concepts. Quite the contrary, his tension of concepts keeps open what Sartori and Riggs hoped to close. Indeed, he gives a reason *other than contest* that definitive conceptual reconstruction cannot succeed.

Pawson on formalism and conceptual certitude

There is another reading of Hesse, represented by Pawson (1989), which I cannot fully rebut until the next chapter on the ontology of the social because it is connected with his scientific realism, but I will mention it now because it has generated a distinctive position on concept formation. Pawson subscribes to both post-empiricism and realism, and in so doing he combines one notion which is central to Hesse's position with another which is the opposite of hers. With Hesse's network model of universals in mind (Hesse, 1974, ch. 2), Pawson tells us that 'Realists . . . stress that scientific terms take their meaning from a network of definitions, relationships and laws' and 'that it is theoretical programmes as a whole which are assessed for correspondence with the world' (1989, p. 7). This is a central feature of Hesse's post-empiricism. He then adds that realists set great store 'by the idea that science does not operate by simply unearthing patterns and regularities in the occurrence of events, but explains by coming to an understanding of the underlying mechanisms that generate and constitute these regular sequences' (p. 7). There is no warrant for this in Hesse and it is confusing that he should imply otherwise.

Pawson associates formal concepts with network models and underlying regularities and makes these what sociology is about, in contradistinction to verbal reasoning and experience of events which is what ordinary life is about. His Rule III states that

> Empirical testing is at its most powerful in those disciplines employing formal networks of co-ordinated explanation. This allows for conceptual certitude as well as conceptual extension, so that precise linkages can be made between relatively speculative ideas and certain other concepts which are understood well enough to control and measure. Sociological theory must refrain as far as possible from ordinary language formulations and link certain of its basic notions to form an abstract calculus of formally defined concepts. Further extension of concepts, to portray a range of social systems, should take the form of hypothesis-making within generative formal models. (1989, p. 324)

According to Pawson, the alternatives in concept formation are thus not contestabilism versus reconstructionism but contestabilism versus formalism.

Pawson asks rhetorically whether 'class' is a knot concept (a point of intersection in one or more networks of definitions, relationships and laws) or a contestable concept, and concludes predictably that it is properly regarded as principally the former. But the question poses a false alternative. 'Class' is both. It turns up in different definitions, axioms and propositions, in both formal and verbal networks, and may thereby be said to tie them together, and it remains not just contestable but contested. What Pawson wants to do is set that contest aside and privilege one set of formal concepts by invoking underlying realities. I shall argue in the next chapter against the ontology of the social that that requires. For the moment I will just say that Pawson's ambition is also the antithesis of Hesse's post-empiricism. She holds that 'the language of theoretical science is irreducibly metaphorical and unformalizable' (1980, p. 173); he demands formalism.

Conclusion: beyond essential contestability and definitive reconstruction

Social scientists and philosophers of social science have been arguing about concept formation for a century and it is instructive to note some of the recurrent themes.

Social world and natural world   When forming concepts social scientists and natural scientists have different situations to contend with in so far as the social world is preconstituted and pre-interpreted by the objects of which it is composed (ordinary and not-so-ordinary men and women) whereas the natural world is not. Whilst there is no prospect of objects in nature changing their behaviour in the light of what natural scientists say about them there is just such a prospect with the objects of social scientific inquiry.

Primary and secondary concepts   The terms primary and secondary concepts often oversimplify. Different classes and class fractions, genders and generations, ethnic groups and nations, local and re-gional communities, sometimes give currency to alternative, and not necessarily compatible, concepts and accounts of the world. Also governments, managements and other authorities sometimes use concepts at variance with both those current among persons whose thinking they seek to penetrate and those favoured by social scientists. The British government's concept of unemployment, for example, was revised repeatedly under Mrs Thatcher to yield a lower figure for the total unemployed than would otherwise have been the case. No member of the public could possibly keep up with the changes and no social researcher adopting the latest definition could hope to publish before it was changed again. In short, primary concepts are seldom shared by everyone and are often contentious.

Schutz argued that social scientists must respect the postulate of adequacy but are otherwise free to introduce factors relevant only to social science in their constructs. Thus they may attend to conditions and consequences of action unknown to the actors concerned, or they may have cause to classify them in ways of no relevance to them. This approach has much to commend it because it does not limit social scientists to reproduction of members' own accounts or deny them a critical role – provided always that it be remembered that social scientists' concepts, too, are, for good reasons and bad, seldom shared by all social scientists, often contested and nearly always contestable.

Incommensurability and translation   Kuhn has had to explain that his celebrated, or notorious, incommensurability of paradigms does not preclude comparison between them. Comparison does, however, involve difficulties similar to those associated with translation between languages; quick multiple language translations risk distortions, whilst sensitive ones are laborious. I would make a similar point about concepts; quick reviews of the theoretical and research literatures in a field like class and stratification risk almost certain distortions whilst sensitive ones are achievements in their own right.

Openness and closure   Parsons, those who seek normal science in the Kuhnian sense, Sartori and COCTA all seek closure in the formation of conceptual systems in the belief that without it social sciences will never be able to formulate laws and law-like generalizations comparable to those which are the glory of natural science. In opposition to them I would argue that closure is a denial of the essential openness of the social world itself, its unending and unendable capacity for reconstitution. I also do not think it is possible to circumvent the unending variation of social forms by arguing that all forms are composed of combinations of elements in some closed analytical system, as Parsons tried to do with his analytical realism.

Symbolic interactionists and other interpretive sociologists have generally made sensitivity to a variegated and ever changing social world one of their strengths. Where they also retain 'theory-building' ambitions, however, incoherence can result as the case of grounded theory illustrates.

Finitists, such as Hesse and Barnes, give a reason other than contest why definitive conceptual reconstruction cannot succeed. They also provide a challenge to the one alternative path to conceptual certitude to that of the definitive reconstructionists, namely the formalism represented in this chapter by Pawson. Pawson's formalism is inseparable from a scientific realist ontology. For the moment, I will just say that the conceptual certitude he seeks is possible only in closed systems. Ideal-typifications and other models can provide closed systems, but only under what Weber called utopian conditions; how these utopias can serve explanation and understanding of the real world is still a matter for debate. What scientific realists do is posit closure in systems which underlie the open systems of surface phenomena and events – the ones we actually observe. How these can serve explanation and understanding of the real world is still a matter for debate. When it comes to explanation and understanding, there is thus perhaps more of a symmetry between utopian methodology and scientific realist ontology than partisans of the latter have sometimes been willing to admit. But these are matters to which I shall return in the next chapter, on ontologies of the social.

Cognitive and practical interests   Weber and the essential contestabilists stress that alternative concepts play their part in alternative constitutions of society. Definitive reconstructionists argue that social scientific concepts can and should rise above the battle. For them, as for Schutz, the social scientific world is completely separate from the everyday world. This is clearly untenable. Social scientists cannot hope to articulate some system of purely secondary and analytical concepts detached from all consideration of how the world is and how it could be because there is a two-way tie, Giddens's double-hermeneutic, between such concepts and those in ordinary discourse. In their formation, social science concepts always have some connection with natural language concepts; and in their use they always have some capacity, actual or potential, mediated or not, to inform ordinary discourses and practices. Social scientific discourses can therefore never be emptied of moral and political content and consequence. Alternatively put, social scientists have a practical interest, actual or potential, in the object of their studies as well as a cognitive one. On occasions it may suit them to adopt Kariel's indicative mode and play this interest down, but even then they may find themselves drawn into the transactional mode in spite of themselves.

Reconstruction and contest   The definitive reconstructionists put one in mind not just of Hempel but of the Vienna Circle. The whole movement towards a post-empiricist philosophy of science seems to have passed them by. As Bernstein comments:

> In the philosophy of science, and more generally in contemporary analytic philosophy, we have witnessed an internal dialectic that has moved from preoccupation (virtually an obsession) with the isolated individual term, to the sentence or proposition, to the conceptual scheme or framework, to an ongoing historical tradition constituted by social practices – a movement from logical atomism to historical dynamic continuity. (1983, p. 24)

For all their references to semantic fields, definitive reconstructionists still seem obsessed with individual concepts and terms.

By contrast, essential contestabilists move easily from individual terms to ongoing historical traditions constituted by social practices. Indeed Gray (1977) goes so far as to argue that 'essentially contested concepts find their characteristic uses within conceptual frameworks which have endorsement functions in respect of definite forms of social life' (p. 332). But this invites consideration of a question posed by Stehr (1982): 'is the reduction of . . . multiple discursive formations in sociology either possible or desirable?' (p. 51). The definitive reconstructionists consider it desirable and cling to the notion that it is possible despite the evident difficulties. The essential contestabilists argue that, at least as far as some concepts are concerned, it is neither possible nor desirable. Stehr's own view is that 'sociological discourse may be conceptualized as embedded in the life-world and as reflecting the life-world. A basic feature of all discourse thus is its context-dependence. The lack of unanimity among sociologists therefore has deeper roots than is usually assumed' (p. 53). I agree with Stehr that conceptual uniformity in sociology would depend upon conceptual uniformity in ordinary discourse, and that the latter is both improbable and inhuman in so far as it entails a single undifferentiated world language community and the end of history.

What are we to do about conceptual variations in the social sciences? My proposal is simple to state but difficult to execute. We eschew unnecessary conceptual variations and we endorse the rest. One does not have to subscribe to the old empiricist project of a quasi-natural science of society to find the impediments to routine comparison and cumulation of research findings posed by the non-availability of a categorial system irksome. Variation of concepts without good reason obstructs communication and is to be deplored. By contrast, variation of concepts with good reason testifies that societies are ever open to new possibilities and to reconstitution; it affirms our very humanity and is therefore to be welcomed. Who but cravers after the final realization of the idea, the heirs of Hegel and Rickert, could object to that?

The essential contestabilists limit contest to concepts with an appraisive component. Some concepts have a more obviously appraisive component than others; democracy, for example, is more obviously appraisive than administration, and leader more than individual. But it is very difficult to think of concepts which could never have an appraisive content in any circumstances. Thus though there may be limited empirical contestedness at any given time, only the practical imperative of communication places limits on theoretical contestability. To detach oneself from past usages without giving persuasive reasons is to speak into a void. To attach oneself to past usages, or to relate to them reflectively, is to make connections. Definitive reconstruction and reconceptualization may attract would-be thought police; lesser modes of reconstruction justify themselves if they encourage social scientists to vary concepts only after due deliberation and with good cause. In sum the most appropriate guiding principle in matters of concept formation is one of *limited contest and justified reconstruction* only.

3

The Constitution of Society: Agency and Structure

As sociologists we want to say that every distinct society has a particular relational structure, that it exhibits a certain order, a specific interconnectedness of the diverse elements, or spheres, of social life; and most of us would want to claim further that beyond or behind the unique structures of particular societies there are more general structural 'types' – that there are 'tribal', 'feudal', 'capitalist', 'socialist', 'industrial', and perhaps even 'post-industrial', forms of society. The real problem is to formulate a conception of social structure which does justice to these elements of regularity and order in social life, while not neglecting the flow of historical action by individuals and social groups which sustains, recreates, revises, or disrupts this order.

Bottomore, 'Structure and history' (1975)

Introduction

The 69th meeting of the American Sociological Association, in 1974, had as its theme 'Focus on social structure'. The papers given at the plenary sessions were published a year later under the title *Approaches to the Study of Social Structure* (Blau, 1975b). There is, of course, not much point in a symposium in which everyone says the same thing, and Blau, the organizer of the plenaries, no doubt chose his contributors with an eye to the generation of debate. It is nevertheless striking how little the different approaches had in common. 'Structure', it would seem, is something very many sociologists speak about without there ever having been agreement as to what it is. Now it could be said that this is true of most concepts in sociology, so why single out structure for comment? The answer, I think, has to do with the long-held view that social structures provide sociology with its distinctive objects of inquiry. Ambiguity about post-industrialism, class or charisma does not call in question the integrity of sociology as a distinct discipline; by contrast, ambiguity about structure seems to cast doubt on what sociology is and does.

It could be argued that, even so, equivocation about 'structure' is not worth agonizing over in that sociologists have clearly produced interesting researches and analyses in spite of it and can be expected to continue to do so provided that they do not succumb to the paralysis of theoretical doubt. There is much to be said for this posture, there being, after all, no agreed alternative vocabulary to that of structure; even the apparently anodyne 'society' has no agreed referent (cf. Frisby and Sayer, 1986). The difficulty with it, however, is that sociology is not just a private diversion; it is also a discipline with applied ambitions which it cannot abandon because they are what commend it to so many of its paymasters and -mistresses. Effective application, in turn, is connected with adequate working assumptions about the constitution of society.[1] Argument about the constitution of society is thus not a recondite activity which most sociologists can safely ignore.

In the first part of this chapter, I shall briefly review the classical legacy of Marx, Durkheim, Weber and Simmel, before moving on to the (mostly American) work that dominated thinking from the late 1940s to the late 1960s – the age of structural functionalism. I shall discuss this material only cursorily as it must be some of the most familiar in all sociology. The main import of my brief treatment will be that it did not settle very much – hence Bottomore's problem. In the much longer second part, I shall take a more extended look at what Americans most often call the micro–macro debate and Europeans the problem of structure and agency – unquestionably one of the big issues in sociology over the last two decades and more. This will allow me to review a number of attempts to supersede the dualisms of micro and macro or agency and structure, including Elias on figurations, Bourdieu on habitus, Habermas on lifeworld and system, Bhaskar's transformational model of social activity, and Giddens on structuration. In the course of these discussions it will emerge that the constitution of society is about not only structure and agency but also structure and process and structure and chaos or amorphousness. Ontologies of the social also raise questions about both the constitution of the person and relations between the actual, the real, the ideal and the virtual. I shall conclude by recommending an approach to the constitution of society which acknowledges the futility of phenomenalism (where that is taken to forbid reference to anything other than actual phenomena and events) without embracing scientific realism.

The classical legacy of Marx, Durkheim, Weber and Simmel

Marx's version of the constitution of society contains three main elements. The challenge of rendering each unambiguous and consistent with the others is responsible for many of the strands in the exceedingly variegated Marxist tradition. First, there is the model of material base and superstructure, with the former determining the latter in the last instance. Second, there is the concept of modes of production which transcend (state) boundaries, contain contradictions and have a partly concealed character. Third, there is the formula that men and women make their own history out of circumstances which are not of their choosing. This rich mixture has proved highly unstable. The base–superstructure model does not specify sufficiently what the base consists of: what count as forces of production, what count as relations of production, and what the connection is between the two, are all unclear. In sum, the determinant of the superstructure is as ambiguous as the notion that, whatever it is, it *ultimately* determines the superstructure. The concept of a mode of production involves connection of its underlying realities with historical and contemporary actualities in all their complications. Evidence for the unobservable underlying mode is one aspect of the problem; the unit of analysis – delimitation of a mode that transcends societal boundaries or societies as bounded by sovereign states or jurisdictions – is another. Contradictions, too, are not self-evidently so; indeed they are disputed. Finally, the formula about men and women and the making of history – with its appealing combination of voluntarism and determinism – is unclear as to who can do what, when, with whom and to whom. Precisely because this is a heady mixture, it is hardly surprising that different writers, explicitly or implicitly finding their own solutions, should have produced accounts of great power and persuasion. But equally, nor is it surprising that these selfsame accounts should be contested, not only by non-Marxists but also by other Marxists.

Durkheim's version of the constitution of society has four main elements. First, there is the characterization of society as a reality *sui generis* and of social institutions and social currents as things external to individuals which constrain them. Second, there is the conviction that society is a moral community which normatively regulates the individual. Third, there is the idea that crystallizations of social forces in 'legal and moral rules, popular sayings, or facts of social structure, etc.', which it is the job of sociologists to attend to, are separable from individual acts and facts, which it is not (Durkheim, 1895, p. 82). Fourth, there is the idea that 'The primary origin of all social processes of any importance must be sought in the constitution of the inner social environment [*milieu social interne*]' (p. 135). Each of these elements presents major difficulties. The conception of social facticity in terms of externality and constraint accommodates the routinized, the conforming, the crystallized, the institutionalized, the established and the fixed, but not the innovatory, the non-conforming and the yet-to-be, or even never-to-be, institutionalized and established. By treating structures as constraining, but not enabling, it opposes society to the individual and obscures any capacity men and women may have to remake their own world. Society as moral community connects with notions of society as the source and object of moral life reminiscent of Hegel; it also leads Durkheim to the contentious conclusion that God is society transfigured. The separation of social facts from individual facts and acts leaves unclear how the one is related to the other. Lastly, like Marx on the material base, what the inner social environment, the social substratum, includes and what it excludes are insufficiently specified. In addition, the meaning of primary origin is far from clear, and the use of the notion sometimes dubious – as when Durkheim and Mauss (1903) explain away exceptions to the law relating social organization to primitive classification as the product of historical deflections. Given the absence of a theory of action, I do not consider Durkheim's version of the constitution of society to be as rich a mixture as Marx's, but it has left plenty of room for differences of opinion. Those taking Durkheim as a resource, from Radcliffe-Brown to Parsons, to Lévi-Strauss, to Goffman, to Habermas are diverse indeed.

Frisby and Sayer (1986) have perceptively argued that society is an absent concept in Weber and Simmel, but this does not mean that the latter have no conception of the constitution of society. Weber's version has four main elements. First, he rejects the idea of societies and structures as realities *sui generis* and as collective actors, and concentrates on individual actors and the meanings, motivations, mutual orientations and consequences of their actions. Tendencies towards communitization and sociation in action, as distinct from community and society considered apart from action, give the tenor of Weber's sociology. Second, he treats social relations and organizations in terms of the probabilities of certain courses of action being repeated; structuring is an ongoing accomplishment and not something to be taken for granted. Third, society and other boundaries have to do with the extent to which the authority of the state is acknowledged in practice, or the extent to which judicial writ actually runs, or whatever – and not the sovereign territory claimed by the state or the jurisdiction pronounced by a constitution. Fourth, ideal-types are indispensable in the analysis of social life. All of these bring problems. Weber's self-styled methodological individualism brings with it all the problems of nominalism. The idea of structuring as ongoing accomplishment underestimates experience of institutions as external and intractable, and the open attitude towards boundaries makes it hard to specify units within which individual action and its consequences are to be examined. Finally, rules for the formation of ideal-types are conspicuous by their absence, and relations between idealizations and the actual historical world are correspondingly unclear. Connect all of these with Weber's variant of the theory of value relevance and one ends up with a version of the constitution of society which shelters solipsists and lauds contestedness. As with Marx and Durkheim, a legion of interpreters and more or less inventive descendants have devised their many splendoured ways of coping with the problems the master left behind – in consequence of which (neo-)Weberian has become even less informative a label than (neo-)Marxist.

Even more than Weber, Simmel opposed the reification of society. His version of the constitution of society has two basic elements. First, society consists of individuals and their interaction. It is what emerges from sociation – the co-operation, association and coexistence of individuals. Second, the forms of sociation – such as competition and conflict, leadership and subordination, dyads and triads – are distinguishable from the contents in which they recur – such as firms, or religious orders or political alliances. The problem with the first is that it is hard to say what does emerge if it is inseparable from processes of sociation. The problem with the second is to know whether the forms are idealizations or real entities which enjoy some kind of ontological priority, and, either way, how they relate to contents. Perhaps part of the enduring appeal of Simmel is his elusiveness; pinning him down demands considerable invention.

In sum, the legacy of Marx, Durkheim, Weber and Simmel is varied, profound, fascinating – and also inconclusive. No wonder American and other advocates of structural (functional) sociology in the 1940s, 1950s and 1960s (who in any case were not always as well informed about the classical legacy as Europeans, at least, are now) were moved to offer new formulations of their own.

Structural sociology

Like the classics, structural functionalism and systems theory are already very familiar to most sociologists – so I shall content myself, here, with a few summary remarks on Parsons, Merton and others. I shall, however, also comment on a less hackneyed topic – notions of structure which figure in American empirical social research. Again the thrust of my argument will be that the problem identified by Bottomore in the passage at the head of this chapter was not solved to general satisfaction.

Blau has described two contrasting conceptions of social structure, the first of which he associated with Radcliffe-Brown and the second with Lévi-Strauss:

> The first view holds that social structure is a system of social relations among differentiated parts of a society or group, which describes observable empirical conditions and is merely the basis for a theory yet to be constructed to explain these conditions. The second view holds that social structure is a system of logical relationships among general principles, which is not designed as a conceptual framework to reflect empirical conditions but as a theoretical interpretation of social life. (1975a, p. 220)

I think these were indeed the two main conceptions of structure in the period in question. Blau subscribed to the first; so did Merton, with the proviso that the conditions and consequences of socially structured alternative courses of action are not always apparent to the actors concerned (Merton, 1957d). For Merton, as for Durkheim, structures constrain. By contrast, Parsons adopted a variant of the second view. Parsons's model of the social system is analytical in his own terms, but utopian in the eyes of a critic like Dahrendorf (Parsons, 1951; Dahrendorf, 1958). The social system consists of institutionalizations of values and norms which govern people's expectations. As such it underlies, but must not be confused with, actual patterns of interaction. That Parsons's structures enable as well as constrain is most easily seen in his functional theory of power (1963a, 1963b).

Blau has also commented on the micro–macro problem with regard to structure, with Parsons, Merton and others offering macro approaches, Homans, Garfinkel and Goffman offering micro approaches and a few figures, such as himself, trying to elucidate macro–micro connections. Perhaps the most important of the micro approaches is that of the symbolic interactionists, according to which, in Rose's words:

> The term structure will be used to refer to a cluster of related meanings and values that govern a given social setting, including the relationships of all the individual roles that are expected parts of it. Structures may be fairly small or temporary ones, such as a conference committee, or a large and 'permanent' one, such as a state or society. (1962, p. 10)

The two conceptions of structure, the social and the logical, are also each subdivided into those which treat conflict and change residually and those which treat them integrally.

It is commonly said that American sociology in the 1940s, 1950s and 1960s was dominated by structural-functionalism. Giddens, for example, has written of the orthodox consensus which combined functionalism with naturalism (1979, ch. 7; 1987, ch. 2). This is probably true of the theoretically conscious at that time, but in their different ways the Willers (1973) and Warshay (1975) have argued that the mass of American work has been empiricist and largely devoid of theory (cf. Bryant, 1985, pp. 168–73). Where theories do appear, they are, according to Warshay, 'small theories' – such as differential opportunity theory in the sociology of crime and delinquency, reference group theory in social psychology and status crystallization theory in the sociology of stratification – rather than 'large theories', such as functionalism, conflict theory, interactionism or exchange theory. Wells and Picou (1981), in their content analysis of the *American Sociological Review* from 1936 to 1978, bear this out. They conclude that theory in most American sociology has been driven by a methodological preoccupation with multivariate statistical applications and survey and census data sources. The nearest America has to a dominant paradigm, and it is already quite near and getting nearer, is 'quantitative structuralism', in which structures refer to actual connections between variables. As such it may be regarded as an empirical variation on Blau's first conception of structure. Empirical variations on his second conception are harder to come by but Lazarsfeld's (1968) latent structure analysis is one candidate.

Finally, it should be noted that there were those inside and outside the interpretive tradition who protested that prevailing images of society and structure presented individuals as always determined and never determining. Wrong (1961) protested at the oversocialized conception of man and Garfinkel (1967) deplored the depiction of men and women as cultural dopes.

All in all, the age of structures and functions and structures and systems, with its semi-submerged alternative tradition of symbolic interactionism, and its all too evident accompaniment of empiricist social research, again failed to come up with a generally accepted version of the constitution of society. Bottomore's challenge of accommodating the unique structures of particular societies *and* structural types, order *and* the flow of individual and collective actions which sustains, revises and disrupts it, is clearly not easily met. It is even harder if one adds in another of his requirements, that one allow for continuity *and* discontinuity in history. It is, nevertheless, a challenge which a variety of scholars has accepted in the last two decades and more. I shall argue that they have not laboured in vain.

The micro–macro and agency–structure debates

The shortcomings of earlier ontologies of the social invited correction and from the 1970s onwards numerous writers have set out to supply it. Their efforts have generated a major debate which in America is more often called the micro–macro debate and in Europe the agency–structure debate. Symposia edited by Knorr-Cetina and Cicourel (1981), by Alexander, Giesen, Münch and Smelser (1987), and by Sztompka (1994) explore the issues. There are also a number of writers who have reconsidered what they call the microfoundations of macrosociology; they include Collins (1981), Hechter (1983) and Coleman (1990). Those attempting revised ontologies of the social include Elias (1939, 1968, 1970), Gurvitch (1958), Touraine (1965, 1973), Bourdieu (1972, 1980), Habermas (1973a, 1981), Bhaskar (1975, 1979, 1986), Giddens (1976, 1979, 1984), Archer (1982, 1988), Sztompka (1991) and Mouzelis (1992). Elias first formulated his position long before the present period but it has only recently been taken up by others and discussed widely. Gurvitch also wrote well before the period in question; he seldom figures in the debate but he was the first to use the term 'structuration' in sociology. Touraine's 1965 book had little follow-up and has not been translated. None of these three can therefore be said to refute the claim that the *debate* about the ontology of the social is a feature of the 1970s onwards.

The time has now come for a systematic review and evaluation of all these contributions. The task is large, however, and as yet no one has attempted it.[2] Certainly I cannot hope to do so here within the confines of a single chapter. Instead I shall consider the five figures who have arguably been most influential in reformulating the ontology of the social: Elias, Bourdieu, Habermas, Bhaskar and Giddens (although in the case of Habermas the ontology is a by-product of a methodology). This is the order in which their first major contributions appeared. I will then compare them on a series of issues before reaching a considered position of my own.

Elias on figurations

Elias's distinctive approach to sociology is still most often known as figurational sociology (as in the 1987 special double number of *Theory, Culture and Society* entitled 'Norbert Elias and Figurational Sociology') even though Elias himself came to prefer process-sociology in protest at what Mennell calls the reification of 'figuration' by both friend and foe (Mennell, 1989, p. 252). Elias first uses the term 'figuration' in the original German edition of *The Civilizing Process* (1939). He defines a figuration as 'a structure of mutually oriented and dependent people' (vol. 1, p. 261). What he means by this is illustrated by a passage discussing the territorial ambitions of early French kings in connection with something once said of an early American pioneer: 'He didn't want all the land; he just wanted the land next to his' (vol. 2, p. 160). Elias comments that

> This simple and precise formula expresses well how from the inter-weaving of countless individual interests and intentions – whether tending in the same direction or in divergent and hostile directions – something comes into being that was planned and intended by none of these individuals, yet has emerged nevertheless from their intentions and actions. And really this is the whole secret of social figurations, their compelling dynamics, their structural regularities, their process character and their development; this is the secret of their sociogenesis and relational dynamics. (vol. 2, p. 160)

In the first German edition, however, there is no articulation of a theory of figurations as such, just passing references to the thinking which underpins a work of historical sociology. In any case, publication, on the eve of the Second World War, passed largely unnoticed. Elias won significant recognition only in retirement with the publication of a second German edition in 1968, and a two-volume English translation in 1978 (*The Civilizing Process*) and 1982 (*State Formation and Civilization*). There is an explicit statement of the theory of figurations in the Introduction to the second German edition, which appears as an appendix to volume 1 of the translation, some comments in the final chapter of volume 2 (from which the quotation above is taken) and another brief but helpful comment in a new endnote to volume 2 (1982, no. 128, pp. 354–6). In addition, there are, of course, Elias's *What is Sociology?* (German, 1970; English, 1978) and comments in the stream of works published up to and beyond his death in 1990. Elias did not consider himself a theorist, however, and a full appreciation of his distinctive approach to sociology can be obtained only by reading his substantive works.

Writing in the 1970s Goudsblom (1977b) attributed neglect of Elias's figurational sociology in the English-speaking world to his marginality in British academic life. Elias taught not at the University of Oxford or of Cambridge or at the London School of Economics (LSE) but at the University of Leicester, and then only from 1954, and he retired in 1962, just as Neustadt was promoted to the foundation chair of sociology, with his major work still untranslated and much else unpublished and sometimes unfinished. I am not convinced by this explanation. In the 1960s and 1970s Leicester became one of the biggest teaching departments of sociology in Britain and the network of former Leicester students and teachers in other universities and colleges is probably second only to the LSE's in its scale and penetration. Elias did retire just before the big expansion of the Leicester department placed its graduates seemingly everywhere, but even so he continued to come into the department on his return from Ghana in 1964 in order to talk to colleagues, participate in staff seminars and teach graduate students. Potentially there were plenty of people to spread the word, so why was the word not spread? Part of the answer had to do with the non-availability of recent German editions of his work and the inability of most British colleagues to read them even if there had been (though it has also to be said that Elias placed considerable obstacles in the way of those who wanted to translate him). The greater impediment to Elias's reception, however, was not practical but intellectual – and I comment as one who was an undergraduate in the department from 1962 to 1965 and an MA student and tutorial assistant for a further year. Although the general influence of Elias showed in the distinctive developmental emphasis of the Leicester undergraduate curriculum in sociology (cf. R. K. Brown, 1987), and also in the inclusion of psychology taught from within the department, no attention was given to the theory of figurations, or the thesis of the civilizing process or any other specific feature of Elias's work. There seem to me to have been two reasons for this. First, Elias had failed to articulate the principles of his figurational sociology with sufficient clarity to commend it to his colleagues; the principles were (and arguably remain) too vague and too detached from contemporary developments in sociology. Second, and more importantly, Elias may be regarded as a man before his time. He wanted to supersede the dualisms of individual and society, order and change, agency and structure, and objectivity and subjectivity in a manner which is now respected, even expected, but which was not then. Moreover he did so in ways which then seemed idiosyncratic and without firm foundations. It was thus only in the context of the intensifying micro–macro and agency–structure debate, and even more the resurgence of historical sociology in the late 1970s and the 1980s (cf. Mennell, 1990), that the value of Elias's work came to be widely acknowledged. Recognition has been greatest in the Netherlands and Germany but is now significant in Britain also (cf. Mennell, 1992).

Elias's theory of figurations rests on two simple points, his rejection of sociological analyses which take as their object states rather than processes (Parsons is his *bête noire*) and opposition both to analyses which reify society (Durkheim's mistake – at least in his cruder moments) and to those which absolutize the individual (Weber's mistake). Even analyses which consider individuals-in-society at a single point in time mislead in their presentation of a stable structure, for that moment in time freezes relations which are always in flux. These relations pertain to interdependencies between individuals. Society apart from these networks of interdependencies is a reification; likewise, the individual closed off from social formation ('*homo clausus*') and the social context of action is a myth. Accordingly, the object of sociological inquiry should be what Elias calls figurations.

Layder is right to complain that objections to the false dichotomy of individual and society are hardly new. Indeed he cites lines from Cooley which make the point as well as any in Elias: 'a separate individual is an abstraction unknown to experience, and so likewise is society when regarded as something apart from individuals' (Layder, 1986, p. 373; Cooley, 1902, p. 36). The persistence of the dichotomy in spite of long-standing objections to it, however, itself calls for an explanation. Elias offers one by recalling Whorf's thesis about the subject–predicate structure of Western languages (Whorf, 1956). This structure disposes us to think of substantives in states of rest. To say 'the wind blows', for example, suggests that the wind is separable from its blowing. It also inclines us 'to express all change and action by means of an attribute or a verb, or at least as something additional rather than integral' (Elias, 1970, p. 112). Elias objects that:

> This constant process-reduction results in the changeless aspects of all phenomena being interpreted as most real and significant. It extends to spheres where it imposes a totally false limitation. Whorf mentions how we draw involuntary conceptual distinctions between the actor and his activity, between structures and processes, or between objects and relationships. (p. 112)

Elias's concept of 'figuration' is intended to avoid process-reduction. Even so it is only its connections with interweaving, bonding and long-term developments which make it more than a new term for an old idea.

Interweaving refers to the way action is constrained and conditioned by, is orientated towards, and has intended and unintended consequences for, others. Elias gives the example of two groups of hunters and gatherers whose competition over dwindling sources of food extends into mutual killing. Each conditions the other's existence and their interdependence exhibits a clear structure. Much more often some conduct at least is normatively regulated. Elias uses the 'didactic model' of the game. The more people in the game, and the more levels at which it is played, the more complex the figurations and the longer the chains of interdependence.

By 'bonding' Elias simply refers to the forging of interdependencies, affective, political, economic, etc. He also treats both functions and power as integral elements of all relationships. Power has to do with the capacity of one party to deny another something it lacks. Function has to do with the capacity of one party to do something for another whether that something is intended or unintended, or wanted or unwanted, by either or both. Functions are about functional relations between parties, not between individuals and society or parts and the whole. Dysfunctions therefore play no part in Elias's scheme. Elias also emphasizes that relations are rarely perfectly balanced or symmetrical. For Durkheim exercise of the power of disruption by a party within an extended division of labour is evidence of a pathology. For Elias it is confirmation that powers and functions occur together, and a reminder of the emptiness of debates in which conflict theory is pitted against functional theory. Perhaps the best definition of figuration is thus that of a Dutch commentator: 'Configurations are networks of interdependent human beings, with shifting asymmetrical power balances' (van Bentham van den Bergh, 1971, p. 19, quoted in Bogner, 1986, p. 393).

Layder (1994) criticizes Elias for overlooking that the defining characteristics of institutions are not to be found in the mere connectedness of people but in the character of the connections: 'it is the nature of the ties (pecuniary, altruistic, contractual, and so on) and the resources that underpin them (law, money, property) that are of crucial importance in understanding work relations, political involvements and power conflicts between groups' (p. 123). But if Elias sometimes says less about different kinds of tie than one might wish, resources like law, money and property have a great deal to do with shifting asymmetrical power differences.

Elias addresses the succession of figurations in the long as well as the short term, but he distrusts all presentations of developments as inevitabilities. There is a sense in which, looking back, a figuration can always be seen to have realized a developmental tendency contained in its predecessor. Looking forward, however, one can never be sure which of the possible courses of development a figuration will actually take. Contingency precludes prediction. All that Elias can suggest is that we 'keep in mind the key idea that every relatively complex, relatively differentiated and highly integrated figuration must be preceded by, and arise out of, relatively less complex, less differentiated and less integrated figurations' (1939, vol. 2, p. 161). This onward and upward characterization of figurational change has similarities with Durkheim's thesis of the division of labour in society. Both ill-prepare one for cases which go the other way such as the decline and fall of the Roman Empire.

Bauman (1989) has pointed out important differences between interdependencies in Elias's figuration theory and the unacknowledged conditions of action in Giddens's structuration theory. The latter refer to conditions of action of which the actor is ignorant (or, better, unaware); the former to conditions of action which are irretrievably beyond the actor's control irrespective of his or her knowledge (or, better, awareness). 'Interdependencies' refer to the ties that actors have to others including the resources they share, such as language, and the differences their action makes to others. 'Knowledge', Bauman stresses, 'has . . . considerable bearing on what the actors do; but not on what they may do nor what the outcome of their doing might be' (p. 41). Participants in a zero-sum game, such as four candidates competing to fill a single job vacancy, cannot change the 'figurational logic' which demands that the failure of three is a condition of the success of one, and that co-operation between them is impractical, however knowledgeable they may be.

Knowledgeability might also in principle be evened out. (One could imagine Habermas welcoming this.) By contrast, Bauman argues, the concept of interdependencies, or, better, networks of dependencies, 'couples the preconditions of action from the start to the recognition of the differentiation of actors and their capabilities in virtue of their involvement in the figuration' (p. 41). Interdependency involves differential constraint, and a good deal can be learned about the possibilities of action and its outcomes from analysis of the figuration prior to any hermeneutic scrutiny of the actors. Bauman clearly approves of this feature of figurational sociology but it is connected to another which he had earlier criticized and which I shall shortly come to.

The possible tracings of interdependencies, if not infinite in number as Weber would have claimed, are at least very numerous, but Elias has nothing to say on which tracings should be followed and why. He is, in fact, even less helpful on the specification of figurations than Weber is on the formation of ideal-types. This makes where one figuration ends and another begins seem arbitrary. One way out of this arbitrariness would involve acknowledgement and justification of the values and interests which enter into the specification of particular figurations. Elias rules this out, however, by arguing that figurations have no reality apart from the real historical interdependencies of which they are composed. This also has the effect of denying any reality to culture independently of social structure. After likening figurations to social dances, for example, Elias comments:

> One can certainly speak of dance in general, but no one will imagine a dance as a structure outside the individual or as a mere abstraction. The same dance figurations can certainly be danced by different people; but without a plurality of reciprocally oriented and dependent individuals, there is no dance. (1968, p. 262)

As Layder (1986) has pointed out, it is one thing to oppose the notion that dances are mental constructs and nothing more, and quite another to suggest that they are never mental constructs. Indeed one could go further and say that without our capacity to imagine the dance as a structure outside the individual we would never be able to dance at all, and Elias would never have been able to communicate his metaphor of the dance. Culture is locatable between the situated activity Elias attends to and the reified objects he dismisses. Elias allows his opposition to reification to turn into a distrust of all abstraction. Yet figurations involve abstraction just as surely as do Weberian idealizations or Schutzian typifications.

Rojek (1986) and van Krieken (1990) have both made comparisons between Elias and Foucault. In each there is a decentring of the subject. In van Krieken's words, 'Elias . . . looks for changes in the nature of social relationships, in social figuration, which in themselves "require" different forms of behaviour, different personality structures' (1990, p. 360). This being so, what kind of applied sociology does figurational sociology allow? Elias warns that 'The social fabric . . . forms the substratum from which and into which the individual constantly spins and weaves his purposes. But this fabric and the actual course of its historical change as a whole, is intended and planned by no-one' (1982, p. 356). Few, these days, would dispute that. But the tone of Elias's work invites a resignation which no one who believes in the utility of applied sociology could accept.

Liberals like Adam Smith, Spencer and Hayek at least associate the hidden hand with the generation of the best of all possible worlds. Elias just refers to the factual order in a matter-of-fact way. In Bauman's (earlier) words:

> Elias's sociology reconciles itself to the role of a wise outsider finding out what people have done while they were doing what they thought they were doing. Nowhere in Elias's reflections the thought that sociology may perhaps play some active part in shaping human actions and influencing their outcomes, visibly influences the form or the content of the social sciences he postulates. (1979, p. 124)

The sociologist is a destroyer of myths and as such may help individuals better orient themselves in the world, but better orientation may still amount to resignation rather than active engagement with transformative intent.

Elias dedicated the second edition of *The Civilizing Process* to the memory of his parents; he believes his mother died in Auschwitz in 1941. The state of Israel may not have turned out as anyone intended but it is testimony to the determination of Jews after the Holocaust never again to face genocide without any means of resistance. The state of Israel affirms that individuals, singly and in concert, can sometimes achieve more than local and immediate goals – but then Israel is more than a figuration, it is also a project and an idea. How ironic that Elias of all people should promote an ontology of the social which is insensitive to that.

In choosing to pay special attention to Elias, Bourdieu, Habermas, Bhaskar and Giddens, I have highlighted the contributors to the micro–macro and agency–structure debate who have had the most influence, but Elias's influence is unlike that of the others. Elias has devoted followers in the Netherlands, Germany, Britain and elsewhere ever ready fiercely to defend the master, but he is still ignored by most other sociologists. Those like Bauman who treat Elias as one valuable resource among others are disappointingly rare. The reasons for this are too complicated to examine properly here, and I will confine myself to one remark which is most easily expressed in Kuhnian terms. With *The Civilizing Process* Elias provides an exemplar but the other elements in his disciplinary matrix for sociology are under-theorized. In deference to Elias's unusual powers of synthesis, Mennell (1989) concludes (the first edition of) his otherwise superb book on Elias with the aphorism 'only connect'. 'No-one else', he says, 'has so coherently drawn the connections between manners and morals, power and violence, states, war and peace through human history' (p. 269). Well, maybe; but in another respect the most obvious deficiency in Elias is his failure to connect. Figurational, or process, sociology involves, or perhaps implies, nothing less than a distinctive ontology of the social and of the person, a distinctive epistemology and a distinctive methodology. Its originator demonstrated them in use in *The Civilizing Process* and elsewhere but he chose not to elaborate them systematically and comprehensively. There are relevant comments in plenty but there are also many omissions; and in any case the comments are offered mostly in detachment from reflections on the sources of his own thought and in self-defeating isolation from the work of others and the debates of the day.[3] When Elias does connect, his interlocutors are all too often yesterday's straw men. As a consequence he invites misunderstanding and the sectarian keepers of the word have continually to leap to his defence. 'Only connect'; I only wish he had! What I would now like is sociologists generally to rise above the prickly protestations of the sectarians, read Elias for themselves and make their own connections.

Bourdieu on habitus

Like Elias, whom from time to time he cites approvingly, Bourdieu considers himself as first and foremost a substantive researcher. His theoretical formulations are an outgrowth of his substantive work and he is hostile to theorists who do nothing but theorize. Like Elias he also has his dedicated followers – in the Centre de Sociologie du

Collège de France, and the pages of the *Actes de la recherche en sciences sociales*, in particular – but beyond them, ironically, he appears more often a figure of interest to theorists than an inspiration to researchers. This may change as translations of his work become more widely known, but I have my doubts. One of the reasons Giddens's structuration theory is now being used by researchers in different countries and disciplines who have no personal connections with him is that he has taken great care to define his terms. The summaries, the diagrams and the glossaries have helped researchers to put structuration theory to work in numerous inquiries. Bourdieu's theoretical formulations, by contrast, are richly suggestive but exasperatingly difficult to pin down. It is much easier for theorists to debate them than for researchers to apply them. Where Elias is under-theorized, Bourdieu is enigmatic.

Bourdieu introduced the notion of habitus in 1967, but the main sources for his formulations of structure, habitus, practice and field are *Outline of a Theory of Practice* (1972) and *The Logic of Practice* (1980). His answers to Wacquant's questions in Bourdieu and Wacquant (1992) are also very revealing. Bourdieu rejects the dualism of objectivism and subjectivism, and the notions of the actor as rule follower or norm respecter (favoured in structuralism and functionalism) or rational calculator (favoured in classical economics and in rational choice, or as he prefers, rational action, theory). Instead he places at the centre of his theory 'habitus', which variously means in Latin condition, character or disposition. Bourdieu uses it idiosyncratically as 'an acquired system of generative schemes objectively adjusted to the particular conditions in which it is constituted' (1972, p. 95). But how is it acquired, where is it lodged, what does it generate and how is its objective adjustment secured? It is difficult to get consistent unambiguous answers to these questions, but I will risk the following: it is acquired via socialization, it is inscribed in the minds (and bodies) of actors, it generates practices (i.e. what people do) or, rather, it regenerates past practices thereby ensuring that what people do is what can be done. Wacquant (Bourdieu and Wacquant, 1992) has offered the simple notion that 'habitus consists of a set of historical relations "deposited" within individual bodies in the form of mental and corporeal schemata of perception, apperception, and action' (p. 16). Bourdieu's own elaboration is harder to grasp:

> The conditionings associated with a particular class of conditions of existence produce *habitus*, systems of durable, transposable dispositions, structured structures predisposed to function as structuring

structures, that is, as principles which generate and organize practices and representations that can be objectively adapted to their outcomes without presupposing a conscious aiming at events or an express mastery of the operations necessary in order to attain them. Objectively 'regulated' and 'regular' without being in any way the product of obedience to rules, they can be collectively orchestrated without being the product of the organizing action of a conductor. (1980, p. 53)

What we seem to have here is an analogue to Giddens's duality of structure in which structure is the medium and outcome of the conduct it recursively organizes, except that in one respect it is more complicated.[4] For Bourdieu structures produce/deposit habitus which generates practices which reproduce structures – three features (structures, habitus and practices) where Giddens has only two: systems and structures. Structures, moreover, belong to an objective, not a virtual order as in Giddens, and habitus, as a durable system of dispositions, combines what Giddens separates – the actor and what the actor draws upon when acting.

Jenkins (1982, 1992) suggests that Bourdieu's scheme sometimes appears overly determinist. 'Strategies', what actors reasonably do given who they are and where they are, are forged in the interaction of the dispositions of the habitus and the objective possibilities and the constraints of the 'field' or arena – strategy without a strategist. Individuals seem to be habitual dopes caught up in a cycle of reproduction which only ever repeats itself. Bourdieu concedes that he is hyperdeterminist in so far as he takes account of the effects of both position and disposition, but he adds that this is not the whole story (Bourdieu and Wacquant, 1992, p. 136). Determinisms operate to the full only, he says, with the complicity of the unconscious; in other words, what Giddens would call the reflexivity of actors can make a difference. Habitus is 'an *open system of dispositions* that is constantly subjected to experiences' (p. 133; author's italics). Also Bourdieu emphasizes that the structures of different fields – the arenas in which struggles or manoeuvres take place over things of value (such as cultural goods, distinction, power or land) – vary and thus so does the habitus associated with each. Dispositions, however, are transposable – potentially transferable from one field to another – and this may lead to clashes or prompt reflection. Patriarchy at home, for example, might clash with educational opportunity for girls and women at school and university. Bourdieu's scheme does not assume a closed system forever repeating itself. Even so, Bourdieu's scheme is more determinist than Giddens's.

There can be no doubt that Bourdieu's central concept of habitus has informed research of considerable interest, if sometimes mixed quality, such as his studies of reproduction in education (with Passeron, 1970), taste and distinction (1979) and French academia (1984). The concept remains too obscure, however, for widespread use by social researchers, but not obscure enough to deter social theorists (cf. the responses to Bourdieu in Calhoun, LiPuma and Postone, 1993). Claims like the following are an invitation to interpreters but a rebuff to researchers:

> The *habitus* – embodied history, internalized as a second nature and so forgotten as history – is the active presence of the whole past of which it is the product. As such, it is what gives practices their relative autonomy with respect to external determinations of the immediate present. This autonomy is that of the past, enacted and acting, which, functioning as accumulated capital, produces history on the basis of history and so ensures the permanence in change that makes the individual agent a world within a world. The habitus is a spontaneity without consciousness or will, opposed as much to the mechanical necessity of things without history in mechanistic theories as it is to the reflexive freedom of subjects 'without inertia' in rationalist theories. (Bourdieu, 1980, p. 56)

Jenkins (1992) comments that Bourdieu is good to think with. There is, indeed, pleasure in Bourdieu like there is in working out what Marx's *Theses on Feuerbach* mean or Sartre's aphorism that 'I am what I am not, and I am not what I am'. Whether there is something that one can use in research of one's own is quite another story.

Habermas on lifeworld and system

Critical theory is central to the concerns of the next chapter but Habermas's lifeworld/system scheme also raises issues comparable to those associated with Elias, Bhaskar, Giddens and Bourdieu which it is appropriate to consider now.

Habermas has referred to both lifeworld and system, and to the tensions between them, at least since *Legitimation Crisis* (1973a). It was not until *The Theory of Communicative Action* (1981), however, that they were discussed at length; the key section is the 'intermediate reflections' on system and lifeworld in volume 2. Following a review of Durkheim and Mead, Habermas argues that there is a basic distinction between society conceived 'from the perspective of acting subjects as the *lifeworld of a social group*', and society conceived from the perspective of an uninvolved outsider 'as a *system of actions* such that each action has a functional significance according to its contribution to the maintenance of the system' (1981, vol. 2, p. 117). What he wants is to make possible the *simultaneous* conception of societies as systems and lifeworlds (p. 118). His aim is thus more methodological than ontological, and this marks him off from other writers discussed in this chapter.

Habermas argues that we must go beyond the treatment of the lifeworld in terms of a philosophy of consciousness associated with Husserl, Schutz and Luckmann, and instead think of it as 'represented by a culturally transmitted and linguistically organized stock of interpretive patterns' (p. 124). But even this is too 'culturalistic'; the world of shared experience also includes social relations, institutions, and personality structures. That experience is, however, symbolically mediated – which returns us to communicative action.

I will say more about language and communicative action in the next chapter. For the moment, it is enough to acknowledge that Habermas distinguishes (a) *communicative action* which is oriented towards reaching understanding with others from (b) *instrumental action* whose orientation to success (achievement of goals) involves calculation of what others may do without seeking to influence them and (c) *strategic action* whose orientation to success also involves influencing rational opponents who could deny one success. Both instrumental action and strategic action are, says Habermas, egological, but the former is non-social in so far as it does not involve communicative exchange whereas the latter is social because it does. He further argues that the means–end schema associated with instrumental and strategic action and with the atomistic and nominalist modes of thought so prominent in our own age in economics and beyond (such as in rational choice theory) loses sight of the mutual understandings necessary to co-ordinated action. Durkheim once reminded us that the non-contractual elements in contract are fundamental to it. What Habermas does is insist that the communicative elements in purposive action are fundamental to it. Quoting Kangiesser (1976), he tells us that 'From a sociological point of view it makes sense to begin with communicative action. "The necessity for coordinated action generates in society a certain need for communication, which must be met if it is to be possible to coordinate actions effectively for the purpose of satisfying needs"' (Habermas, 1981, vol. 1, p. 274). Communicative action has a kind of priority; the analysis of strategic action abstracted from communicative action can only be distorting.

It is in this context that we can appreciate the very strong claims made for communicative action.

> Under the functional aspect of *mutual understanding*, communicative action serves to transmit and renew knowledge; under the aspect of *coordinating action*, it serves social integration and the establishment of solidarity; finally, under the aspect of *socialization*, communicative action serves the formation of personal identities. The symbolic structures of the lifeworld are reproduced by way of the continuation of valid knowledge, stabilization of group solidarity, and socialization of responsible actors. The process of reproduction connects up new situations with the existing conditions of the lifeworld; it does this in the *semantic* dimension of meanings or contents (of the cultural tradition), as well as in the dimensions of *social space* (of socially integrated groups), and *historical time* (of successive generations). Corresponding to these processes of *cultural reproduction*, *social integration*, and *socialization* are the structural components of the lifeworld: culture, society, person. (Habermas, 1981, vol. 2, pp. 137–8: author's italics)

In a later essay, Habermas set out the reproduction processes in table 3.1. The structural components call to mind Parsons's action systems, but Habermas's detailed and critical appropriation of Parsons's systems theory yields a distinctive position of his own. According to Habermas, the integration of society involves both social integration and system integration. In the lifeworld, members' 'goal-directed actions are coordinated not only through processes of reaching understanding, but also through functional interconnections that are not intended by them and are usually not even perceived within the horizon of everyday practice' (1981, vol. 2, p. 150). In capitalist societies, for example, the market interconnects the unintended, indeed often unforeseeable, consequences of individual actions. Thus where social integration depends on consensus, whether normatively or communicatively achieved, system integration requires the 'nonnormative steering of individual decisions not subjectively coordinated' (p. 150). If we identify the integration of society with social integration, we reduce society to the lifeworld. In effect, we say that everything about it is known to members and is hermeneutically accessible, and the reproduction of society is a matter only of the maintenance of the symbolic structures of the lifeworld.

If, by contrast, we equate the integration of society with system integration, we opt, Habermas argues, for the presentation of society as a self-regulating system seen from the perspective of an external observer. But this forgets that the structural patterns of action systems

Table 3.1 Contributions of reproduction processes to maintaining the structural components of the lifeworld

Reproduction processes	Structural Components		
	Culture	Society	Personality
Cultural reproduction	Interpretative schemata susceptible to consensus ('valid knowledge')	Legitimations	Behavioural patterns influential in self-formation, educational goals
Social integration	Obligations	Legitimately ordered interpersonal relations	Social memberships
Socialization	Interpretative accomplishments	Motivation for norm-conformative actions	Capability for interaction ('personal identity')

Source: Habermas (1982), p. 279

are not identifiable from without as if they were the systems of other species. On the contrary, they must first be identified 'as the lifeworlds of social groups and understood in their symbolic structures' (p. 151). Habermas's whole purpose in *The Theory of Communicative Action* is to connect the two conceptual strategies represented by lifeworld and system and thereby acknowledge that 'societies are systemically stabilized complexes of action of socially integrated groups' (p. 152).

I no more want to discuss Habermas's theory of modernity as such here than I do those of Bourdieu or Giddens, but I will have to introduce a few points about it before I can properly pass comment on Habermas's lifeworld/system scheme. Habermas argues that modernity has involved the disenchantment and rationalization of the lifeworld (a Weberian theme), and the elaboration of structural differentiation (a Durkheimian theme). The former has implications for social integration in terms of the justification of norms and the capacity to reach agreements or the lack thereof. The latter involves the uncoupling of systems from the lifeworld and makes the role of steering media like money and power both more necessary and more difficult:

> modern societies attain a level of system differentiation at which in-
> creasingly autonomous organizations are connected with one another
> via delinguistified media of communication: these systemic mecha-
> nisms – for example, money – steer a social intercourse that has been
> largely disconnected from norms and values, above all in these subsys-
> tems of purposive rational economic and administrative action that, on
> Weber's diagnosis, have become independent of their moral-political
> foundations. (Habermas, 1981, vol. 2, p. 154)

Their penetration of the lifeworld, what Habermas calls its 'mediatization', can impair the internalization and institutionali-
zation of value orientations and the ability and the willingness to reach understandings and agreements. These are the pathologies of the 'internal colonization' of the lifeworld. There are nine of them, including delegitimation, demotivation, anomie and alienation. The internal colonization of the lifeworld, however, is not irresistible. Indeed new social movements, such as the greens and the women's movement, are in the forefront of criticizing, resisting, sometimes even repelling it.

Habermas's ontology of the social is a by-product of a methodology. He wants to combine two methodological artefacts of dis-
tinguished provenance in social science – lifeworld and system – but never gets beyond biperspectivism; what the observer identifies as system changes feed into the structural components of the lifeworld which members understand for themselves, or not, as the case may be. It is hard to see how it could be otherwise without setting lifeworld and system aside and reconsidering the ontology of the social anew. There is, then, no analogue in Habermas to Elias on figuration, Bourdieu on habitus, Bhaskar on reproduction/transformation, or Giddens on structuration. Habermas attends to both lifeworld and system but he does not indicate how men and women simultaneously reproduce both in what they do.

Habermas's distinction between lifeworld and system is not a variant of the micro–macro distinction. The lifeworld includes the structures of culture, society and personality in so far as ordinary members understand them. System exceeds lifeworld, however, in so far as it refers to systemic connections between structures – connections sometimes conceived in terms of functional interdependencies and sometimes in terms of the unacknowledged conditions and the unintended, and sometimes unacknowledged, consequences of

action. One objection to this is that Habermas, as much as Parsons, starts from the assumption of a bounded system and so treats both boundedness and systematicity as axioms when they are better regarded as variables. For all his emphasis on the hermeneutic provenance of the lifeworld concept, he also risks the displacement of action by system. In connection with this, Crespi (1989) argues that Habermas omits to allow for the mutifaceted character of individual relations to the symbolic forms of the lifeworld. Real actors variously and to varying degrees internalize, acknowledge, contest, misunderstand and ignore the symbolic forms of the lifeworld whereas Habermas's too often only embrace them. Crespi goes 'in search of action' but in Habermas fails to find it.

The other side of the same coin is Habermas's tendency to attribute agency to systems, as in 'Social systems regulate their exchanges with their social and natural environments by way of coordinated interventions into the external world' (1981, vol. 2, pp. 159–60). Giddens anathematizes such attributions. How seriously Habermas intends them is often confused by his transmutation of ontology into perspectivism, as in the following passage from Habermas's next paragraph:

> What appears from the perspective of participants to be a task induced division of labor, presents itself from the system perspective as an increase in societal complexity. The adaptive capacity of an action system is measured only by what the aggregate effects of action contribute to maintaining a system in a given environment; it matters not whether the objective purposiveness of the action consequences can be traced back to purposes of the subjects involved or not. From systemic points of view as well, *power* and *exchange relations* are the dimensions in which action systems adapt themselves to the requirements of the functional specification of social cooperation. (p. 160; original italics)

In sum, Habermas sometimes appears to reproduce the very extinction of action by system that he laments in Parsons, but he then defuses the issue by suggesting that what is at stake is only how one *sees* things. Where Parsons proposes analytical *realism*, Habermas succumbs to biperspectivism.

The Theory of Communicative Action is a massive work – over nine hundred pages in translation. (There is a brilliant short summary and criticism of it in Giddens (1982b) and an impressive longer discussion in White (1988).) Its primary purpose is a reworking of critical theory via the ambivalences of the rationalization of the lifeworld (a goal and a process which I will consider in the next chapter); as it only indirectly affords an ontology of the social it is not surprising that this is not where its influence mainly lies. On the other hand the stature of its author has seemed to endorse the lifeworld/ system scheme. After all, working within that scheme Habermas has thrown out dozens of ideas which others have picked up, and it could be argued that that is justification for it enough. I disagree because I think that the constitution of society has proved too basic an issue to ignore and that the lifeworld/system scheme requires a greater justification than biperspectivism.

Habermas's scheme also has a more mundane limitation as far as the empirical research of others is concerned. Habermas elaborates his distinctions way beyond the basics discussed here in a succession of complicated figures. Theorists who do this tend to generate discussion among theorists but risk forfeiting the attention of empirical researchers (cf. Menzies, 1982). Parsons's more complicated figures defied incorporation in the research designs of others; Habermas's invite the same fate.

Bhaskar's transformational model of social activity and scientific realism

Scientific realism arose out of dissatisfaction with positivist and conventionalist epistemologies. Its advocates accuse positivists of phenomenalism, that is, of supposing that opposition to metaphysics requires the exclusion from science of unobservable entities both as objects of inquiry and as causes of observable phenomena and events. By contrast, scientific realists claim that specification of underlying realities is indispensable to the explanation of observable phenomena and events in both the natural and social worlds. They thus make a point of distinguishing naturalism, the generic idea of the unity of science, which they approve, from positivism, with its particular conception of the unity of science, which they reject. Conventionalists give different offence. They are said to open the way to relativism by arguing for the underdetermination of theory by data and the irreducibility of competing theoretical explanations to one by reference to empirical evidence alone. Instead conventions, according to Duhem, Quine, Kuhn, Feyerabend and others, play some part in both the theoretical constitution of data and the formation and selection of theories themselves. Scientific realists tend to regard conventions as arbitrary, and the problems they address as avoidable once recourse is permitted to unobservable entities. Post-empiricists disagree; they

Source: Bhaskar (1979), p. 40

regard conventions as not arbitrary but justifiable, and they refuse to privilege unobservable entities.

Scientific realism has some affinities with structural linguistics after Saussure, structural anthropology after Lévi-Strauss and structural Marxism after Althusser. It has been promoted by Harré and Secord (1972), Keat and Urry (1975), Bhaskar (1975, 1979, 1986), Benton (1977), Sayer (1984), Outhwaite (1987), Pawson (1989) and others, although as early as 1983 Stockman was able to point to important differences among its advocates. I shall concentrate on Bhaskar, paying particular attention to *The Possibility of Naturalism* (1979), because his version has the most explicit social ontology and is therefore the most instructive for my purposes. Bhaskar is probably also the single most important figure in a 'school' which has had great influence in Britain, some in Europe and an occasional impact beyond. I shall argue that Bhaskar's 'transformational model of social activity' offers a satisfactory way of conceptualizing the constitution of society provided the notion of ontological depth which accompanies it is modified and provided that certain conventions are given their due. Bhaskar would, of course, disown this manoeuvre. I will also consider whether Pawson (1989), in the latest major contribution to scientific realism, avoids what I object to in Bhaskar.

Bhaskar rejects three earlier models of the society/person connection attributed to Weber, Durkheim, and Berger and his associates (Berger and Pullberg, 1966; Berger and Luckmann, 1967), before putting forward his own. As I am here interested only in setting the context for Bhaskar's own model, I shall not discuss whether the first two attributions are fair and will comment only very briefly on the third. In Model I (see figure 3.1), 'social objects are seen as the results of (or as constituted by) intentional or meaningful human behaviour' (Bhaskar, 1979, pp. 39–40); this model provides for actions but not conditions. In Model II (see figure 3.2), social objects 'are seen as possessing a life of their own, external to and coercing the individual'

(p. 40); this model provides for conditions but not actions. Bhaskar further claims that 'the various schools of social thought – phenomenology, existentialism, functionalism, structuralism, etc. – can be seen as instances of one or other of these positions' (albeit with a little stretching) as can the varieties of Marxism. Not surprisingly, attempts have been made to synthesize the two models 'on the assumption of a dialectic in society between action and conditions' (p. 40). Model III (see figure 3.3) is the most plausible; it posits a continuous dialectic in which 'society forms the individuals who create society' and it makes no distinction between action and conditions (p. 40). Bhaskar's objection to it is that it merely compounds the vices of Model I – voluntaristic idealism – with those of Model II: mechanistic determinism. The internalization of society and the externalization of men and women are not, he complains, two moments in a dialectic because they are not related dialectically, but are, rather, 'two different kinds of thing' (p. 42). Although correct this does not do justice to Berger and Luckmann (1967); the escape they promised from the false alternative of voluntarism or determinism may not have worked but they succeeded in making the quest for an escape a priority among social theorists. One could say that the contemporary micro–macro and agency–structure debates began with them.

Bhaskar argues that men and women do not create society out of nothing; instead they work on a society which is already there. And societies do not form the individual as if he or she is a perpetual *tabula rasa*; rather, they more or less subtly reform them. Thus

> both society and human praxis . . . possess a *dual character*. Society is both the ever-present *condition* (material cause) and the continually reproduced *outcome* of human agency. And praxis is both work, that is conscious *production*, and (normally unconscious) *reproduction* of the conditions of production, that is society. One could refer to the former as the *duality of structure*, and the latter as the *duality of praxis*. (1979, pp. 43–4: author's italics)

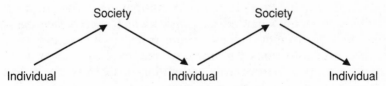

Figure 3.3 Model III: the 'dialectical' conception: 'illicit identification'
Source: Bhaskar (1979), p. 40

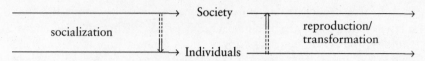

Figure 3.4 Model IV: the transformational model of the society/person connection

Source: Bhaskar (1979), p. 46

Bhaskar acknowledges Giddens (1976) as the source for 'duality of structure', and goes on to summarize his model of the society/person connection as follows:

> people do not create society. For it always pre-exists them and is a necessary condition for their activity. Rather, society must be regarded as an ensemble of structures, practices and conventions which individuals reproduce or transform, but which would not exist unles they did so. Society does not exist independently of human activity (the error of reification). But it is not the product of it (the error of voluntarism). Now the process whereby the stocks of skills, competences and habits appropriate to given social contexts, and necessary for the reproduction and/or transformation of society, are acquired and maintained could be generically referred to as '*socialization*'. It is important to stress that the reproduction and/or transformation of society, though for the most part unconsciously achieved, is nevertheless still an *achievement*, a skilled accomplishment of active subjects, not a mechanical consequent of antecedent conditions. (1979, pp. 45–6)

Despite his insistence that there is a difference in kind between society and people, Bhaskar's transformational Model IV (see figure 3.4) retains the symmetry of the dialectical Model III. There is a difference in kind in so far as 'purposefulness, intentionality and sometimes self-consciousness characterize human actions but not transformations in the social structure' (p. 44). There remains a symmetry, however, in that just as conditions set limits but do not determine, so actions have consequences which exceed their agents' intentions. One cannot read off actions from conditions, but neither can one explain actions without reference to them; similarly, one cannot read off structures from action, but neither can one account for their reproduction without reference to them.

Bhaskar (1986) later reworked his transformational model of the society/person interconnection as the transformational model of social activity (TMSA) with acknowledgements to Giddens (1976) and Bourdieu (1972). Figure 3.4 is now said to represent the 'existential interdependence of society and individuals', and the new figure 3.5 represents 'the duality of structure and praxis'.

Figure 3.6 sets out the transformational model of social activity. It displays how 'unintended consequences [cf. 1] and unacknowledged conditions [cf. 2] may limit the actors' understanding of their social world, while unacknowledged (unconscious) motivation [cf. 3] and tacit skills [cf. 4] may limit his or her understanding of him or herself' (1986, p. 126). Fortunately he complements this portrayal of human haplessness with a claim that social science offers an emancipatory benefit at each of the four cognitive limits. At (2) and (3) it can reveal the social and psychological conditions of praxis, and at (1) and (4) the effects and forms, thereby 'identifying opaque social structures and hidden motivational springs, and disclosing counterfinality and latent or unrecognised powers, etc' (pp. 126–7).

So far I have outlined Bhaskar's transformational model but I have not said anything about his conception of society as such. He derives it from Marx and calls it 'relational'. Societies, we are told, consist neither of the sum of the individuals nor of the groups within them

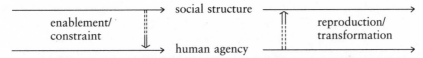

Figure 3.5 Duality of structure and praxis of the TMSA
Source: Bhaskar (1986), p. 126

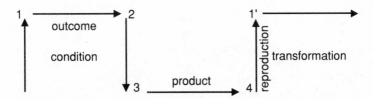

NB: 1,1' = unintended consequences
    2 = unacknowledged conditions [properties of practices]
    3 = unconscious motivation
    4 = tacit skills [properties of agents]

Figure 3.6 The transformational model of social activity
Source: Bhaskar (1986), p. 126

but, rather, of the relations between them. This may sound a bit like Elias's figurations but it is not because it is related to a notion of the stratification of reality quite unlike anything in Elias.

All action, in that it involves acting in and on a social world that is already there, reproduces or transforms that world; it is located within relations of production. Bhaskar bases himself on a passage in the *Grundrisse* in which Marx says that 'Society . . . expresses the sum of interrelations, the relations within which individuals stand' (Marx, 1857–58, p. 265). Whether Bhaskar is right to construe these ensembles of social relations not only as generative structures but also as ontologically stratified and still plead Marx in aid is open to debate. My concern here, however, is with the validity of Bhaskar's notion of ontological depth, not its provenance.

Ontological depth and the stratification of reality make their entrances in Bhaskar's characterization of explanation. Explanation involves 'the building of a model . . . of a mechanism, which *if* it were to exist and act in the postulated way would account for the phenomenon in question' (1979, p. 15). The generative mechanism postulated 'must then, of course, be subjected to empirical scrutiny' (p. 15). Once this is done, the generative mechanism must itself be accounted for in the same way. One thus has in science a three-phase schema of development in which, in a continuing dialectic, science identifies a phenomenon (or range of phenomena), constructs explanations for it, empirically tests them, and thereby identifies the generative mechanism at work which in turn becomes the next phenomenon to be explained, and so on. Science it would seem is trapped in an infinite regress, forever seeking to identify the mechanism that connects the mechanism that connects the mechanism . . .

Bhaskar summarizes this process as follows.

> Knowledge of deeper levels of reality may correct, as well as explain, knowledge of more superficial ones. In fact one finds in science a characteristic pattern of explanation and redescription of the phenomenon identified at any one level of reality. But only a concept of *ontological* depth (depending upon the concept of real strata apart from our knowledge of strata) enables us to reconcile the twin aspects of scientific development, viz. growth and change. . . . Moreover, only the concept of ontological depth can reveal the actual historical stratification of the sciences as anything other than an accident. For this can now be seen as grounded in the multi-tiered stratification of reality, and the consequent logic – of discovery – *that* stratification imposes on science. (1979, p. 16; author's italics)

It is hard to imagine a more striking example of the foundationalist desire to submit to what Rorty calls 'compulsion from the object known' (Rorty, 1980, p. 159; see above pp. 6–7).

I shall not question whether the object-world of the natural scientist is 'stratified' in the manner Bhaskar claims (although I would say that the geological metaphor is an odd choice in that the composition of one geological stratum in no way governs the composition of the stratum above it), but I do doubt whether the object-world of the social scientist is stratified quite as Bhaskar supposes. I would first emphasize something Bhaskar mentions only in passing, namely that 'Social structures, unlike natural structures, may be only relatively enduring (so that the tendencies they ground may not be universal in the sense of time-space invariant)' (1979, p. 49). As a consequence, social scientists are less likely to be engaged in identifying ever deeper levels of reality, and more likely to be concerned with new social phenomena and the structural realities which generate them. Indefinite, if not infinite, regression is less likely to beckon because investigation of new phenomena often (seems to) promises a better return on the intellectual effort invested.

Bhaskar rightly stresses that societies are open systems in which the constant conjunctions of events demanded by the Humean concept of causal law rarely occur. On the contrary, most events and phenomena in the 'actual' world that is the object of experience can be explained only in terms of a multiplicity of causes. He also argues that 'science employs two criteria for the ascription of reality to a posited object: a perceptual criterion and a causal one'; the latter has to do with 'the capacity of an entity . . . to bring about changes in material things', i.e. in the world itself as distinct from our idea of it (1979, pp. 15 and 16). It is the causal criterion which justifies reference to the reality of structures which cannot be perceived but which are capable of generating phenomena for which explanations are sought. It is very important to grasp what this capacity to generate does and does not entail. To have the capacity to generate is to govern but not to determine. It is, argues Bhaskar, in the essential nature of something that it has the capacity to generate the effects it does, but whether it actually does so generate them or not depends on whether or not other mechanisms are also at work in what are open systems. It also depends on the extent to which agents reproduce or transform the relations of production in which they are implicated.

What the social scientist has to do is identify the structures which, were they to exist, would account for the events and phenomena of the actual world. I have two objections to this. First, it implies that the actual world is wholly open and that the structures beneath the surface are relatively durable. It would, I think, be more appropriate to treat the degree of openness and closure of social systems, and the degree of durability of (any) underlying structures, as variables. Second, and crucially, it leaves unclear what the empirical work necessary to test for a posited underlying structure could consist of given that the latter does not *determine* events and phenomena in the actual world. It is, of course, Marxists of various persuasions who have most often invoked underlying realities to explain surface phenomena; but Marxists themselves differ about the structure of the capitalist mode of production and the precise nature of the mechanisms which generate both the apparent relations of capitalist and worker to each other and to the market and the (mis)understandings actual actors have of them. Take into account different types of capitalism and stages in the development of capitalism and there is added room for dispute. If non-Marxists were also to play this game, we would soon have still more alternative claims about the realities which underlie the 'same' events or phenomena, limited means of testing them empirically, and only (disputed) conventional means of reducing them to one, or of settling which reality was operative on any given occasion. Clearly the assumption of objective existence matters to a Marxist, but it would make no difference to the explanatory power of the supposed underlying reality if one were to treat it as, say, an ideal-type – which is exactly how Weber did propose to deal with Marx's formulations.

I would also challenge the heterodox character of Bhaskar's conception of an internal relation. According to Bhaskar, 'A relation R_{AB} may be defined as *internal* if and only if A would not be what it essentially is unless B is related to it in the way that it is' (1979, p. 54). Internal relations express a thing's essential nature. Now the ensembles of social relations which make up the stratified realities of the social world are all composed of internal relations. In the capitalist mode of production, for example, the relationship of bourgeoisie to proletariat is an internal one in that each would not be what it is without the other. But then so are the connectives, the causal relations which connect a deep structure with something on the surface and a deeper structure with a deep one. Indeed the connectives are treated as inherent tendencies or powers in the underlying structures. I think it is confusing to treat both relations within structures and relations between underlying structures and surface phenomena – the real and the potentially real – in the same way. There is also a tension here between a realist tendency towards totalization (as in the relation of innumerable features of modern Britain to the capitalist mode of production) and an actualist acknowledgement of contingency.

Finally, and most fundamentally of all, the geological metaphor of ontological depth, of the stratification of surface actualities and beneath-the-surface realities, is misleading. There is but one geological stratification of Salford, the city in which I work, but there is no reason to assume that there can be but one stratification of social reality there. It is one thing to argue that things seen can be explained by reference to things unseen, but it is quite another to argue that all things unseen are arrangeable in a single stratified order which has an objective existence. The privileged explanatory status of the capitalist mode of production as described by Bhaskar, for example, is not an ontological discovery but a practical convention – something justifiable in terms of the purposes it serves. As one considers what could generate an entity capable of generating some actuality, one constitutes a new object of inquiry but one does not necessarily reach greater ontological depth. Working out connections is just as often a matter of (overlapping) contexts, of extension rather than depth.

Perhaps the most valuable contribution of scientific realism will prove to be not to social ontology but to methodology. Scientific realists reject attempts to deal with the *ceteris paribus* problem by using the elaboration techniques associated with multivariate methods (Bhaskar, 1975, ch. 2). Lieberson has stated the problem as follows:

> In one form or another, we constantly encounter the following argument: 'The investigator did not control for X_{14}; had such a control been made, then the influence of X_8 on Y would be quite different from the results obtained by the investigator'. In addition, if control variable X_{14} cannot be measured adequately or is not used for some reason, someone disinclined to accept the empirically determined influence of X_8 can claim that the observed effect would be radically different if X_{14} were tossed into the statistical hopper. (1985, p. 121)

As Pawson (1989) has pointed out, 'not only is statistical closure arbitrarily drawn (the X_{14} problem) but the dilemma over whether to "partial out" or "calculate in" the effects of additional variables leaves us with ambiguity over the very meaning of a closed system' (p. 210). Realist closure differs from actualist closure in that it aims to connect actual events and phenomena not with other actual events and phenomena but with underlying realities and their generative mechanisms. These realities are assumed to be time-and-space specific and their connection to actual phenomena and events has to do with their inherent character and powers. In other words, closure is logical not physical (as in laboratory conditions) or statistical. Given that underlying realities are said to govern but not determine actual events and phenomena, their empirical confirmation presents difficulties. But these difficulties are no different from those which accompany attempts to establish the utility of any ideal-type or logical construction, such as those of classical economics, in the explanation of the actual social world or the real economy in the economists's sense of 'real'. What scientific realism can do is bring those who have turned aside from ideal-typification or classical economics or other intellectual constructions because they object to the substantive content and political import of frequently cited exemplars into greater methodological alignment with those who continue to use them.

This is one strand in Pawson's (1989) enigmatically complex, perhaps ultimately incoherent, alternative to the variable analysis he so wittily and comprehensively demolishes in his manifesto for an empirical sociology. Pawson critically endorses scientific realism; the problem is to know what his underlying realities consist of. Pawson wants to substitute generative mechanisms for variables in sociological explanation, and he makes the ontological claim that they are the basic constituents of the world (p. 154) but he refuses to endorse the notion of deep, underlying or basic structures (p. 171). Instead he locates his generative mechanisms in generative models (p. 171), i.e. in Bhaskar's terms, not in real things but in our idea of them. These models take the form of networks of related concepts (cf. the discussion of Pawson on conceptual formalism in chapter 2). But this does not of itself indicate what makes them different from non-realist models, such as those in classical economics, which also contain networks of concepts. Pawson's answer is 'that certain properties will figure prominently in scientific discourse, simply because they have so many threads converging on them'. But is this convergence generated internally by the structure of the discourse or externally by the world the discourse purports to be about? Pawson implies, but never quite says, that it is the latter. He does, after all, cling to the goal of conceptual certitude. (I am reminded of Parsons's announcement that *The Structure of Social Action* (1937) is an empirical work because the theoretical convergence upon which it builds could have occurred only because the theorists concerned were converging on how the world is.) Both Bhaskar's and Pawson's scientific realisms make additional ontological assumptions for no additional explanatory benefit – contrary to the principle of Ockham's razor. What Pawson does offer, but Bhaskar does not, is shrewd guidance on how to do sociological research.

Giddens on structuration

Giddens first referred to (class) structuration in his 1973 book *The Class Structure of the Advanced Societies*. He progressively developed it into a fully elaborated theory of (social) structuration in a series of subsequent works beginning with *New Rules of Sociological Method* (1976) and culminating in *The Constitution of Society* (1984). Of the intervening writings, the most important is *Central Problems in Social Theory* (1979), which gives the first extended treatment of issues of time and space.

Giddens picked up the term 'structuration' from the French of Piaget and Gurvitch. His use of it is different from each of theirs but passages like the following from Gurvitch would seem to have planted an idea.

> La structure sociale est un processus permanent: elle est comprise dans un mouvement de déstructuration et de restructuration perpétuelle parce qu'elle est un aspect de la société en acte, qui, en tant qu''œuvre', ne peut subsister sans l'intervention de l''acte': effort d'unification et d'orientation toujours à recommencer. (1958, p. 206)

But what does Giddens do with the notion of structuration?

Like Elias and Bhaskar, Giddens rejects the dualism of the individual and society, associating sociologies which build from the sovereign individual with subjectivism and voluntarism and sociologies which posit the priority of society with objectivism and determinism. He similarly criticizes the philosophy of action and most interpretive sociologies for concentrating on 'production' to the exclusion in practice and in comprehension of reproduction, and thus for 'not developing any concept of structural analysis at all' (1976, p. 121). Likewise, he accuses functionalism, structural Marxisms and structuralisms of treating reproduction as 'a mechanical outcome, rather than as an active constituting process, accomplished by, and consisting in, the doings of active subjects' (p. 121). Instead he insists upon the duality of structure. In his *New Rules*, rules B1 and B2 indicate what he has in mind. Echoing Marx's opening to the '18th Brumaire', B1 states that 'The realm of human agency is bounded. Men produce society, but they do so as historically located actors, and not under conditions of their choosing . . .' (Marx, 1852, p. 247;

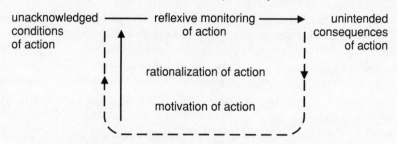

Figure 3.7 Stratification model of the agent and consciousness

Source: Modification of combined figures from Giddens (1984), pp. 5 and 7, as in Bryant and Jary (1991), p. 9

Giddens, 1976, p. 160). B2 specifies, contra Durkheim, that 'Structures must not be conceptualized as simply placing constraints upon human agency, but as enabling' (p. 161). Giddens adds that 'To enquire into the *structuration* of social practices is to seek to explain how it comes about that structures are constituted through action, and reciprocally how action is constituted structurally' (p. 161).

In order to clarify the character of action, Giddens presents his stratification model of the actor or, as he later prefers, the agent (see figure 3.7). This distinguishes between the motivation of action which may be partly unconscious but is not necessarily so, the rationalization of action (agents' articulated reasons for action), and the reflexive monitoring of action (agents' knowledge of what they are doing). Rationalization always involves discursive consciousness, or verbalization; reflexive monitoring involves either or both of discursive consciousness and practical consciousness, or unverbalized awareness. Giddens claims that many other theories have ignored practical consciousness, or what actors know but cannot put into words.

This may seem to suggest that structures are similar to the systems of which functionalists speak, but very definitely they are not. Systems, in Giddens, refer to 'The patterning of social relations across time-space, understood as reproduced practices' (1984, p. 377). They vary greatly in their 'systemness' and internal unity, but they all have an actual existence (or a real existence in the economist's sense of real); put another way, they involve 'the situated activities of human agents, reproduced across time and space' (1984, p. 25). Structures, by contrast, refer to 'systems of generative rules and resources' (1976, p. 127), or as Giddens later put it, to 'rule-resource sets, implicated in the articulation of social systems' (1984, p. 377). Structure exists only in its instantiation in interaction and in the 'memory traces' of actors.

Structures thus have only a virtual existence, 'out of time and space' (1976, p. 127). (The source for this notion of the virtual is Ricoeur (1971).) Giddens has acknowledged that his systems are like Elias's figurations – though he sees no merit in Elias's term (1989, p. 254); there is, however, no analogue to Giddens's virtual order of structures of rules and resources in Elias. It can now be seen that the 'duality of structure' means 'that social structures are both constituted *by* human agency, and yet at the same time are the very *medium* of this consti-tution' (Giddens, 1976, p. 121); or, as later formulated, the duality of structure refers to 'Structure as the medium and outcome of the conduct it recursively organizes' (1984, p. 374).

The structuring or 'structuration' of social interaction, or social relations, across time and space always involves 'three elements: the communication of meaning, the exercise of power, and the evaluative judgement of conduct' (1977, p. 132) as represented in figure 3.8. Taking the top line first, 'Structure as signification involves semantic rules; as domination, unequally distributed resources; and as legit-imation, moral or evaluative rules' (p. 133). Rules and resources are the properties of communities and collectivities; the modalities of the middle line have to do with the modes in which actors can draw upon rules and resources in the production of interaction. ' "Interpretive schemes" are the modes of typification incorporated within actors' stocks of knowledge, applied reflexively in the sustaining of commu-nication' (1984, p. 29). Facilities include command over people and resources, and norms include normative expectations of actors.

Rules, both semantic and moral, are the 'techniques or generalizable procedures applied in the enactment/reproduction of social practices' (p. 21). Resources divide into allocative, or material, and authoritative, or non-material; the former derive from dominion over things, the latter from dominion over people. Both are involved in the generation of power, the capacity to do; there is also, however, a dialectic of control whereby the controlled, and not just the control-lers, have an effect on the relation between them and the situation they share. 'The most deeply embedded structural properties, impli-cated in the reproduction of societal totalities [i.e. groups, organiz-

structure	signification	domination	legitimation
(*modality*)	interpretive scheme	facility	norm
interaction	communication	power	sanction

Figure 3.8 Dimensions of the duality of structure

Source: Variation on Giddens (1976), p. 122; (1979), p. 82; (1984), p. 29

S–D–L	Symbolic orders/modes of discourse
D(auth)–S–L	Political institutions
D(alloc)–S–L	Economic institutions
L–D–S	Legal institutions

where S = signification, D = domination, L = legitimation

Figure 3.9 Structures and institutional orders
Source: Giddens (1984), p. 32

ations, collectivities, societies]', he calls, '*structural principles*. Those practices which have the greatest time-space extension within such totalities can be referred to as *institutions*' (p. 17). Different institutional orders all involve signification, domination and legitimation, but in different proportions, as figure 3.9 shows. Time–space refers not to some framework, or set of co-ordinates, within which interaction occurs, but to the ways duration and extent enter into the constitution of social practices. Writing, for example, affords communication at a distance and over time, and clock timing affords the commodification of labour power.

Bhaskar and Giddens have each noted some similarity between the transformational model of social activity and the duality of structure (Bhaskar, 1979, pp. 44 and 50; 1986, pp. 123 and 127; Giddens, 1984, p. 26; 1985, p. 170). Even so, it is wrong to try to enlist Giddens for the realist camp as Outhwaite (1990) does. It is notable that Giddens has nowhere endorsed scientific realism. It is also significant that he has changed the way he represents the dimensions of the duality of structure. Figure 3.8 follows the third and most recent version in making structures the top line instead of the bottom as in the first two; Giddens would hardly have changed to placing structures on top if he had regarded them as underlying realities. But then, virtuality and underlying reality are not the same.

In 1982 Archer complained that structuration theory is unhelpful when trying to account for variations in the proportions of voluntarism and determinism and in degrees of freedom and constraint. In *The Constitution of Society* Giddens responds by distinguishing different senses of 'constraint' and by reminding us that there are no natural laws of society. He adds that: 'The nature of constraint is historically variable, as are the enabling qualities generated by the contextualities of human action. It is variable in relation to the material and institutional circumstances of activity, but also in relation to the forms of knowledgeability that agents possess about those circumstances' (1984, p. 179). This, however, does not deal with Archer's complaint. Are all these variations historically contingent, or can structuration theory say something about (some of) them? Giddens gives a partial answer, but it is only partial, in terms of structural principles and structural sets. Structural sets, or structures (in the plural), refer to rules and resources which hang together to make a set. Take, for example, the following, very familiar, example of capitalism:

private property: money: capital: labour contract: profit

The items in the set are internally related. One can also move from the set both to (a) the more abstract structural principle of capitalism, or class societies ('the disembedding, yet interconnecting, of state and economic institutions' (p. 183)), and to (b) the less abstract structures, the rules and resources, which, via the dimensions or axes of structuration (signification, domination and legitimation), are involved in the institutional articulation of capitalist societies. In assessing what options actors had or have, much depends on the strength of the internal connectives within the structural set and between it and the rules and resources upon which actors draw. The options which actors perceive/conceive and enact can vary greatly in number and scope. However, as Thompson (1989) has pointed out, one cannot grasp why rules and resources are setted as they are by invoking further rules and resources. There is more to structures than rules and resources and what that extra is is not captured by the notion of structural principles. Rather, it has to do with the *connections* between different rules and resources.

Structural principles and sets are only a partial answer to Archer's problem, because of the extraordinary combination of the historical and the virtual which Giddens employs. Capitalist structures are not underlying realities; quite the contrary, they belong to a virtual order. Nor are they ideal-types, as in Weber's revisions of both Marx and Menger. What they are is a historically privileged virtual order, the one which Giddens's reading about the origins and development of the modern world disposes him to think has, more than any other, been involved in its institutional articulation.

Giddens stresses that the duality of structure refers to structure as the medium and outcome of the conduct it recursively organizes. Recursion, in turn, refers to actors knowing how to follow a rule, or better, and more generally, how to go on.[5] Now if 'To study structures, including structural principles, is to study major aspects of the transformation/mediation relations which influence social and system integration' (1984, p. 377), as Giddens says it is, what has knowing how to go on got to do with transformation?

Together, these two points say something about the limits of Giddens's theory of structuration. On the one hand, it has little to say about the formation and distribution of the unacknowledged and acknowledged conditions of action or about the differential knowledgeability of actors. On the other, it has little to say about individual and collective *transformative* projects, and the differential capabilities of actors to see projects through successfully including the capacity to cope successfully with unintended consequences.

Whatever its deficiencies, structuration theory is being widely used. In *The Constitution of Society* Giddens lauded works by Willis (1977) on working-class schoolchildren in Birmingham learning to labour, Gambetta (1982) on educational opportunity in Piedmont, and Ingham (1984) on relations between the finance capital of the City of London, industrial capital and the state, all of which conform to the principles of structuration theory although they were conducted independently of it. In a later essay (1991) Giddens pointed to researches which had made some explicit use of it in a manner which he approved: viz. Burman (1988) on unemployment in Canada, Connell (1987) on gender relations in Australia, and Dandeker (1989) on surveillance, bureaucratic power and war. Users of elements of structuration theory are now too numerous to list in full. Shotter (1983) in psychology; Riley (1983), Spybey (1984), Whittington (1992), and Yates and Orlikowski (1992) on management and organizations; Roberts and Scapens (1985) and MacIntosh and Scapens (1990) on accountancy; Lee (1992) and Mellor (1993) on religion; and Shilling (1992) on education provide just some of the more notable applications.

The actual, the real, the ideal and the virtual

By way of conclusion, I shall first recover certain themes which recur in the work of Elias, Bourdieu, Habermas, Bhaskar and Giddens and then put forward a proposal of my own for dealing with the constitution of society.

Bourdieu, Habermas, Bhaskar and Giddens obtain much of the persuasive force of their ontologies from the relations they posit between two or more constituents or levels. Elias, by contrast, refers only to figurations (in which the real is identified with the actual). Figurations are dynamic – Elias abhors process reduction – but are not to be accounted for in terms of something else. Figuration is a good term because of its flexibility, as Giddens's opposition to it perversely confirms. The latter dismisses it because it adds nothing to his idiosyncratic notion of systems in which the assumption that systems are highly integrated and clearly bounded is rejected – systems without system as it were (Giddens, 1989, p. 254). But as Habermas confirms, this is precisely the assumption about systems which is usually made in both social scientific and lay discourse; anything else dissociates system from systems. Giddens's choice of term would thus seem perverse.

To say that figuration is a good term, however, is not to say that it is sufficient for an ontology of the social. Elias may abhor process reduction but he perpetrates a kind of culture reduction when, for example, he claims that without dancers dancing there is no dance. What is an unperformed choreography if it is not a dance? Is a national dance proscribed by an invading power no longer a dance? Bourdieu and Giddens deal with this issue via their notions of structure. Bourdieu argues that structures produce/deposit habits which generates practices which reproduce structure. Practices are actual, structures are real and habitus connects the two. I dislike Bourdieu's scheme because I find the constitution and composition of habitus obscure and am unsure how to clarify them. Giddens's version may also be considered obscure in so far as it refers to the virtual but I think it is possible to reformulate it and thereby remove the obscurity. For Giddens structures refer to cognitive and moral rules and to allocative and authoritative resources. They are virtual, not real, in that they exist only in instantiations in action and in memory traces. This amounts to saying that things are real only when they are activated. It is half-way to Elias's culture reduction, but only half-way in so far as it distinguishes structure from system, denies it reality but accords it virtuality. Rather than puzzle about the status of the virtual, I would prefer to say that the actual is real (as economists do in their notion of the real economy) but not all realities are actualities; and that in order to grasp the actual one often has to take into account other realities.

Treating the virtual as a kind of reality helps to dispose of the objection to Giddens's treatment of structures, made forcefully by Archer (1982, 1988), that it is incapable of specifying when there will be more determinism and when more voluntarism. Giddens's structures refer to rules and resources. Archer prefers to call rules the cultural system and notes that in Giddens it has only a virtual existence outside time and space and is operative only when instantiated by actors. She then argues that 'Since what is instantiated depends on the power of agency and not the nature of the property, then properties themselves are not differentially mutable' (1988, p. 88). In other words, rules do not constrain because agents can conform to, modify or reject them at will. She calls this 'the ontological diminution of culture', and notes that it involves denial of the autonomy of the cultural system. Giddens's response (1990) is to say that of course structures, resources as well as rules, differentially enable and constrain but they do either only as mediated by agents' reasons. Structural constraint cannot enforce like a causal force in nature. Even Marx's wage labourers forced to sell their labour power can, and on occasions do, reject one employer's labour contract for another, strike, go slow and organize politically. Structures are virtual, it seems, not just because they are out of time and space but also because they do not determine. To this I would counter that structures are real because, by Giddens's own admission, they differentially enable and constrain. Giddens's system–structure differentiation works well (although I would prefer figuration–structure) but the differential potential for enablement and constraint in his structures cannot be grasped only by reference to agency. On the contrary, the potential is also contained within the structures themselves (a point with which Bhaskar would concur). One realist axiom says that something is real if it has real effects. If this is accepted, structures are real, not virtual. On the other hand, Giddens at least provides for active and reflective agency; in Elias and in Bourdieu there is the danger of, if I may invent a term to parallel Archer's, the ontological diminution of the actor.

Although the real is more complicated than Giddens allowed, it is not necessarily stratified in the way that Bhaskar claims. Bourdieu, Bhaskar and Giddens differ from Elias in that they believe analysis of actual societies involves going beyond the actual. I have accepted Pawson's argument that actualist closure is often impossible, but I have contested Bhaskar's response to it in so far as it depends on the notions of ontological depth and the stratification of reality. In other words, I reject the false dichotomy between actualism and Bhaskar's realism in favour of the notion that there is no one way of responding to open systems which is right in all circumstances. In particular, I want to insist, contra Bhaskar (1975), that construction of ideal-types, or indeed models generally, is neither abstract nor arbitrary. Nor does it entail subscription to the thesis that the actual is more real than whatever is idealized or modelled and held to account for it, and neither does it require endorsement of nominalism or methodological individualism. To reverse a point made earlier, establishing the utility of an ideal-type or logical construction, such as those in classical economics, in the explanation of the actual social world or what economists call the real economy, is a task comparable in form and difficulty to confirming empirically the presence of an underlying reality which governs but does not determine actual events and phenomena.

I have identified what I believe to be the most influential attempts to rethink the constitution of society. I have also indicated that there are many others, and that the time has come for book-length systematic comparisons and assessments of them all. What I do not think would be helpful would be for more contenders to step forward in full or partial detachment from those already in the field, coining new terms, generating their own coteries of interpreters and users and making contemporary social scientific discourse even more complicated and fragmented than it already is. Instead I would like to encourage the abandonment of perverse usages, such as Giddens's 'system', obscure notions like Giddens's on the virtual and Bourdieu's on habitus, and schemes (often represented in figures) which are too complicated for others, especially empirical researchers with limited time, to grasp and use, such as some of those in Habermas (1981) and Bhaskar (1986).

Switching to the positive, I want to claim that any satisfactory ontology of the social has to deal with the actual, the real and the ideal, and that Elias, Bourdieu, Habermas, Bhaskar and Giddens are all relevant to this. I also suggest that social scientists will properly want to refer on occasions to societies, systems, figurations, structures, underlying realities, models and idealizations, but I doubt whether it is possible to specify in advance which will be the most relevant in what circumstances. I also suggest that it is a mistake to reserve 'structure' for either social or logical connections. Instead one should consider the various ways in which societies, systems, figurations, structures, underlying realities, models and idealizations all accommodate the dualisms/dualities of structure and agency and structure and process.[6] At the same time, I see little point in encumbering research reports with ontological elaborations. Giddens is surely right to regard structuration theory as largely a matter of sensitization, and I can understand the hostility of Elias and Bourdieu to theorizing and metatheorizing independently of empirical research even if I do not share it. In addition to the issues posed by the duality of agency and structure, the different perspectives of lifeworld and system, and the linkage of micro and macro, one has to be alive to the unlikelihood of actualist closure, the possibility of underlying (but not necessarily stratified) realities, and the more or less continuous

extension of practices and patterns of interaction and their consequences beyond conventional demarcations of time and place.

In the end, then, there are no formulaic answers to the real problem
of social structure to which Bottomore refers in the quotation at the
beginning of this chapter. Instead, ways of dealing with it appropriate
to the work in hand have always to be found and fashioned. Between
them Elias, Bourdieu, Habermas, Bhaskar and Giddens have done a
great deal to show what this is likely to entail.

4

Values in Social Science: Decisions, Justifications and Communities

[A]ll scientific theories are underdetermined by facts, . . . this being the case, there are further criteria for scientific theories that have to be rationally discussed, and . . . these may include considerations of value.
Hesse, 'Theory and value in the social sciences' (1978)

I suggest that the proposal of a social theory is more like the arguing of a political case than like a natural-science explanation. It should seek for and respect the facts where these are to be had, but it cannot await a possibly unattainable explanation. It must appeal explicitly to value judgements and may properly use persuasive rhetoric.
Hesse, 'Theory and value in the social sciences' (1978)

Introduction: the Weberian legacy

Few social scientists today subscribe in principle to any simple distinction between facts and values, but in practice many continue to conduct their research and analysis as if they did because they do not know how to address questions of value. Neither the positivist nor the Weberian traditions are much help to them. The original French positivist ambition of movement from a positive science to a positive polity, which began flamboyantly with Saint-Simon and culminated circumspectly with Durkheim, is now generally perceived to have depended upon an indefensible notion of social laws and has thus become largely a historical curiosity (Bryant, 1985, ch. 2).

More importantly, the 'Weberian' separation of facts and values to which most social scientists in consequence retreated omits to provide for rational judgement about values even when correctly formulated, in the light of Weber's modification of Rickert's theory of value relevance, as a distinction between, on the one hand, values and, on the other, facts in whose formation values enter and which are thus never value-free (1985, ch. 3). To acknowledge that values enter into the constitution of facts is to say nothing, Weber insisted, about the validity of the values concerned. Rejection of crude misreadings of Weber in favour of a distinction between valuations and value-related facts still does not indicate how questions of value should be addressed.

In chapter 2 (pp. 20–24) I noted that both Rickert and Weber argued that the 'objectivity' of a historical account is limited by the empirical currency of the value to which it is related in the community of which the investigator is a member. There is, however, a crucial difference between them. Where Rickert viewed different national accounts with equanimity whilst passing over the possibilities of different sectional accounts within the national community, Weber seems positively to have welcomed competing sectional and individual accounts and the consequent interminable rewriting of history. Where Rickert conserved, Weber subverted. And where many since have conceived the maturity of a social science in terms of the subscription of all its practitioners to a common set of principles and practices (a Kuhnian paradigm or disciplinary matrix), Weber delighted in the prospect that the historical sciences are among those 'to which eternal youth is granted' (Weber, 1904, p. 104). In short, Weber refuses to justify the values which inform objects of inquiry by referring to tradition or community – precisely the practice to which MacIntyre (1981) would return us (see below) if only the historical conditions in which it were possible had not been displaced. Indeed, in the interests of intellectual innovation, Weber famously proposed the appointment of an atheist to a chair in theology and an anarchist to a chair in law.

Despite his exclusion of value choice and justification from science, Weber did not argue that empirical sciences can contribute nothing to the making of moral and political choices and the formulation of responses to practical problems. On the contrary, they can help by recommending how given values and ends may best be realized (compare the idea of 'optimum means'); they can identify alternatives forfeited once resources are devoted to a particular course of action (compare the idea of 'opportunity cost'); and they can clarify the consequences of a given course of action oriented towards a given end (compare the idea of 'cost–benefit analysis'). They cannot, however, justify judgements as to what is a benefit and what a cost; nor, most emphatically, can they establish what any individual or collectivity should want, or what his, her or its values should be. Science can, it is true, point up inconsistencies in the elaboration of value standpoints; it can expose conflicts in the simultaneous subscription to two or more values; and it can generally help the individual to make up his or her mind, or the collectivity reach a decision, by bringing order to matters which are often confused or contradictory. Even here, however, it can never absolve the individual of responsibility for deciding his or her own commitments.

In Weber's view, advocates of a particular policy may recommend it on the basis of testable propositions ('it will have the following effects') but even if these propositions prove false they can always embrace an ethic of conviction in which certain values and standards are endorsed as the basis of right action regardless of the consequences. Conversely, it is usually possible to conceive more than one policy which is consistent with any given set of social scientific findings. Practical action, the formation and execution of policies, according to Weber, always involves choices. Social scientists can never remove the citizen's obligation to choose.

Weber returned to the issues of the responsibilities of social scientists and citizens in the two Munich addresses to students published in 1919. In the science address Weber agrees with Tolstoy that 'Science is meaningless because it gives no answer to the question, the only question important for us: "What shall we do and how shall we live?"' (1919b, p. 143). We have no alternative but that 'each finds and obeys the demon who holds the fibres of his very life' (p. 156). Not everyone, however, answers to the same demon, not everyone embraces the same value: in consequence, struggle between the *dévotés* of different values is inevitable. Weber conceives politics in terms of power, domination, conflict, violence and legitimacy, and struggle between those who embrace different values lies at its very heart. Science can assist in the ways mentioned above, but that is all. As Weber presents ultimate values as warring gods, as demons, almost as Durkheimian sacred things, beyond the reach not only of science but of rational discourse, it is hardly surprising that, after the horrors of the Third Reich, the Frankfurt School should have rejected this Nietzschean view of politics. It is not, however, the whole story.

Weber tempered his politics with an ethic of responsibility. In the politics address, Weber contrasts such an ethic with an ethic of conviction. The latter posits an end which must never be compromised, it justifies the means to that end, and it absolves the individual of responsibility for the consequences of acting in accordance with it. Weber gives as examples the Christian who does rightly and leaves the results with the Lord, and the convinced syndicalist who closes his mind to the likelihood that his action will prove counterproductive (1919a, p. 120). An ethic of conviction, or ultimate ends, holds unconditionally, and those who adhere to it are merely the instruments of God's will, or the servants of history, or whatever. By contrast, an ethic of responsibility requires the individual to assess an end in the light of the means necessary to its realization, and to take responsibility for the consequences of any action in pursuit of it. It is therefore much more calculating and much more dependent upon nomological regularities, including those pertaining to human frailties and irresolution; there is an affinity, then, between an ethic of responsibility and instrumental knowledge that affords control over social processes.

Weber abhors the prospect of men and women in general – and politicians in particular – without convictions, he acknowledges that without pursuit of the impossible the possible would often not be attained either, and he agrees that we must all have some sticking point at which we can only declare, as Luther did, 'Here I stand, I can do no other.' But he also prefers that an ethic of conviction always be overlaid by an ethic of responsibility. In Weber's judgement, to negotiate, to compromise, to conclude that means, costs, consequences are, in the circumstances of the day, out of proportion to ends is not to betray those ends; rather, it is to act realistically. Others may have perverted *Realpolitik* into unprincipled opportunism or the *de facto* formula that might is right, but in Weber's eyes it offers the possibility of acting responsibly. There is for Weber as much honour in heeding the consequences of one's actions as there is in any ethical politics in which it is assumed that ultimately good always flows somehow or other from acting rightly. There is also less danger because those who can compromise with honour are less likely to visit suffering on their fellows than those who cannot.

In practice, what Weber does here is advance a reasonable and persuasive case for an ethic of responsibility as a means of accommodating different primary values. Commitment to the secondary value of accommodation is arguable, it seems, even when commitment to primary values, such as his own nationalism, brooks no argument. Weber's legacy thus turns out to be more complicated than it first appears. On the one hand there is the claim that values ultimately rest beyond the pale of rational discourse; on the other there is the reasonable and persuasive case made for the value of accommodation in the context of an ethic of responsibility.

The first part of the legacy, the notion that values ultimately rest beyond the pale of rational discourse, is both the more familiar one and the one repeated in different guises in subsequent debates about 'is' and 'ought' in twentieth-century social science and moral philosophy. It was an American advocate of a critical sociology, C. Wright Mills, who expressed most graphically the limits to reason in those, like Weber, who reject the 'naturalistic fallacy' and deny that ought can be derived from is:

> We cannot deduce – Hume's celebrated dictum runs – how we ought to act from what we believe is. Neither can we deduce how anyone else ought to act from how we believe we ought to act. In the end, if the end comes, we just have to beat those who disagree with us over the head; let us hope that the end comes seldom. In the meantime, being as reasonable as we are able to be, we ought to argue. (1959, p. 77)

If all else fails, violence, or the threat of violence, is what brings others into line. It is also significant that Mills assumes that subscription to values and norms is a matter of individual choice.

Mills's position is similar to what in moral philosophy is called emotivism, as here defined by MacIntyre (1981):

> Emotivism is the doctrine that all evaluative judgments and more specifically all moral judgments are *nothing but* expressions of preference, expressions of attitude or feeling, insofar as they are moral or evaluative in character. . . . [M]oral judgments . . . are neither true nor false; and agreement in moral judgment is not to be secured by any rational method, for there are none. It is to be secured, if at all, by producing certain non-rational effects on the emotions or attitudes of those who disagree with one. (pp. 11–12)

Here agreement on values is still beyond reason, but is connected not to (the threat of) force but to appeals to the emotions (which do, however, include fear). MacIntyre, of course, is disturbed by emotivism and would like to recover an older notion of virtue and the moral life which situates them within tradition and community and connects them to self-realization and the living of an authentic life within terms whose very meaning is sustained by tradition and community. His problem is the irreversible disintegration of tradition and community associated with modernity and perpetrated, above all, by capitalism. In *After Virtue* (1981) he finds it conspicuously difficult to specify what the moral life after virtue could consist of.

Where MacIntyre endorses an alternative to emotivism, Habermas rejects 'decisionism' – the treatment of values in Weber and others as axioms which are beyond reason, and the reduction of norms to the arbitrary decisions of individuals. Decisionism supposes that 'decisions relevant to the praxis of life, whether they consist in the acceptance of values, in the selection of biographical [*lebensgeschichtlich*] design, or in the choice of an enemy, are not accessible to rational consideration and cannot form a rationally substantiated consensus' (1963, p. 266). Mills endorsed argument about values but had nothing to say about the forms it could take. Habermas has, I shall indicate, had a great deal to say about rationally substantiated consensus; unlike MacIntyre, he is not haunted by a world we have lost but, rather, retains his faith in the possibilities of reason.

The second part of the legacy, the demonstration that reasonable and persuasive cases can be made for particular values, is the one I want to explore further in this chapter. First, I shall offer brief comments on Rawls on justice, Habermas on discourse ethics, and some feminists on epistemology. Then I shall argue a position on the relationship between social science, moral inquiry and political philosophy. Three themes will run through both, the pros and cons of republics of the head and habits of the heart, the use of normative counterfactuals, and relations between primary and secondary values. The notion of 'republics of the head' comes from Wolfe (1989), the notion of 'habits of the heart' originates with Tocqueville (1835 and 1840), and the distinction between primary and secondary values figures in MacIntyre (1967).

Rawls on justice

Rawls's theory of justice as fairness has been articulated in a number of essays from 1958 to 1975 and beyond, but his *magnum opus* is *A Theory of Justice*, published in 1971. It has generated a massive critical literature, of which Barry (1989) is a particularly distinguished example. Rawls's theory makes use of a distinctive restatement of social contract and rational choice theories:

> the guiding idea is that the principles of justice for the basic structure of society are the object of the original agreement. They are the principles that free and rational persons concerned to follow their own interests would accept in an initial position of equality as defining the fundamental terms of their association. (1971, p. 11)

In the original position, individuals are supposed to think instrumentally about justice in terms of the rules which should govern the pursuit of individual self-interest, without knowing what their own interests, talents, social positions, even gender, are. About these they remain behind 'a veil of ignorance'. Rawls's theory is, as he says himself in his seminal article, 'Justice as fairness', a development within the tradition which treats justice as a pact between rational egoists (1958). In Rawls's version of justice as fairness, rational egoists are presumed to recognize two notions of justice, justice as mutual advantage and justice as impartiality; the (abstract) principle of justice should appeal to everyone, the restraints of justice being preferable to the war of all against all, and the (actual) principles of justice should be chosen impartially, that is, without favouring the interests of some over others.

Rawls supposes that under the conditions of the original position we can all recognize that rational individuals would agree to two principles of justice, those of equality and difference, which he initially states as follows:

> First: each person is to have an equal right to the most extensive basic liberty compatible with a similar liberty for others.
>
> Second: social and economic inequalities are to be arranged so that they are both (a) reasonably expected to be to everyone's advantage, and (b) attached to positions and offices open to all. (1971, p. 60)

The first principle ascribes to individuals rights to free speech, assembly, political activity, conscience, personal property and the rule of law. The second proposes that the distribution of wealth, income, power, authority and status should be for the benefit of all, and leads on to the proposition that no change in distribution can be justified unless there is a benefit for all including the least advantaged or worst off. It bears upon such fundamentals as access to power and influence; the acquisition, accumulation and transmission of personal and corporate property; educational and other opportunities to acquire the means of entry to advantaged social positions; and the operation of the fiscal system.

The original position is a normative counterfactual. No claim is made that principles of justice have ever historically been arrived at in this way; what is being claimed is that principles which it is reasonable to suppose would have been arrived at under these conditions are thereby fair. The veil of ignorance ensures that no one is naturally or socially advantaged when choosing principles of distributive justice, and no one can choose principles which favour their own particular interests and circumstances because they do not know what they are. On the other hand, Rawls does assume that it is rational to cover against the possibility that one will be one of the least advantaged rather than gamble on the probability that one will not.

The device of the original position is open to fundamental objections which I shall come to in due course, but I want to make one point in its favour immediately. It underwrites the difference principle and this has provided a critical standard of some purchase in the 1980s. Thatcherite liberalization of the economy, including the reduction of the top rate of income tax in Britain from 83 to 40 per cent, was justified by its advocates in terms of the accelerated economic growth, from which all would benefit, which would follow. The gap between rich and poor would widen but trickle-down would ensure that the poor were less poor (absolutely) than they were before. By contrast, it is now confirmed that in Britain the incomes of the poorest 20 per cent of households have declined absolutely since the Conservatives came to power in 1979.[1] Rawls's difference principle allows inequality but adjudges this aspect of 1980s neo-liberalism unjust.

For all its intellectual challenge, there are two fundamental flaws in Rawls's theory of justice – it is intolerably paradoxical (some might say incoherent) and it is unsociological. Somewhat like Kohlberg (1963, 1969), Rawls argues that morality passes through three stages. In the first, that of authority, we accept moral precepts from our superiors, as children do, because we are not able to judge them for ourselves. In the second, that of association, we do what is expected of us; we honour our obligations because we know that the associations of which we are part and from which we benefit require that we should. In the third, that of principle, we neither do as we are told by our elders and betters nor conform to the expectations inscribed in role or association; rather, we embrace abstract standards and principles – such as those of justice. The last two stages are a little like the other- and inner-directed character types described by Riesman (1950) except that Rawls's development is from other to inner, the opposite of Riesman's, and Rawls characterizes principle in a special way. The principles to which we subscribe in our moral maturity, according to Rawls, are those consistent with 'natural human attitudes in a well-ordered society', namely those for which consent would be given in the original position (1971, p. 490). It is thus hard to know what the 'original' in the original position means as the latter can be imagined as the founding moment of justice only in conditions of moral maturity. The persons without qualities who occupy the original position are presumed to have a prior interest in principles of justice which is itself a product of lengthy moral maturation – apparently there can be no beginning until the end. What we seem to have is an enchanting thought experiment for clever grown-ups in a disenchanted age.

This is not the only paradox of the original position. Justice, by definition, places limits on individual self-interested action. But persons without qualities in the original position are held to seek and arrive at the principles of justice by conforming to an instrumental rationality and self-interest restrained only by the veil of ignorance. They have no interest in the interests of others. Justice would thus seem the ironic product of persons deemed to have acted without reference to it.

In Rawls's well-ordered society there are divisions of labour, interdependence, co-operation and solidarity, but, as Wolfe notes, there is 'little or no sociology to provide the glue of moral obligation' (1989, p. 124). It is about a human nature and a universal justice that know nothing of the particularisms of real cultures and real societies, real social relations and real encounters. Men and women love not other men and women, but humankind. 'Rawls's moral vision is one in which we are all tied together by our common intellectual respect for the rules of justice. This', Wolfe concludes, 'is a republic of the head, not the heart' (p. 124).

Rawls's theory is unsociological because it tries to justify a theory of justice by transcending how real people generate and sustain notions of justice, fairness, reciprocity and loyalty in the circumstances of real life. Real men and women, however, are not just rational egoists. This prompts Wolfe to complain that Rawls's theory

> teaches people to distrust what will help them most – their personal attachments to those they know – and value what will help them least – abstract principles that for all their brilliance, are a poor guide to the moral dilemmas of everyday life. By upholding a world of perfect thinkers, it has little of relevance to say to imperfect doers. (p. 125)

The reason for this, Wolfe continues, is that Rawls thinks of individuals as the alternative to government when he should have thought of civil society. His, like other liberal theories without society, leaves individuals to look to the state to satisfy their needs and wants when they cannot meet them themselves, and to complain indignantly when it fails to do so. It overlooks civil society and has the state formulating policy in more and more areas not formerly its concern. Without civil society, the strong state, however ironically, is bound to end up the accompaniment of the free economy. Yet it can disappoint only those who expect so much of it. If I understand Wolfe rightly, it is, in

Durkheim terms, like expecting the state to guarantee all the non-contractual elements in contract. Or, to echo Tocqueville (1835 and 1840), the generation of real justice from generation to generation involves habits of the heart – in this case appreciations of fairness, reciprocity, loyalty and decency acquired in the experience of real social relations and exchanges. In other words, what Rawls calls the morality of (universal) principle is in reality always mediated by experience of (particular) associations.

The theory is also unsociological in so far as it takes no account of time and space. The difference principle says that there should be no losers in changes of distributive justice. Chancellor Kohl said there would be no losers in the unification of Germany in 1990. In the short term there have been, especially among the unemployed in the former East Germany. In the longer term there may not be. Application of Rawlsian principles in real time is not straightforward. The same can be said about real space. No real societies (or associations or organizations) are wholly self-contained: when the Thatcherite governments in Britain in the 1980s reduced the percentage of gross domestic product spent on overseas aid, there were no British losers but there were losers in the Third World. The omission of time–space in Rawls's theory impairs its application in real circumstances in which time–space has always to be considered.[2]

I have suggested that Rawls's theory of justice is flawed. The paradoxes of the original position render it less compelling to intellectuals than it first appears, and the attempt to transcend the untranscendable, human association, ensures that it does not speak to the experience of ordinary citizens. Even so, it does show brilliantly that, with the aid of a normative counterfactual, values can be brought within the terms of rational discourse.

Habermas's discourse ethics

The 'ideal-speech situation' is central both to Habermas's theory of knowledge and to his ethics. He now largely avoids the term because, he says, it has been hypostatized by others (1990, p. 164); but he still subscribes to the notion to which the term refers and I will go on using it. The ideal-speech situation is also, in my view but not in his, a normative counterfactual only. I shall therefore have to justify a different view of its critical value. There are interesting discussions of Habermas's discourse ethics in White (1988), Rasmussen (1990) and Poole (1991).

Habermas regards truth as the product of rational consensus, and as such it is universal and objective. Rational consensus is the outcome of an ideal-speech situation: that is, a situation in which all parties have equal opportunities to speak and equal competence in speaking, there are no asymmetries of power and influence between them, and where, freed from both internal and external forces (of compulsion and repression), they are persuaded by the 'unforced force of the better argument' (quoted in McCarthy, 1978, p. 292; also Habermas, 1990, p. 163).

What is the status of this idealization? It is, after all, at variance with a modern world in which, Habermas insists, many practices, including many integral to capitalism, depend upon the systematically distorted communication associated with manipulative half-truths and deception, unequal access to knowledge and inequality of both communicative opportunity and competence. Habermas (1973b) argues that the ideal-speech situation can be thought of as a normative counterfactual (like Rawls's original position), or a Kantian regulative idea, but is better acknowledged for what it really is – something transcendental anticipated in all speech and thus in all discourse. 'The ideal speech situation would best be compared with a transcendental illusion were it not for the fact that . . . this illusion is also the constitutive condition of rational speech' (quoted in McCarthy, 1978, p. 210). The reasoning behind this claim becomes clearer in Habermas's essay on universal pragmatics:

> anyone acting communicatively must, in performing any speech action, raise universal validity claims and suppose that they can be vindicated [or redeemed: *einlösen*]. . . . The speaker must choose a comprehensible [*verständlich*] expression so that speaker and hearer can understand one another. The speaker must have the intention of communicating a true [*wahr*] proposition . . . so that the hearer can share the knowledge of the speaker. The speaker must want to express his intentions truthfully [*wahrhaftig*] so that the hearer can believe the utterance of the speaker (can trust him). Finally, the speaker must choose an utterance that is right [*richtig*] so that the hearer can accept the utterance and speaker and hearer can agree with one another in the utterance with respect to a recognized normative background. (1976, pp. 2–3: square brackets inserted by McCarthy, the translator)

Communicative action can continue undisturbed only if the parties believe that the four validity claims which they reciprocally raise – viz. (grammatical) comprehensibility or intelligibility, truth, the truthfulness or sincerity of the speaker (who would otherwise not be believed even when speaking the truth), and rightness (choice of utterances appropriate to context or the speaker will not be listened to) – are justified. Habermas acknowledges that communication is often distorted, even systematically distorted, but he holds that communication, and thus human life, would be impossible if the four validity claims were not redeemable most of the time. The lie, for example, can succeed only where most utterances are true. In this way, Habermas (1983) privileges what would otherwise be a normative counterfactual by claiming a 'transcendental-pragmatic' status for the ideal-speech situation and undistorted communication. It should also be noted that whereas Rawls's original position makes no assumptions about the interaction of the participants – the pact between rational egoists is apparently spontaneous – the ideal-speech situation cannot be other than social because it has to do with communicative interaction.

There is much which is contestable about Habermas's theory, but there is also a lot to be said for a modified version of it which makes fewer claims and connects more easily to real life. It was the American pragmatist, Peirce, who provided Habermas with the key to the ideal-speech situation. Peirce originated the notion that the possibility of scientific truth presupposed a counterfactual scientific community of interpreters, 'extended ideally in social space and historical time', which could judge the validity of scientific truth claims (Habermas, 1991, p. 53). In other words, there is an inescapable procedural element in scientific truth. Claims to truth have to do not only with correspondence with reality but also with appeals to others judged fit to assess them. What Habermas has done is to articulate the conditions in which a community of truth seekers reaches a consensus solely on the merits of the better argument, and to claim that our use of language cannot do other than anticipate such a possibility.

I want to set aside the transcendental claim for two reasons, the first of which I can only assert here.[3] I contend that our use of language does not anticipate anything; instead it serves our current practical purposes. For these the paradigm case is not the perfectly rational consensus but, rather, the agreement sufficient for the purpose in hand – an agreement which seldom needs, let alone obtains, perfect rational consensus. Indeed I suspect there is much to be said for Baudelaire's aphorism that 'If, by some misunderstanding, people understand each other, they would never be able to reach agreement' (quoted in Poole, 1991, p. 78). Even if I am wrong in my challenge, however, there is another reason for setting the transcendental claim aside: it is unnecessary in that a modified version of the ideal-speech situation as a normative counterfactual has more use as a basis for practical criticism.

Habermas assumes that undistorted communication in an ideal-speech situation will always issue in rational consensus. By contrast, I cannot see why it should not sometimes issue in rational dissensus. I cannot see why, even after emancipation from internal compulsion and external repression, reason should be able to dissolve all differences of language and value. But I also think this matters less than Habermas does. Habermas wants to equate objectivity with a universal rational consensus. Rational consensus, so defined, is thus different from a freely negotiated compromise between subscribers to two or more particular constructions. Well, so it may be, but I think the secondary value of accommodation which freely negotiated compromise best embodies is worthwhile in its own right and is of greater practical application because it does not suppose there are even counterfactual conditions in which all differences of language and value can be dissolved.

Habermas grounds his ethics in the same way as his theory of truth. 'If rightness as well as truth can qualify as a discursively redeemable validity claim, it follows that right norms must be capable of being grounded in a way similar to true statements' although the structure of argumentation will be different (quoted in McCarthy, 1979, p. 311).[4] No one should be excluded, everyone should be able to make their claims and criticize those of others, and the only valid norms are those which it is agreed regulate common interests. Argumentation differs in so far as it involves not the logic of necessity but the rhetoric of cogency and persuasion, but it is still the unforced force of the better argument which should prevail.

Favouring an objectivist approach to ethics, Habermas seeks a principle of universalization for moral and practical discourse. He argues that every valid norm has to fulfil the following condition: '(U) All affected can accept the consequences and the side effects its general observance can be anticipated to have for the satisfaction of everyone's interests (and these consequences are preferred to those of known possible alternative possibilities for regulation)' (1983, p. 65). But can norms be so justified? Habermas's principle of discourse ethics – '(D) Only those norms can claim to be valid that meet (or could meet) with the approval of all affected in their capacity as participants in a practical discourse' (p. 66) – is idle if they cannot. Habermas says that discourse ethics has to assume that normative validity claims have cognitive meaning and can be treated like cognitive validity claims, and that real discourse – dialogue not monologue, communicative action not the individual calculation of a Rawlsian rational egoist – takes place.

The first of these assumptions is easier to sustain than the second. Norms regulate legitimate chances for the satisfaction of needs. Argument about norms centres on the consequences for different people and groups with regard to the satisfaction of generally accepted needs; in other words, normative claims are open to cognitive validation. Only those norms about which there is *rationally motivated consensus* are valid – which is a very different matter from Rickert's empirical currency. Rationally motivated agreements of this kind may not justify the norms which actually exist and may prompt the demand for others. This, for Habermas, gives practical discourse an objectively justified critical standard. But how does one get the rationally motivated, and thus binding, agreed standard in the first place? Habermas is informative on what would count as objectively valid norms, but uninformative on their achievability under real conditions.

Habermas (1983, 1990), like Rawls, has been influenced by the developmental psychology of Kohlberg. He has also modified his own position to take account of the objection to Kohlberg raised by Carol Gilligan. This episode throws interesting light on the practical value of discourse ethics. As already mentioned, Kohlberg (1971) described three levels of moral development which occur in all cultures. At the pre-conventional level, the child responds to rules about right and wrong, and good and bad, in terms of rewards and punishments. At the conventional level, there is conformity to the expectations of one's family, group or nation out of loyalty and a wish to sustain its integrity. At the post-conventional level, there is an attempt to define values and principles of general validity and application which transcend the individual's own affiliations. This last is what discourse ethics aims to generate.

Gilligan (1982) contrasts the Kantian 'ethic of justice' favoured by Kohlberg following experimental research on the moral thinking of men – an ethic which centres on rights, fairness, balancing claims, separation and individual autonomy – with the 'ethic of responsibility and care' indicated by her work on the moral thinking of women – an ethic which hinges on compassion, avoidance of harm, context-sensitivity, connectedness and interdependence (cf. White, 1988, pp. 83–4). Given the gendering of experience, this second voice of morality has, since Kant, spoken mostly, though not exclusively, through women. Habermas acknowledges the significance of Gilligan's research and has modified his own theory accordingly – a process facilitated by Gilligan's claim that in mature moral thinking 'dialogue replaces logical deduction as the mode of moral discovery' and that in dialogue there is 'a process of communication to discuss the other's position and discern the chain of connections through which the consequences of action extend' (1983, p. 45).

Habermas (1983) argues that the two voices of morality represented by Kohlberg and Gilligan are better viewed as two aspects of a single richer voice. Put another way, it is necessary to synthesize two aspects of morality: moral principles (*Moralität*) and ethical life (*Sittlichkeit*). *Moralität* is about 'universalistic criteria of justice and the abstract judging of different institutional orders'; *Sittlichkeit* deals with 'concrete relationships and value configurations peculiar to given forms of life' (White, 1988, p. 84). In the modern rationalized lifeworld, moral questions are first questions of justice. Thinking about them in these terms, however, does not necessarily yield implementable solutions in real conditions of conflict. It takes hermeneutic skill and 'sensitivity to context' to relate general criteria to specific situations. As Habermas says, 'Moral issues are never raised for their own sake; people raise them seeking a guide to action. For this reason the demotivated solutions that postconventional morality finds for decontextualized issues must be reinserted into practical life' (1983, p. 179). In view of this, it is appropriate that he should have entitled his second book on discourse ethics *Justification and Application* (1991). Justification aims at universalization and objectivity; application requires appropriateness in context (which, one might add, is more easily invoked than justified). Habermas's response to Gilligan (and Benhabib, 1987) has also pointed up how he differs from Rawls. Where Rawls is unsociological, Habermas draws very heavily upon the sociological tradition.

The distinction between morality and ethical life has also enabled Habermas to minimalize the claims made for discourse ethics.[5] Morality is universal; it has to do with what is equally good for all, in other words with justice. The modern world is pluralist, and 'what is capable of commanding universal assent becomes restricted to the *procedure* of rational will formation' (Habermas, 1990, p. 150). If we want to settle questions of everyday coexistence, not by overt or covert force, 'but by the unforced conviction of a rationally motivated agreement, then we must concentrate on those questions that are amenable to impartial judgement' and an appeal to generalizable interest (p. 151). These are few compared with the mass of evaluative questions with which life confronts us. Were we to follow Habermas, the objectivity of discourse ethics could triumph only at the expense of its usefulness.

Viewed as a normative counterfactual only, the devices of the ideal-speech situation and undistorted communication themselves constitute a critical standard which can be applied in real conditions. One does not have to believe in the possibility of the full realization of the ideal-speech situation to examine whether changed practices and policies have taken those involved nearer to a situation in which the unforced force of the better argument prevails. Nor does one have to assume that the ideal-speech situation would yield the rational consensus about truth, right or goodness for which, in the name of objectivity, Habermas craves – for the device also specifies the conditions for freely negotiated compromise. Of course it may then serve to justify only the secondary values of accommodation and compromise, but that has real worth in a world of different ideologies and religions – as Habermas himself concedes. In this amended form Habermasian ideas already have extensive currency. Giddens (1992), for example, identifies democracy in all contexts from personal relations to polities large and small with openness, dialogue, negotiation, compromise where necessary, and the autonomy of the participants – in short with discussion and 'the chance for the "force of the better argument" to count' – without citing Habermas (Giddens, 1992, p. 186). But what one cannot do is identify particular rationally motivated and binding norms in advance of achievement of undistorted communication. That achievement may credibly be secured in very local contexts of place and association, and it may sometimes be approximated elsewhere – but not closely and not often, as Habermas's own analysis of the contemporary public sphere confirms (Habermas, 1962).

Lessons from feminism

Femininist writing in the social sciences and philosophy is highly diverse and much contested by feminists themselves, let alone anyone else (cf. Stanley and Wise, 1983; Stanley, 1990; and the responses of Ramazanoglu, 1992, and Gelsthorpe, 1992, to a male commentator, Hammersley, 1992, on feminist methodology). My aim here is not to review this complex literature, but to extract from it some contributions which, taken together, indicate a more justified way of responding to the Weberian legacy, from which we all can learn, than emotivism and decisionism.[6]

Lengermann and Niebrugge-Brantley (1990) argue that feminist sociological theory applies three standards when assessing the truth of a proposition or 'knowledge construct': evidential base (connection to lived experience); theoretical congruity (connection to feminist sociology's model of gender stratification and social production); and practical effectiveness in addressing problems viewed as central by the theoretical community (principally the elimination of all forms of domination and the equal empowerment of differentially situated actors).

The third of these, it seems to me, combines value-relatedness and practical value, and is developed in a way which refers to all who are disadvantaged. In the case of women, the value which informs feminist social science is woman-centredness, i.e. sensitivity to the situation, experience and potential of women. This requires opposition to patriarchy. The concept of patriarchy is contestable in a number of ways but I suggest that at a minimum it refers to the determination of women's life chances by men, or, perhaps better, by practices and institutions which have served the interest of male domination and which are to be found in all societies. In effect, feminists supply reasons, which are examinable in debate and the light of research evidence, why woman-centred social science should be pursued. These have to do not just with abstract notions of equity but also with the benefits for all, men included, which would flow from the overcoming of patriarchy. One example here would be the generation of a morality which combines the ethics of justice and of care and responsibility – a project whose very conception has depended on an opening up to the different voice to which Gilligan's research on the moral thinking of women attends (cf. Phillips, 1992). In short, feminist social science, so conceived, is intrinsically transformative in intent. Its critical mission is the advancement of women for the benefit of all humankind.

The position I have just outlined is consistent with a sophisticated-standpoint epistemology but not with a crude one. Feminist epistemology insists that all knowledge is situated. It argues that empiricist science aimed at an objective knowledge in which the identity and interests of the knower had no place – what might be called the view from nowhere. In social science this was associated with 'positivism' and the emulation of natural science. Much feminist epistemology can be seen as one contributant to the broader development of a post-empiricist alternative. Much, too, embraces the principle, which is also a sociological commonplace, of the social construction of knowledge or 'naturalistic epistemology'. And in social science many 'feminist' criticisms of 'positivism' have as often been made by men. There are thus numerous similarities, sometimes acknowledged, sometimes not, with arguments put forward by Marx, Weber, Wittgenstein, Duhem, Quine, Kuhn, Feyerabend, Hanson, Habermas, Rorty, and the Edinburgh School in the sociology of science (Barnes, 1974; Bloor, 1976; etc.) – and also Hesse, a woman but not a feminist; as Alcoff and Potter (1993) concede, the feminist orientation towards mainstream views involves appropriation and respect as well as criticism and rejection. Having said all that, some feminists are instructive on what precisely the alternative to the view from nowhere is.

According to Harding (1993), standpoint theories start research off from the objective social location of the subordinated, disadvantaged and marginalized. Starting off from women's lives, for example, provides the grounding for less partial and distorted accounts of women's lives, men's lives, and indeed the whole social order, than starting off with the understandings of dominant groups. Women's standpoint is epistemologically advantaged and thus provides a necessary, though not sufficient, condition for the maximization of objectivity by the researcher. One is reminded of the claims for epistemic privilege made by Marx and Lukács on behalf of the workers as a universal class (rather than claims for the intellectual innovation to be expected from appointment of an atheist to a chair of religion, or an anarchist to a chair of law, made by Weber). The trouble with this approach, as Bat-Ami Bar On (1993) has pointed out, is that one ends up with multiple claims for epistemic privilege on the part of numerous groups disadvantaged by gender, class, ethnicity or any other factor in the structuring of social inequality, and multiple idealizations of their particular practices. This, she continues, ought to prompt abandonment of all claims for epistemic privilege; claims for epistemic privilege have, however, served to empower movements of oppressed people by giving them belief in their authority to speak and might in these circumstances be deemed to have been justified.

Cain (1990) has offered a way of defending feminist standpoints (in the plural) without claiming epistemic privilege. She connects the location of the subject to the knowledge produced (by, *inter alia*, invoking arguments about the social construction of knowledge and the constitution of objects of inquiry) without claiming that the first determines the second. She then justifies knowledge acquisition by reference to claims for both the shared character of the standpoint and the utility of the knowledge gained for those who share it. Theory and politics, as she puts it, go together. More controversially, she locates the concept of standpoint within a realist philosophy (after Keat and Urry (1975) and Bhaskar (1979)) – but hers is a soft realism without ontological or epistemic privilege. Where Bhaskar, for example, makes underlying realities, intransitivity and generative mechanisms three related and distinguishing features of his scientific realism, Cain stresses only intransitive realities. She makes no claim for the stratification of reality and ontological depth (see chapter 3). What she does do is insist that there are realities which impact upon us regardless of our knowledge or ignorance about them, i.e. intransitively. For example: 'The humble realist . . . may relate observed teenage mating customs to any or all of domestic structures and ideologies, labour markets, religious beliefs, patriarchy or social class' – intransitive realities all (1990, p. 131). It is not in the nature of any of these intransitive realities, however, that they contain mechanisms which, under even tightly specified conditions, *automatically* generate observed phenomena of any kind. With an honesty which is both rare and brave, Cain argues that there are links between intransitive realities and observed phenomena but what they are is captured neither by 'causes' (if by that be meant determinants) nor by 'mechanisms' (if by that be meant the generative mechanisms favoured by scientific realists), *nor by any other concept yet available*. Her strategy is to go on describing the links in particular cases, enjoin others to do the same, and trust that in the fullness of time someone will define the 'explanatory devices' at work appropriately and find terms for them. In sum, Cain justifies (feminist) standpoints pragmatically, but without claiming epistemic privilege, and associates them with a realist philosophy (understood largely in terms of intransitivity), which makes no attribution of generative mechanisms.

In another revision of standpoint theory, Longino (1993) advocates as an alternative to both the unconditioned or universally conditioned subject (the view from nowhere), and the conditioned subject (the view from somewhere), the diversity of conditioned subjects (views from many wheres perhaps yielding the view from everywhere). She connects this to a conception of the scientific community as an 'interactive dialogic community' which, in my view, combines elements of the sociology of scientific communities (cf. Hagstrom, 1965; Latour and Woolgar, 1979) and Habermas's ideal-speech situation. She holds that a 'community's practice of inquiry is productive of knowledge to the extent that it facilitates transformative criticism' (p. 112). For transformative discourse to be possible:

1 There must be publicly recognized forums for the criticism of evidence, of methods, and of assumptions and reasoning.
2 The community must not merely tolerate dissent, but its beliefs and theories must change over time in response to the critical discourse taking place within it.
3 There must be publicly recognized standards by reference to which theories, hypotheses, and observational practices are evaluated and by appeal to which criticism is made relevant to the goals of the inquiring community. . . .
4 Finally, communities must be characterized by equality of intellectual authority. What consensus exists must not be the result of the exercise of political or economic power or of the exclusion of dissenting perspectives; it must be the result of critical dialogue in which all relevant perspectives are represented. (pp. 113–14)

Point (3) introduces non-cognitive standards of evaluation. Whilst empirical adequacy may be common to all communities, standards appropriate for particular communities include both the cognitive virtues of accuracy, coherence and scope and such social virtues as the meeting of technical or material needs 'or facilitating certain kinds of interaction between a society and its material environment or among the society's members' (p. 112). Point (4) is similar to the Habermasian unforced force of the better argument, but Longino does not assume her interactive dialogic communities will necessarily generate rational consensus; coherent and empirically adequate alternative accounts of parts of the social world cannot always be reduced to one because 'cognitive needs can vary and . . . this variation generates cognitive diversity' (p. 113).

Feminist writings such as these are instructive because they give reasons for subscription to both the primary value of the advancement of women (in terms both of equity and of the benefits for all humankind) and the secondary value of an interactive dialogic community (in which agreements and negotiated compromises are forged). The standpoints of women (for women are differentially located in relations of domination and inequality) are starting points for dialogue along with the starting points of other participants, but they are not endpoints or there would be no dialogue – just people talking past each other. This sophisticated version of standpoint theory does not imply closure but, rather, an opening up to others. It thus holds no brief for that balkanization of social science of which Merton (1972) complained in which only women are deemed able to study women, blacks study blacks, and black women study black women, etc. At the same time, and contrary to Habermas, it is not assumed that even the unforced force of the better argument will dissolve all differences of value and language and issue in rational consensus. It thus provides for particularism, but not sectarianism, within a universal commitment to dialogue.

The justification of values

The part played by values in the formation of concepts and the determination of theory, and the part played by the conceptualizations of ordinary members and social scientists in the constitution of society, demand that values themselves be rationally assessed. Very many social scientists have found this difficult and deemed it beyond the bounds of social *science*. Consideration of Weber on ethics of principle and responsibility, Rawls on justice, Habermas on the ideal-speech situation and undistorted communication, and feminists on feminist standpoints and dialogue, at least shows this exclusion to be unwarranted.[7] In each of these cases questions arise about the connection of a normative counterfactual – exclusive subscription to an ethic of principle, the original position and the veil of ignorance, the ideal-speech situation and undistorted communication, and the interactive dialogic community – to present actualities and future scenarios. Republics of the head are unsociological where they take no account of the formation and reformation of the habits of the heart. At the same time habits of the heart are seldom universal. It is therefore no wonder rational considerations of values so often justify pragmatically the secondary values of open communication, mutual understanding and compromise which afford the accommodation of difference, and no wonder, too, that they so often place a premium on the arts of persuasion. Style and rhetoric matter. Clearly there are continuities, too, between the justifications for cognitive, moral and political pluralism.

Hesse's network model of theories treats theories as constructions which are not only unfinished and unfinishable, but also forever reconstructable. Empirical adequacy constrains the theories which can be constructed but it does not determine them. Values also play their part, more so in the social sciences. And in any case truth does not have to be equated with instrumental knowledge that enables us to manipulate people and things. It can also – echoes of the early Habermas – embrace hermeneutic knowledge which enables us to come to a mutual understanding with others, and critical knowledge which helps us to overcome the manipulations of others in the interests of self-determination. That, too, is a matter of value. Metaphors, with their different value implications, continually figure in theories. Theories also always involve learning to see some things as similar and others as different not because they naturally are so but because that is what it is currently conventional to attend to.

In so far as moral discourse is about qualities, connections and consequences, it too involves construction of a network of relations. Cognitive and moral models of the human world have more similarities than might once have been supposed. Cognitive models cannot exclude values, and moral models which refer to qualities, connections and consequences cannot dismiss empirical adequacy. The making and accepting of truth claims and moral claims both involve persuading others freely to reach a consensus or freely to accommodate differences or negotiate a compromise.

'What we hope from the social sciences', writes Rorty, 'is that they will act as interpreters for those with whom we have difficulty talking' (1983, p. 169). But then he, like Dewey, is a pragmatist, in that he regards knowledge not as a representation of the (social) world but as a way of coping with it, and part of coping is figuring out what to do. Put like this, social science cannot be other than moral inquiry (cf. Haan et al., 1983).

5

Models of Applied Social Science:
Engineering, Enlightenment, Interaction and Dialogue

Researchers need to be aware that the work they do, no matter how applied in intent and how practical in orientation, is not likely to have major influence on the policy decision at which it is purportedly directed – at least not if policy actors' interests and ideologies are engaged.

Weiss, 'Research and policy-making: a limited partnership' (1986)

Introduction

Provision of sociology degree courses by universities increased greatly in the 1960s and 1970s in North America and in Europe. The same period saw a big expansion of social research funded from public sources in general expectations of an applied pay-off. There were certainly some successes (cf. Bulmer, 1990). In the mid-to late 1970s, however, expansive hopes gave way to disappointment, disillusionment, even recriminations, at the apparently limited application, actual and potential, of much of the research completed (Weiss, 1977, 1983, 1986; Thomas, 1985; Cherns, 1986; Nelson, 1987). Analyses and empirical research in America have related this to the inadequacies of the research and the inadequacies of the users – but also to the multiple inputs to most decision-making and policy formation of which research is but one, and the limited tractability of many of the problems addressed. Out of this reassessment a new way forward is emerging. The deficiencies of one erstwhile commonplace model for applied social research, the social engineering model, are now widely recognized, and the deficiencies of perhaps its most trumpeted successor, the enlightenment model, are also becoming plainer. Accordingly, attention has now passed to the emergent third possibility, the interactive model. In America Scott and Shore (1979), Lindblom and Cohen (1979) and Weiss with Bucuvalas (1980), among others, did the initial work showing that development of an interactive model was both necessary and possible. In Britain Bulmer (1982) also made an early contribution to the cause.

I shall proceed first by outlining the characteristics of the social engineering and enlightenment models, and then by indicating how and why the interactive model overcomes some of their deficiencies. The movement from interaction to enlightenment was first described in those terms by Janowitz (1971), and the further movement to interaction was first added by Bulmer (1982). I shall depart from Bulmer, not only in emphasis and nuance, but also in some of my responses to the modes of social scientific inquiry with which they are associated, and I will draw attention to some of the ironies of Habermas (1968, 1981). I shall then point up the consistency between Giddens's post-empiricism, his theory of structuration and the interactive, or, as Giddens prefers, the dialogical model of applied social science. Dialogue figures prominently, too, in the approaches of Gustavsen (1986) and Kalleberg (1992). It also returns us to the concerns of the last chapter.

Social engineering

Given that the French positivist tradition originated with Saint-Simon, that it was dedicated to advancement from positive philosophy to a positive polity informed by its principles and conclusions, and that civil engineers were prominent in the wider Saint-Simonian movement in the Second Empire, one might have expected Saint-Simon or one of his followers to have first coined the term 'social *engineering*'. So far as I am aware, however, none of them did. Instead the term first comes to prominence in the work of Popper (1944). Popper distinguishes utopian social engineering, in which utopians (capture the state as the instrument with which to) remodel all society in accordance with a guaranteed blueprint for the future, from piecemeal social engineering, in which liberals implement limited reforms in particular institutions according to the best knowledge available but without any certainty that the effects will be only those desired. Popper associates the first with closed minds, closed societies, historicism and inevitable failure. The second he associates with open minds, open societies, an indeterminate future and modest chances of success for those able to amend their initiatives in the light of experience. It is thus no surprise that he condemns the first and endorses the second. Even if Popper made the notion of social engineering familiar, however, few social scientists so labelled themselves. Yet, as Cherns (1976a) conceded, this was effectively how many applied researchers sought to operate.

The social engineering model depends upon sharp distinctions between pure and applied research and between existential and normative statements. The basic social science which the engineering model applies is empiricist in the sense discussed in chapter 1; it is conceived in terms of 'a logico-deductive system of hypotheses and propositions' (Janowitz, 1971, p. 3). The engineering model is also a linear one (Coleman, 1972). Bulmer (1982, p. 43) represents it as a five-step sequence: (a) definition of social problem, is followed by (b) identification of missing knowledge, is followed by (c) acquisition of social research data and relationships, is followed by (d) interpretation for problem solution, is followed by (e) policy change. The model lends itself to what the 1971 Rothschild Report on British government research and development in the natural sciences called the customer–contractor principle (Rothschild, 1971). The customer or client wants information about, or an analysis of, something, and the social scientist is contracted to provide it. The customer has an objective and the social scientist helps to engineer it by using his or her expertise in research design and instrumentation to obtain relevant information and by drawing upon the stock of social scientific knowledge in order to move from analysis to advice on how it might best be achieved. Third parties, perhaps even the public at large, are just there to be manipulated. Of course, the scale and ambition associated with the customer–contractor principle are much smaller than those integral to the French positivist movement from positive philosophy to the formation and operation of a positive polity. To modify terms supplied by C. Wright Mills (1959), the social scientist is more the king's adviser, or the minor princeling or magnate's adviser, than the philosopher-king.

There are distinguished examples of applied social research which have conformed to the engineering model. Durkheim's contributions to teacher training served the cause of the French Third Republic and represent an attempt at cultural engineering (cf. Coser, 1971, pp. 167–72).[1] The Hawthorne experiments, conducted in the early 1930s by Mayo and his colleagues for the Western Electric Company in Cicero, near Chicago, in order to help the company raise worker productivity, provide another much discussed example

(Roethlisberger and Dickson, 1939). The surveys of Stouffer and others for the US Army's Research Branch between 1941 and 1945, which provided the army with attitudinal data on its soldiers on an unprecedented scale, and which were later reanalysed in the series *The American Soldier* (Stouffer et al., 1949), are similarly famous (cf. Bryant, 1985, pp. 157–62). But then again, the social engineering model often does not work in practice. In particular, the customer-users of research are often inadequately specified; where they are specified, or have indeed contracted the research, they often do not know what they want (they may even have commissioned the research as an alternative to deciding what they want); social scientific research is never incontestable in the way the engineering model supposes in so far as values inform all terminologies and methodologies; and third parties seldom prove totally predictable and manipulable. At best the engineering model is authoritarian or managerialist; at worst it is irrelevant.

Janowitz (1971) has pointed to the institutionalization of the engineering model in the Bureau of Applied Social Research which Lazarsfeld founded at Columbia University in 1944 and in its many imitators (cf. Bryant, 1985, pp. 149–57). The bureau had great success, and continues to this day as the Center for the Social Sciences, but has always been controversial. C. Wright Mills, a colleague at Columbia, and Horowitz, promoters both of a new critical sociology in the early 1960s, voiced early complaints. Mills (1959) thought that intellectual craftsmanship and sociological autonomy were threatened by the 'bureaucratic ethos'. The only interests which could afford to pay for expensive team research were government and business. They welcomed a version of social science dedicated to prediction and control which offered them the undemocratic prospect of 'human engineering'. Mills wanted a sociology which would democratically enable ordinary men and women to understand better the connections between the 'personal issues of milieu' and the 'public issues of social structure' and allow them better to determine their own futures. More bitingly, Horowitz deplored the practice of 'sociology for sale' (1963b) and raged that ' "Who pays how much and for what" . . . best explains the dominant *motif* in American sociology. And what pays are survey design, communication and influence analyses, studies of leadership and organized behavior, etc.' (1963a, p. 164).[2]

At least the university base of the Columbia bureau and other such institutes of applied social research offered some counterbalance to the bureaucratic ethos. If research moved off-campus altogether into government and business in-house research units, or into private commercial social research firms, there would be no such counterbalance – although the researchers so placed might find it easier to be of influence. Early on Merton and Lerner (1951) recognized the dilemma facing the social scientist:

> If he is to play an effective role in putting his knowledge to work, it is increasingly necessary that he affiliate with a bureaucratic power structure in business or government. This, however, often requires him to abdicate the academic privilege of exploring policy possibilities which he regards as significant. If on the other hand he remains unaffiliated to a power structure in order to preserve fuller freedom of choice, he usually loses the resources to carry through his investigations on an appropriate scale and the opportunities of getting his findings accepted by policy makers as a basis of action. (p. 292)

The danger they perceived grew significantly in America in the 1970s when the number of commercial social research firms willing to do what they were contracted to do on time and to budget, and without asking those who contracted them unsettling questions, increased sharply at the same time as political and public confidence in the applied pay-off of publicly funded research fell (Horowitz, 1979). It would also have been no surprise to them that a senior social researcher in a British government department should describe it to me in the late 1980s as a gilded cage. By university standards resources were generously available, but freedom to pursue lines of inquiry whose conclusions might be inconsistent with certain Thatcherite views loudly proclaimed by ministers there was not. Baritz called her book on the use of social scientists' work in American industry *The Servants of Power* (1960), but the term would apply equally well to government use of social scientists.

Where the American critical sociologists of the 1960s were unremitting in their criticism of the bureaucratic ethos and sociology for sale, the critical theorists of the Frankfurt School offered a more sophisticated critique of instrumental reason. All of them objected to the eclipse of substantive reason by instrumental reason or the calculation of the technically most appropriate means to pre-given ends. Habermas's position, however, is worthy of special note. Initially it involved a distinction between three knowledge-constitutive interests. According to Habermas, the positivist tradition of empirical-analytical sciences is founded upon an instrumental interest. It springs from the subject's desire to manipulate and control an objective world, a world of objects separated from the subject, and it issues in statements of laws and generalizations. In the social sciences, it has prompted the formulation of numerous nomological regularities although these have often been misconceived as natural laws of society. The alternative tradition of historical–hermeneutic sciences is founded on a quite different practical interest in understanding and communication within a community. Again, much valuable work has been done although insufficient attention has been paid to misunderstanding and distorted communication and insufficient notice has been taken of the conditions of action with which actors are obliged to contend. The critical tradition which supersedes the other two rests, Habermas continued, upon an emancipatory interest in knowledge as an indispensable aid to autonomous and responsible action. This interest incorporates technical and practical interests, in that it places technical control and interpretive understanding in the service of real human needs whilst at the same time freeing men and women from false dependence on hypostatized powers, whether external to themselves, as in the supposedly ineluctable economic forces uncovered by Marxist analysis, or internal, as in the supposedly fixed compulsions revealed by Freudian analysis.

Habermas's critique of the instrumental interest of the empirical–analytical sciences acknowledges the human interest in prediction and control. It may involve the treatment of other human subjects as objects but it is also integral to the routinization of ordinary life. Additionally, it facilitates responsible action; one cannot be responsible for the consequences of one's action if one cannot predict and control what they will be even in part. There are interests in knowledge other than the instrumental, there are kinds of science other than the empirical–analytical, and, most definitely, there are ways of conceiving the regularities which the empirical–analytical sciences posit other than laws which obtain by natural necessity, but, when all is said and done, there remains a necessary human interest in prediction and control. Habermas recognized this more clearly than Mills or Horowitz and built it into his notion of strategic action. What has complicated matters is Habermas's own abandonment of the knowledge-constitutive interests scheme because it could be interpreted as offering a kind of epistemological foundationalism – something which, following Rorty, Habermas explicitly rejects. Instead strategic action figures in the theory of communicative action, aspects of which have been discussed in the last two chapters.

Enlightenment

Given the limitations of the engineering model, it is not surprising that many social scientists have preferred the enlightenment model. Janowitz notes that it largely passes over the distinction between basic and applied research. This is how he describes it:

> The enlightenment model assumes the overriding importance of the social context, and focuses on developing various types of knowledge that can be utilized by policy-makers and professions. While it seeks specific answers its emphasis is on creating the intellectual conditions for problem solving and institution building. (1971, p. 5)

This still casts social scientists as the aides of those in positions of authority and privilege. Later Janowitz adds that the sociological enterprise, especially as advocates of the enlightenment model conceive it, is based on rational inquiry and intellectual debate which in turn require the social and political conditions of academic freedom. Moreover, 'The consequence of effective sociological inquiry . . . is to contribute to political freedom and social voluntarism by weakening myths, refuting distortions, and preventing an imbalanced view of social reality from dominating collective decisions' (1971, pp. 5–6). What is striking is that Janowitz does not then add that social scientists are here conceived not as servants of power but as servants of all citizens (as Mills would have wished). This omission would seem to have been connected to his determination to connect the enlightenment model just as firmly to the logico-deductive method and the professionalization of social science as the engineering model, and to distinguish sharply enlighteners, who work strictly within the bounds of social *science*, from social critics, who do not. It is certainly consistent with his subsequent appreciative analysis of professionalization in sociology, but it unduly circumscribes the enlightenment model (Janowitz, 1972).

Despite its name, which calls to mind the negative philosophy of the eighteenth century, the enlightenment model repeats some of the features of the positive philosophy of nineteenth-century France. Social science brings order where there was confusion, provides scientific knowledge where there was myth, shows the need to adjust to changed circumstances where there was resistance. It also renders the alien less threatening, and the incomprehensible intelligible, by finding the terms to connect them to the understandings and experience of those who deem them so, both social scientists and ordinary citizens. Giddens (1987), for example, refers to the 'anthropological moment of social research' which has to do with 'Showing what it is like to live in one cultural setting to those who inhabit another (and vice versa)' (p. 6). In other words, Janowitz overlooked how often the enlightenment model accommodates work in the hermeneutic tradition of social science, and he underestimated what Shils (1961) called the proper calling of sociology: the illumination of opinion.

Like the engineering model, the enlightenment model sometimes works in practice. Works as different as Myrdal (1944) on race and racism in America, Dahrendorf's *Society and Democracy in Germany* (1965) and McCrone (1992) on nation and civil society in Scotland have illuminated opinion. Indeed, whenever shifts in public opinion occur, the studies of social scientists have usually made some contribution. Attitudes towards minorities – ethnic, religious, sexual or whatever – as well as the latter's own definitions of their identity and estimations of their place and prospects are a case in point. The same is true of at least one majority – women (cf. Rowbotham, 1989, 1992).

The attractive aspect of the enlightenment model is that it promises service to all, not just those in positions of authority or management; the unattractive features are the touch of elitism – the social scientist brings light to the benighted – and the conceit – the social scientist announces and the world responds. Except that all too often it does not, and the problems of how to make social science apply – in the sense of secure specific outcomes – still remain. Nevertheless there is a profound sense in which enlightenment, social science and modernity go together (cf. Giddens, 1987). Social science is integral to the reflexivity which is one of the defining characteristics of modern society. Just as political science offers a running commentary on actual democratic polities which informs the way they operate irrespective of the specifically applied intent of any particular study, so sociology offers a running commentary on the practices and institutions of actual modern societies (cf. Bulmer, 1990, pp. 129–30 on political sociology). This is an important argument. It suggests that social scientists as a collectivity do not have to be lauded and respected as part of an intelligentsia, and do not have to assume the self-appointed responsibilities of an intelligentsia – for there has never been any such formation in Western Europe or North America – to have a diffuse but pervasive bearing on the constitution of modern society.

That sociologists, in particular, often think that no one takes any notice of them does not necessarily mean that their work is of no social consequence. One perverse confirmation of this can be found in East-Central Europe following the extraordinarily quick collapse of communism in 1989. Events there ran ahead of sociological analyses, and sociologists, even in such strong sociological communities as Poland's, found it hard to theorize the course of the would-be transformation (cf. Bryant, 1994). Far from providing a commentary on current events and the course of future developments, they were initially largely silent (cf. Hankiss, 1990). Instead liberal economists, many from the West but some not, pronounced their certainties, filled the vacuum and greatly influenced the new regimes in Poland, Czechoslovakia and Hungary. Vaclav Klaus, a liberal economist who emerged from the Prague Prognostics Institute, a man with a clear story about a rapid transition to capitalism and a withering scorn for suggestions of any alternative, and now the Prime Minister of the Czech Republic, provides the most dramatic example of all. Sociological commentaries do matter, and when sociologists are at a loss for words others will fill the gap.

Interaction

Janowitz (1971) argued that the enlightenment model assumes that social scientists recognize that they are interacting with their subjects and the publics to which they are responsible but did not follow up on his own claim. As it is all too easy to suppose that the social scientist's responsibility to enlighten is discharged by supplying a research report, preferably followed by academic publication and perhaps even by magazine or newspaper articles and radio and television appearances, it is better to move beyond enlightenment not just to endorsement of interaction with publics, or policy makers (as in Nelson et al., 1987), but to elaboration of a distinctive interactive model. The American, Weiss, has done more to achieve that than anyone else, but other contributions are worthy of note beginning with that of a Briton, Donnison.

Donnison (1972) argues that the linear model of science application favoured by Rothschild (1971), which posits a movement from pure research to applied research and development, oversimplifies even when used in connection with the natural sciences and technology for which it was intended, and is of no help at all when used with the social sciences and social policy. Instead of this 'lazy-minded' dichotomy, Dainton (1971) used the trichotomy of basic, strategic and tactical research, but this, Donnison continues, is still grossly insensitive to the complexities of application in the social sciences. Using the examples of income maintenance and distribution, town and country planning and rent regulation, Donnison shows how policy-oriented research impacts depend on the interpenetration of four fields.

> The four fields are: that of *politics* where new policies are approved, major resource allocations made, powers conferred and decisions formally registered; the field of relevant *technologies*, mechanical and social; the field of relevant professional, commercial and administrative *practice* where present policies and programmes are carried out, and new ones formulated and tried out, and the field of *research* in which – as in the other three – the people interested in social security, education (or whatever it may be) are part of a much larger community concerned with other things. Meanwhile those engaged in all four of these fields participate in the larger universe of voters, taxpayers, clients of the policies in question and members of political movements, which together constitutes public opinion. (1972, p. 52)

How the four fields interconnect will vary from case to case, but the system of rent regulation introduced in Britain by the 1965 Rent Act provides one example.

> By 1962, it was clear to *practitioners*, particularly in the Ministry of Housing and Local Government, that things were going wrong in the housing market and that the previous legislation in this field needed amendment. *Political* pressures associated with the Rachman scandals (concerning a London landlord, by then already dead) led to the appointment, in the next year, of a committee of inquiry under the chairmanship of Sir Milner Holland. *Research* workers – in particular a group supported by the Joseph Rowntree Memorial Trust – had been studying these problems for some years. A member of this group was appointed to the committee, two others were seconded to the committee's research team, and others contributed evidence to the inquiry. In the committee they had the opportunity of learning from persons in various fields of *practice* – particularly the then President of the Royal Institution of Chartered Surveyors, who contributed the essential ideas which Mr Richard Crossman, the new minister, needed for the Rent Act his party had promised, during the general election of 1964, to introduce. Enacted next year by the *politicians*, this measure led to the creation of a new system of rent officers and appeals committees – new institutions in the field of *practice*, relying on *technologies* of valuation and rent fixing not hitherto used for this purpose.

Meanwhile *research* began to reveal some of the defects of the measure. (pp. 53–4)

Donnison concludes that in policy studies, things go better when representatives of all four fields meet on equal terms in acknowledgement that all have indispensable skills, expertise and experience to contribute.

In America Scott and Shore reached a less sanguine conclusion in their disturbingly titled *Why Sociology Does Not Apply* (1979). The book examines the use made of sociology in the formation of public policy on domestic affairs at the federal level in the United States. The examples they discuss include the Presidential Commissions on Law Enforcement and Criminal Justice (1968), the Causes and Prevention of Violence (1969), Obscenity and Pornography (1970) and Population Growth and the American Future (1972). From these and other cases they conclude that:

> First, a great deal of sociological research done for application carries no discernible policy implications of any kind; second, in instances where it does, sociology has served as the basis of formulating policy recommendations, less often the basis of enacted policy; and third, most of the recommendations . . . were rejected by policy-making bodies of government as *impractical or politically unfeasible.* (p. 33)

One reason for this is the determination of most 'applied' researchers first to locate their work within disciplinary concerns and only afterwards to cast around for applications. Another is their subscription to a conception of scientific planning which is respected in the academy but inappropriate in the national polity. This conception involves 'a commitment to rationality, a willingness to be persuaded by scientific fact and to be guided by reason, a basic commitment to devise policies based upon scientific determination of what is expedient, [and] a conscious decision to undertake regular assessment and evaluation of programs and to agree to be guided by the results' (p. 63).

What should sociologists do about this? In the name of political realism, Scott and Shore propose that they should concentrate on politically tractable variables that have a bearing on possible marginal additions or revisions to policy, incrementalism being the political rule except in moments of national crisis. This proposal has the drawback, however, that its open adoption would threaten a drastic reduction, not only in the massive public funding of social research, which is dispensed largely in the mistaken belief that it will lead to knowledge usable in policy formation, but also in the accompanying university postgraduate programmes, which tend to render their products insensitive to the only kinds of research that public policy makers are capable of using.

Scott and Shore's idea of making sociology apply is confined to expert advice to the policy maker. In effect, they acknowledge that the standard linear engineering model does not work in interactive practice and try to make pragmatic amendments to it – but without much conviction, given doubt about 'the role which ideas can *ever* play in arriving at policy decisions' (p. xi, my italics). Theirs is a very statist approach which belongs to the period before the revival of interest in civil society. Perhaps a better response to the failures they uncover would be to worry less about Washington and more about everyone else, less about influencing policy directly through the policy makers and more about influencing it indirectly through the constituencies to which politicians look for votes, and less about exerting their influence from the top down and more about influencing it from the bottom up – in sum, to worry less about governors and more about citizens.

It could also be that the gridlock which is said increasingly to characterize American government makes social research application harder there than where politicians can push through radical programmes, such as the Soviet Union under President Gorbachev or Britain under Prime Minister Thatcher. Certainly one of the most influential sociologists in recent times is Zaslavskaya, the 'constructive dissident' from Novisibirsk, who contributed significantly to President Gorbachev's ideas of glasnost and perestroika (Zaslavskaya, 1987; Weinberg, 1992). The four right-wing think-tanks in Britain, in all of which social scientists figured prominently, successfully supplied Mrs Thatcher and her ministers with the thinking behind many of their most radical initiatives. The oldest, the Institute for Economic Affairs, founded in 1957, promoted the ideas of Hayek and Friedman and was associated with neo-liberal economics, monetarism, maximization of the market and a minimization of the state, and hostility to self-serving public sector bureaucrats. The Centre for Policy Studies was established in 1974 by Sir Keith Joseph and Margaret Thatcher explicitly to provide a right-wing counter to a body they distrusted: the research department of the Conservative Party. The third, the Adam Smith Institute, founded in 1979, was described by *The Economist* of 6 May 1989 as a 'cheer leader for radical Thatcherism'. The fourth, the Social Affairs Unit, was set up in 1980 under the directorship of the sociologist, Digby Anderson, to promote individual responsibility and combat welfare dependency. Ideas from these think-tanks were amplified by the Conservative press.

Scott and Shore offer acute comment, *en passant*, on what happens to research application in the complexities of actual policy making and decison taking, but they do not begin to convert it into an alternative model of applied social science. This is what Lindblom and Cohen (1979) do offer. Their interest is in social problem solving, that is, in social processes which, by some standard, eventuate, or offer a prospect of eventuating, in improvement on an existing situation. Any individual or collective subject seeking a social improvement has a problem. What it does about it constitutes a solution. The key question for social scientists is this: in the social construction of problems and solutions ('interactive problem solving'), what place is there for professional social inquiry ('PSI') and professional social inquirers ('pPSI')? Lindblom and Cohen are equivocal. Inputs to the interactive problem-solving process are only authoritative in so far as they are deemed to warrant action to get something done, getting it done being a solution. Unfortunately, PSI seldom warrants anything, at least on its own, such are the awkward ways of both social science and the social world, but pPSI could learn how better to improve the PSI input into interactive problem solving by elaborating their own relationship to it into a research agenda. Lindblom and Cohen do also surmise that the principal impact of policy-oriented studies is akin to a Kuhnian paradigm shift; cumulating studies of inflation, race conflict, deviance, foreign policy or whatever can sometimes move policy makers and decision takers to engage in basic reconsideration of policies and programmes where the studies are hard to square with their decision-making framework, operating political and social philosophy, or ideology.

Lindblom and Cohen offend in so far as they ignore altogether the special claims to knowledge that social scientists seek to make, but they are coldly realistic in placing policy makers and decision takers at the centre of their analysis. Usable knowledge is the knowledge the latter use, and PSI is usually a relatively minor contributant to it. The rarity with which social scientists speak with one voice only reinforces the inclination of policy makers and decision takers to pick and choose what they heed. Lindblom and Cohen seem to condone a sort of take-it-or-leave-it approach to social science which can only demotivate social scientists – certainly Donnison, looking forward, does not anticipate it, and Scott and Shore, looking back, never submit to it – but they can also be read as trying to force social scientists to abandon their conceits and consider more hard-headedly the place of social science in interactive problem solving. Their analysis also applies to all settings and not just the public policy arena.

Weiss: the I-I-I model

If Donnison, Scott and Shore, and Lindblom and Cohen have paved the way for an interactive model of applied social science, it is Weiss who has done most to set out what it consists of. The basic idea was first introduced, albeit briefly, in a paper in 1979. Like Lindblom and Cohen, she places policy makers and decision takers at the centre of her account.

> Those engaged in developing policy seek information not only from social scientists but from a variety of sources – administrators, practitioners, politicians, planners, journalists, clients, interest groups, aides, friends, and social scientists, too. The process is not one of linear order from social research to decision but a disorderly set of interconnections and back-and-forthness that defies neat diagrams. (Weiss, 1979, p. 35)

Three subsequent publications suggest possibilities of order where first there had seemed only disorder (Weiss with Bucuvalas, 1980; Weiss, 1983, 1986).

The first, *Social Science Research and Decision-Making* (1980), reports a major empirical study of the usefulness of social research on mental health as perceived by fifty-one officers of the federal Alcohol, Drug Abuse and Mental Health Administration and three bodies responsible to it, and 104 senior officers in state and local mental health agencies. The authors recognized that their respondents have to contend with three sets of expectations: first, as managers they must respect executive norms for getting things done; second, as professionals in fields that lay claim to a scientific basis, they have to keep abreast of the latest research; third, as senior members of bureaucratic organizations, they have to remain alert to the political need to protect and promote their agencies, programmes, budgets and careers. Against this background, Weiss with Bucuvalas 'hypothesized that decision makers would consider social science research studies more useful to the extent that studies (a) provided implementable conclusions; (b) were methodologically competent; and (c) conformed to users' beliefs and agency policy' (p. 69).

Each respondent was assigned two abstracts of researches on topics of relevance to his or her responsibilities. Respondents rated the abstracts on 129 descriptors. Factor analysis of the ratings yielded three types of factor:

First, there is relevance to issues being considered by one's office (and its related items of priority of the topic and timeliness). Second, there are two factors that provide a basis for trust in a research study. These are Research Quality, which gauges the soundness of a study according to the canons of science, and Conformity with User Expectations, which subjects study results to the test of experience. Third, there are two factors that provide direction. Action Orientation, with its characteristics of explicitness and practicality, offers guidance for incremental change within existing programs. Challenge to the Status Quo, which questions intellectual, organizational, and political perspectives, points towards fundamental change. (Weiss with Bucuvalas, 1980, p. 80)

Weiss with Bucuvalas then used multiple regression 'To test the effects of the research characteristics on decision makers' judgements of the usefulness of research studies' (p. 83). They found that the multiple demands upon decision makers do indeed prompt them to apply multiple standards in their assessment of research usefulness. First, of course, studies have to be relevant. Of the other four factors involved, however, it is notable that the two scientific merit factors count for more than the two practical utility factors. In connection with practical utility, it proved necessary to distinguish between the value and policy positions preferred by the decision makers and those adopted by their agencies – the former often welcoming challenges to a status quo with which they disagreed.

Weiss with Bucuvalas also set up 100 interviews with researchers who had been funded by the federal agencies concerned and members of their research review committees. Both groups made judgements of the usefulness of research broadly similar to those made by the decision makers, although the researchers expressed doubt as to whether decision makers really take much notice of research. Finally, the authors invited respondents in all five groups to comment on selected hypotheses about obstacles to the use of research. Obstacles identified included the unwillingness of decision makers to rely on research that runs counter to their own beliefs or the philosophies of their agencies; the political nature of decision making; the insensitivity of scientists (partly because of different, disciplinary, career imperatives); inadequate communication between decision makers and researchers (despite the best efforts of government research programme officers); and the inability of decision makers to define and specify their research needs.

In conclusion, Weiss with Bucuvalas emphasize that decision makers look to research as much for perspectives, generalizations and concepts that afford them help in defining what it is they are doing as they do for data; diffuse gains in understanding are often as important to them as the acquisition of specific, immediately implementable, findings. (This confirms what Rich (1978) had already called the 'conceptual use' of social research.) In consequence, 'Social science research formulated and carried out by external investigators seems likely to have its effects by modifying the climate of informed opinion' (Weiss with Bucuvalas, 1980, p. 264). Where Shils took the illumination of opinion to be about public opinion, and Biderman (1970) distinguished between supplying knowledge for action at the lowest level of social organization ('information'), supplying knowledge for administration at intermediate levels ('intelligence'), informing broader processes of policy formation ('policy knowledge') and affecting public conceptions ('enlightenment'), Weiss with Bucuvalas prompt the thought that influencing informed opinion is where social science has most impact at all organizational levels and in all organizational settings.[3]

Interestingly, Tijssen (1988), using a research design explicitly derived from Weiss with Bucuvalas, reaches comparable conclusions in her inquiry into how central and local board members of the Royal Dutch Medical Association assess the usefulness of social science research.

In one way, health professionals may be atypical research utilizers. Given that their practice is supposed to have a scientific basis, one would expect them to be particularly attentive to research. In another respect, however, they may be more typical. It is to technical proficiency in research design and execution, and in data analysis, that they look when establishing the scientific credentials of researchers, but it is not to research findings as such but, rather, to theoretical perspectives and concepts that they turn when revising their practice and their understandings of that practice, and these theories and concepts, as often as not, owe nothing in their formation to the technical skills of those who convey them. It is the display of technique that wins the confidence of the research user; it is theories and concepts which the user most often uses.

In 'Ideology, interests and information' (1983) Weiss introduces further elements of order into a process which she had formerly characterized as disorderly. She holds that 'the public policy positions taken by policy actors are the resultant of three sets of forces: their *ideologies*, their *interests* (e.g., in power, reputation, financial reward) and the *information* they have', and the third of these, to which social science is but one contributant, is usually outweighed by the first two, which 'carry higher emotional loadings' (pp. 221 and 222). She outlines the interaction of ideology, interests and information within what she calls the 'I-I-I framework', but which I will call the 3Is framework because it is easier to say. Interaction between each of the Is is deemed to be 'constant and iterative, and policymakers work out the specification of their ideologies and interests in conjunction with their processing of information' (p. 229). She discusses relations between research on the one hand and prior information, ideology and interests on the other; and between interests and ideology; and she stresses that *'The distribution of power determines WHOSE ideology, interests and information will be dominant'* (p. 239; original italics).

The 'organizing construct' of the 3Is framework enables Weiss to treat systematically matters which had hitherto seemed haphazard. Its adoption also promises to help social scientists identify more effectively appropriate points of entry into relations between the three Is whatever the circumstances with which they have to contend. Yet for all that, her conclusions are both low-key and shrewd. She warns researchers to be modest in their expectations of influence and she offers advice on research choice which makes few concessions to the political demands of the moment.

> One suggestion to those who propose, fund, and do policy relevant research is not to spend a heavy share of research money and time on studies designed to answer immediate policy problems. To do such work usefully usually requires accepting the conceptual and practical constraints of government sponsors – that is, limiting research to the variables that the funding bureau has the authority to manipulate and adopting the premises that currently guide the agency's action. If, in fact, even such practically oriented research is likely to run into entanglements with interests and ideologies both inside and outside the bureau, we may serve government better by broadening the scope of the research we do and contributing more critical perspectives on agency activities. Although such research will not have an immediate impact, it probably represents a wiser investment of social science resources. And when alignments of ideology and interests make the information relevant to policymaking, the contribution may prove to be significant. (1983, pp. 241–2)

This may sound like a return to the enlightenment model but it is not. Weiss has abandoned use of the elevated term 'enlightenment' in favour of the rather less dignified 'knowledge creep' (p. 221). She has no illusions about the capacity of social scientists to enlighten anyone.

In a later article, Weiss (1986) supplies further terms with which to combat the disorderliness of the policy process and identify social scientific points of entry. She notes how the academic literature treats decision making largely as an event. Authorized decision makers, at particular times and places, review a problem or opportunity, consider alternative courses of action having calculated the advantages and disadvantages of each, weigh alternatives against goals or preferences, select the most suitable and thereby make a decision. There are five major constructs in this account:

1 *Boundedness*: decision making is set off from the ongoing stream of activity.
2 *Purposiveness*: decision makers have clear goals in view.
3 *Calculation*: decision makers generate, or obtain, a set of alternatives.
4 *Perceived significance*: a decision marks a step of some moment.
5 *Sequential order*: recognition of a problem leads to articulation of alternative ways of dealing with it, which leads to assessment of their relative advantages and disadvantages, which leads to selection of a decision.

Sometimes decision making is like this, but often, Weiss insists, it is much messier. She identifies eight routes to 'non-decisional policy making':

1 *Reliance on custom and implicit rules*: officials do what the agency has always done.
2 *Improvisation*: officials adjust and combine tried procedures to accommodate the unanticipated.
3 *Mutual adjustment*: office-holders without any sense of common purpose adapt to decisions made around them.
4 *Accretion*: officials try again what worked last time.
5 *Negotiation*: where authority is fragmented and agency mandates overlap, office-holders trade off advantages and obligations.
6 *Move and counter-move*: where negotiation breaks down, officials make a move and see how the other party counters.
7 *A window for solutions*: often the solution precedes the problem and officials await the opportunity to implement it.
8 *Indirection*: officials find they have made policy as an unintended consequence of other decisions.

The social scientist who is wise to these routes to policy making may be able to take tactical account of them when seeking to make research apply, but the chances of success are always likely to be unfavourable. The inside knowledge required will probably exceed the reach of the outside researcher, and the shifting balances of factors in the politics, procedures and personnel of the office will probably defy prediction.

Where does the limited applicability of the linear model of decision making leave the researcher? There is something to be said, Weiss argues, for the standard admonitions:

> locate the potential users of research in advance, understand which policy variables they have the authority to change, concentrate the study on the feasible (manipulable) variables, involve the potential users in the research process, establish a relationship of trust, demonstrate the awareness of the constraints that limit their options, report promptly, provide practical recommendations, write results clearly and simply, and communicate results in person. (1986, p. 228)

But, for all the reasons already mentioned, there is still no guarantee of success even when addressing small hierarchical organizations. Given this obstinate reality, social scientists are very often right to do the most rigorous work they can by their own disciplinary standards instead of trying to satisfy unsatisfiable policy makers. Some of their ideas may still filter through and they are as likely to have an effect this way as any other. For example, research provides 'powerful labels for previously inchoate and unorganized experience' and labels like 'externalities', 'aptitude test scores', 'deinstitutionalization', 'white flight' and 'inter-generational dependency' do affect policy and opinion (Weiss, 1986, p. 218; original examples).

Scott and Shore claimed that sociology has not applied because sociologists have failed to place decision takers and policy makers at the centre of their analyses, and I complained that they equated application with influencing governors and forgot about citizens. Be that as it may, Weiss does exactly what they ask – but still concludes that social scientists are unlikely to have the impacts Scott and Shore desire. One reason for this bears repetition. Social scientists find it hard to give government departments and agencies what they want because, by the time they deliver their reports, the latter's perception of what it is that they want has all too often moved on in response to more or less subtle shifts in the ideological, interest and informational factors to which they are subject. In short, and contrary to Tijssen, there is often little point in exhorting social scientists to keep up with the actualities of the organizations that commission their research. To my 'Consider your interaction with all manner of constituencies and citizens, not just people in positions of authority', there can now be added an injunction derived from Weiss: 'Do the best work you can by your own disciplinary standards, and stick to the theoretical perspectives, the long views and the critical outlooks which are the forte of social science.'

I have described Weiss's interactive model of social science application at some length because it is not only sophisticated, it is usable. There are others, but, in my view, they mislead by placing social scientists at their centre and/or are too complicated. Van de Vall (1986) is a case in point. Weiss's model is also consistent with some other interesting studies of policy-oriented research including Bulmer's description of patterns of influence (1982) and Webber's study of legislators in Indiana (1987). In particular, Thomas's study of the aims and outcomes of eleven British social policy research projects contains chapters entitled 'Is anybody listening?' and 'Disappointed hopes'. It also notes that the minority of projects which were taken up by the government departments concerned 'struck a responsive chord within the departments' and all the investigators had worked at some stage within the civil service (Thomas, 1985, p. 62). These researchers, through their connections, conformed to the 'insider' model. Outsiders, however, could sometimes have an effect. Indeed, the 'limestone' model suggests that policy-oriented research can be worthwhile because ideas promoted by researchers do permeate government departments even if it is impossible to predict which, where and how. Thomas also identifies the 'gadfly' model; to be successful gadflies have to have a shrewd grasp of how government works, develop distinctive ideas with some panache, and promote them through meetings, personal networks and the media, in the hope that they will be taken up by policy makers. For independent-minded social scientists the gadfly model can be attractive, but gadflies can find it hard to get research funding and few can easily be shown to have had much impact.

Dialogue

The dialogical model of applied social research is similar to the interactive one except in its approach to methodology and its orientation to ordinary men and women and lay knowledge. Most interactionists, including Weiss and Bulmer, stress the importance of rigorous scientific method to effective policy-oriented research. For Weiss rigorous method is unambiguously empiricist. Bulmer is open to more possibilities but still associates explanation largely with hypothesis testing, variable analysis, scientific laws and the goal of cumulative and uncontested knowledge. In conformity with his post-empiricism, Giddens, who provides a source for a dialogical model, does not. Most interactionists also concentrate their attention on interaction with governors and managers more than with citizens. In acknowledgement of the double-hermeneutic, Giddens does not. Dialogue is similarly a central feature of the models of applied social research developed by Gustavsen and Kalleberg.

Giddens did not formally announce the dialogical model of social science application until a lecture in New York in 1986 (published a year later). It is, however, but a formalization of something that had clearly been in the making since the *New Rules of Sociological Method* a decade earlier. Rule D1, which refers to the double-hermeneutic, includes the germ of the dialogical model:

> there is a continual 'slippage' of the concepts constructed in sociology, whereby these are appropriated by those whose condition they were originally coined to analyse, and hence tend to become integral features of that condition (thereby in fact potentially compromising their original usage within the technical vocabulary of social science). (1976, p. 162)

A later version of the same 'rule' draws attention not to the inevitable contamination of social science concepts (contrary to the ambitions of the definitive reconstructions discussed in chapter 1) but to the penetration of ordinary discourse: 'There is a two-way relation involved between lay language and the language of social science, because any of the concepts introduced by sociological observers can in principle be appropriated by lay actors themselves, and applied as part of "ordinary language" discourse' (Giddens, 1979, p. 248). Variations on how what can happen in principle happens in practice are not spelled out.

Giddens (1979) obtained the notion of dialogue from Gadamer, who uses it to refer to the hermeneutic encounter between traditions, and he subsequently uses Gadamer's term 'dialogical' to refer to 'relations between the social sciences and the lives of the human beings whose behaviour is analysed' (1982a, p. 14). That those analysed can take up social science 'findings' is 'the hinge connecting two possible modes in which the social sciences connect to their involvement in society itself: as contributing to exploitative domination or as promoting emancipation' (p. 14). He does not enlarge on which is more likely in what circumstances. Giddens goes on to stress that human agents are 'knowledgeable' about their society and 'capable' of acting in it (and in speaking of 'action' he alludes to the ineliminable possibility of their acting otherwise). This, in turn, guarantees that social theory is inevitably critical theory. 'Human beings . . . are not merely inert objects of knowledge, but agents able to – and prone to – incorporate social theory and research within their own action' (p. 16). Giddens also adds the term 'dialectic of control' to refer to the knowledgeability and capability which enables even the subordinated to act (1982a). Interestingly, he here complains that Braverman exaggerates the helplessness of the workers in his classic *Labor and Monopoly Capital* (1974).

All these ideas recur in *The Constitution of Society* (1984), where there is also an extended discussion of social science application. Once again Giddens starts by rejecting transfer of the 'revelatory model' of natural science to social science. He then builds upon his distinction between mutual knowledge and common sense (introduced in 1979). 'The first refers to the authenticity of belief or the hermeneutic entrée into the description of social life' (1984, p. 336). The second refers to 'the propositional beliefs implicated in the conduct of day-to-day activities' (p. 337); 'common sense is mutual knowledge treated not as knowledge but as fallible belief' (p. 337).

At this point the distinction between 'credibility criteria' and 'validity criteria' comes into play. Credibility criteria have to do with grasping hermeneutically what it is actors are doing and their reasons for it. Validity criteria concern the assessment of those reasons as good reasons in terms of the criteria of theory and evidence employed by the social sciences. Social sciences provide a critique of common sense by assessing the validity of reasons 'in terms of knowledge either simply unavailable to lay agents or construed by them in a fashion different from that formulated in the metalanguages of social theory' (p. 339). If one then assumes, as Giddens does, that action flows from beliefs, demonstration that a belief is false carries with it practical implications for the transformation of action. As social beliefs are part constitutive of what they are about, 'criticism of false belief (*ceteris paribus*) is a *practical intervention* in society, a political phenomenon in the broad sense of the term' (p. 340; original italics). Additionally, social science cannot but be critical wherever action descriptions are contested by actors themselves.

From all of this, Giddens draws the extraordinarily confident conclusion that 'new knowledge developed in the social sciences will ordinarily have *immediate* transformational implications for the existing social world' (p. 341; my italics). There are, however, the following exceptions: (a) when the new knowledge has to do with past events and social conditions which no longer obtain; (b) when the conduct in question depends upon motives and reasons that remain unaltered by new information; (c) when new knowledge sustains existing conditions; (d) when those who seek to apply new knowledge cannot do so for whatever reason (for example, lack of resources); (e) when new knowledge turns out to be false; and (f) when new knowledge is trivial or uninteresting. Notwithstanding these caveats, what is so striking about Giddens is his confidence in transformative capacity as a human universal (cf. Bryant, 1992).

In his *A Contemporary Critique of Historical Materialism* (1981) Giddens had already argued that there are no universal laws of society (or economy) of the kind often, if contestably, attributed to the natural sciences, i.e. laws which state invariable relations of constant conjunction and temporal succession. The point is developed further in *The Constitution of Society*: 'causal mechanisms in social scientific generalizations depend upon actors' reasons, in the context of a "mesh" of intended and unintended consequences of action' (1984, p. 345). Social science generalizations are unlikely ever to be invariant and universal because the 'content of agents' knowledgeability, the question of how "situated" it is and the validity of the propositional content of that knowledge' all influence the circumstances in which they hold (p. 345). There are, however, two types of 'causal factors that influence action without operating through its rationalization . . . unconscious influences and influences that affect the circumstances within which individuals carry on their conduct' (p. 346). The latter provide the enabling and constraining features of contexts of action and include material and social phenomena.

Generalizations that pertain to outcomes that actors make happen are liable to change. 'Since agents' knowledge about conditions influencing the generalization is causally relevant to that generalization, these conditions can be altered by changes in such knowledge' (p. 346). The causal mechanisms at work are inherently unstable, 'the degree of instability depending upon how far those beings to whom the generalization refers are likely to display standard patterns of reasoning in such a way as to produce standard sorts of unintended consequence' (p. 347). Propositions can prove self-fulfilling and self-invalidating. In sum, generalizations in the social sciences hold only within limits of time and place because they depend upon mixes of intended and unintended consequences of action. They 'may directly reflect maxims of action which are knowingly applied by agents' and they may wittingly or unwittingly feed back into those maxims (p. 347).

Giddens stresses that natural science enjoys a 'technological' re-lation to its object world 'in which accumulated knowledge is "ap-plied" to an independently constituted set of phenomena' (p. 348). By contrast, in the social sciences – and here Giddens quotes Taylor – 'the practice is the object of the theory. Theory in this domain transforms its own object' (Taylor, 1983, p. 74). With this in mind, Giddens uses the example of Machiavelli to illustrate the trans-formative impact of social science. He also gives as an example coroners and court officials whose reading of the social science litera-ture on suicide informs the practices to which suicide statistics refer. In general: ' "Discoveries" of social science, if they are at all interest-ing, cannot remain discoveries for long; the more illuminating they are, in fact, the more likely they are to be incorporated into action and thereby to become familiar principles of social life' (Giddens, 1984, p. 351). But if 'technological' describes the relation of natural science to its object world, what term should be used to describe the relation of the social sciences to their world? In *The Constitution of Society* Giddens does not say; subsequently he has adopted 'dialogical'.

It is following mention of Weiss's work that Giddens first proposes a 'dialogical' model of applied sociology as an alternative to the prevailing 'control' model (1987, p. 46). Like so many others, Giddens argues that much of the post-war development of sociology has been accompanied by a belief that it would underpin better policy making, and that much of the disillusionment with sociology stems from a recognition that all too often it has failed to do so. But the research that has failed has, for the most part, conformed to a model of social science that Giddens believes to be increasingly rejected. This model is based on what natural science is assumed to be like. It aims at a unified conceptual structure, universal laws and ever-increasing incontrovertible knowledge, and it believes objectivity to be indispen-sable to their achievement. By contrast Giddens's post-empiricist alternative rules out the possibility both of a unified conceptual structure and of causal laws that directly determine human behav-iour; instead it stresses the double-hermeneutic and the ineliminably contestable character of social science.

Giddens calls his version of interactive application the dialogical model, believing research most effectively informs policy 'through an extended process of communication between researchers, policy mak-ers and those affected by whatever issues are under consideration' (1987, p. 47). Instead of policy objectives dictating the research to be done, research helps to indicate 'where the most urgent practical questions cluster' and offers 'frameworks for seeking to cope with them' (p. 47). Three suppositions underlie the dialogical model. 'First, social research cannot just be "applied" to an independently given subject matter' (p. 47). Instead it has to be aimed at 'persuading actors to expand or modify the forms of knowledge or belief that they draw upon in organizing their contexts of action' (p. 47). Attempts to persuade will most likely fall short of a Habermasian ideal-speech situation but should include 'direct consultation of a prolonged kind wherever feasible' (p. 47). Second, the 'mediation of cultural settings', i.e. 'the communication, via social research, of what it is like to live in one cultural setting to those in another' (Gadamer's dialogue), coupled with conceptual innovation, is 'at least as significant for the practical outcomes of social research as is the establishing of generalizations' (p. 47). Conceptual innovation is important because 'the will to change things for the better involves positing "possible worlds" of what might become the case via programmes of social reforms' (pp. 46–8), and 'Novel conceptual frameworks open up possible fields of action previously unperceived either by policy makers or by the agents involved' (p. 48). Third, the practical implications of the double-hermeneutic are immense. The most far-reaching practical consequences of social science involve not sets of generalizations which facilitate instrumental control over the social world but, rather, 'the constant absorption of concepts and theories into that "subject-matter" they seek to analyse, constituting and reconstituting what the "subject matter" is' (p. 48). Given this approach to social science application, it is not surprising that Giddens should go on to refer to organizations and social movements as 'the two ways in which reflexive appropriation of knowledge about the social world is mobilized in the modern world', or that he should be attracted to the greater dynamism of social movements (p. 48).

In Giddens's view, despondency about the practical value of social science is a consequence only of subscription to an empiricist model of social science which, most of the time, does not work and cannot work. The prospects for post-empiricist sociology, by contrast, are very good because it is the prime medium of the reflexivity without which societies cannot intelligently modify their institutions in the face of accelerating change. Indeed, 'The degree . . . to which a society fosters an active and imaginative sociological culture will be a measure of its flexibility and openness' (1987, p. 21). This new version of an old message has still to win widespread consent, perhaps because Giddens is not explicit about what is new and what is old. The point can most easily be made by using the terms of Bauman's *Legislators and Interpreters* (1987). Legislators, in what will have to be a somewhat caricatured version of Bauman, are the intellectuals whose special knowledge has enabled them to lay down the law about the development of modernity. Interpreters are the intellectuals whose special skills enable them to interpret between discourses in the age of postmodernity. Legislators aim at universal knowledge; interpreters are satisfied with particular understandings. Giddens argues that ours is a late modern age whose prime medium of reflexivity is a post-empiricist social science which yields understanding not laws. In other words, he associates modernity, albeit late modernity, not with legislators but with interpreters, does not explain himself and fails to strike a chord as often as he might have done. His key interpreters, moreover, are not simply intellectuals, they are social scientists with a special disciplinary competence in the assessment of reasons for action which sets them apart from poets, prophets, journalists and other commentators. Yet he is disinclined to enter the epistemological arguments about social *science* beyond general endorsement of post-empiricism (cf. Bryant, 1992).

Giddens's importance to applied sociology lies not in empirical research on the applications of sociology which adds to the conclusions reached by writers from Donnison to Weiss – for he has not done any; rather, it has to do with his promotion of a post-empiricist model of social science in which applications can only be constituted interactively, in contrast to the empiricist model of social science favoured by the American writers on interactive application in which interaction is at best something imposed on it from the outside and at worst a distortion to be fought. Nevertheless, precisely because dialogue does flow naturally from Giddens's conception of social science, there is a big danger that he will reinforce the old conceit that social scientists have only to publish on topics of social concern for their work to apply. The danger of monologue puffed up as dialogue can only be averted if social scientists consider the actual possibilities of dialogue and do what they can to realize them. Exactly how they should go about this they will have to decide for themselves case by case. They could do worse than to take into account the factors that influence 'the level and nature of the "penetration" actors have of the conditions of system reproduction' (Giddens, 1984, p. 91). These are listed in the section on 'positioning' in *The Constitution of Society* – a section quite separate from the chapter entitled 'Structuration theory, empirical research and social critique' – as:

1 the means of access actors have to knowledge in virtue of their social location;

2 the modes of articulation of knowledge;
3 circumstances relating to the validity of the belief-claims taken as 'knowledge';
4 factors to do with the means of dissemination of available knowledge. (p. 91)

The largely American literature on interactive application also provides a valuable resource upon which they can draw. Without some such supplementation, Giddens on dialogue is criticizable as too general and vague and too removed from what happens in actual cases (cf. Bulmer, 1990). On the other hand, the combination of Weiss's 3Is model and Giddens's dialogical model could prove a formidable one.

I have suggested that the actualities of dialogue have to be considered case by case and regretted Giddens's unconcern to provide examples. By contrast, Gustavsen and Kalleberg, reflecting on action research and interventional social science respectively, do just that. One source for their work is Skjervheim (1973), who had his own version of what Giddens was later to call the double-hermeneutic. In 'Social research as participative dialogue' (1986), Gustavsen discusses research on industrial democracy in which democracy is 'identical to *generative* capacity; to the ability to *create* solutions to problems of technology and organization' (p. 149). Social scientists in Norwegian plants have adopted collaborative research designs in which they offer the workers their concepts, principles and accounts of experience elsewhere and listen to the workers' own understandings, suggestions and criticisms of the research proposed. The aim of what amounts to action research is agreement – Gustavsen invokes Habermas – on changes in the organization of production and the labour process. It is exceptional in so far as research and application proceed bit by bit in tandem rather than the one succeeding the other. Kalleberg (1992, forthcoming) writes more generally of sociology as a constructive science committed not just to interpretation of social reality but also to improvement. He complains about the positivism of American texts on theory building and covering laws, takes a catholic position on modes of explanation and understanding, and gives his sociology a particular constructive turn, an argumentative one. Kalleberg has a long-standing interest in the democratization of organizations understood in terms of procedures for open and rational discursive will formation, and he describes various 'field experiments' by American and Scandinavian industrial sociologists which have arrived at procedures for the conduct of dialogues with and by those from whom changed practices are sought. More generally, however, he commends to social scientists with applied ambitions the role of 'Socratic gadfly'. What he could have added is that it is performable in many more contexts than fieldwork, and that it places an obligation on the social scientist to get the dialogue going.

6

Conclusion:
Impossible and Possible
Sociology

There remains the possibility for rational knowledge in the social sciences even if the empiricist conception of objectivity is abandoned.
Giddens, Social Theory and Modern Sociology (1987)

Only societies reflexively capable of modifying their institutions in the face of accelerated social change will be able to confront the future with any confidence. Sociology is the prime medium of that reflexivity.
Giddens, Social Theory and Modern Sociology (1987)

Sociology in America and Britain

Smelser's compendious *Handbook of Sociology* (1988) offers a summary of sociology as it currently stands – or at least as it very recently stood – in the United States. It opens, as I indicated in chapter 1, with two theoretical overviews which represent incompatible approaches to sociology. The first, by Wallace (1988), embraces a natural-science-inspired notion of theory proper. The second, by Alexander (1988), 'The new theoretical movement', welcomes developments which flow from the linguistic turn and post-empiricism. Anyone reading Ritzer's *Frontiers of Social Theory* (1990b) is likely to conclude that it is contributors to the new theoretical movement who are making all the running. In 1988 the University of Maryland and the American Sociological Association sponsored a conference called 'Sociological theory: current status, near-term prospects'. Nine of the fifteen essays in Ritzer's volume are derived from the conference; the other six have been added to extend the coverage of contemporary developments in social theory. The standard of writing is very high, and the overview of contemporary social theory offered by mostly younger Americans is both sharp and detailed. As many contributors acknowledge, French, German and British writings have dominated many theoretical debates since the 1960s – a point also conceded by Smelser (1988); but these essays reveal the scale, confidence and stature of the new theorizing in America.

Some of the contributors reflect on relations between different paradigms or modes of theorizing, and on relations between theory and American sociology in general. They largely converge on two versions of the same story, the dignified and the down-to-earth. The dignified version notes that, with or without obeisances to Rorty or Lyotard, *dévotés* of most modes of theorizing make non-exclusive claims for their favoured discourse and welcome exchanges and convergences with others: hence the new syntheses of Ritzer's subtitle (and the similar new synthesis to which Giddens (1987, ch. 2) refers in a lecture given in America two years before the Maryland conference). At the same time, they reject any idea of a hegemonic paradigm, grand synthesis or master narrative. American sociology has moved, it seems agreed, from functionalist orthodoxy, through the war of the schools, to a pluralism which is both principled and pragmatic. The only dissenters are Boden, who is much taken with Garfinkel's claim that ethnomethodology is 'an incommensurably alternate sociology' (Garfinkel, 1988, quoted in Boden, 1990, p. 186), and Jonathan Turner, who clings to the 'currently unfashionable presumption that sociology can develop universal abstract laws and assess these laws through systematic empirical tests' (Turner, 1990, p. 371). The down-to-earth version, to which Ritzer himself, and also Wiley (1990), on occasions refer, is similar but adds that most leading theorists find their niches and do their work without regard for the large number of lumpensociologists (my term) who would have welcomed the resurgence of neo-functionalism had they noticed that the original version had fallen into disrepute, and the even larger number of lumpensociologists whose work has no connection at all to theorists' theory.[1]

Theorists' theory has been marginalized in America. I have described elsewhere the 'instrumental positivism' which, I argue, has enjoyed an ever increasing ascendancy in American sociology since the 1930s (Wells and Picou, 1981; Bryant, 1985, ch. 5). It has displayed five main characteristics: a preoccupation with the refinement of statistical techniques and research instrumentation; a nominalist or individualistic conception of society consistent with the sample survey; a view of the cumulation of knowledge as best secured by induction, verification and incrementalism; a linkage of a (false) dichotomy of facts and values with a (mis)conception of value-free-dom; and a commitment to team research and the development of centres of applied social research. There is no doubt that this tradition, which has many admirers in Europe and elsewhere, has been aligned to the pursuit of 'theory proper' in so far as it has attended to theory at all. There is a danger, then, that what I have presented as post-empiricism, and what Alexander calls the new theoretical movement, has only served to detach theorists' theory more sharply than ever from the prevailing research practice in the society in which sociologists have been most numerous.

The same point can be made the other way round. The most lauded contribution to the articulation of 'theory proper' in recent years would seem to have been J. S. Coleman's massive *Foundations of Sociology* (1990). Like Merton before him, Coleman complains that most 'social theory' is really the history of social thought, especially nineteenth-century social thought, and as such it provides a poor basis for the analysis and explanation of a world undergoing an organizational revolution. For that a new robust theory of action is required, and, pulling together the threads of a twenty-year personal project, Coleman heroically sets out to provide it himself in both discursive and mathematical forms. In the course of nearly a thousand pages, Coleman makes innumerable shrewd points about contemporary social phenomena but his researchers' theory is impervious to the linguistic turn, the double-hermeneutic and the preoccupations of post-empiricist philosophy of science. It belongs to a time-warp; it avoids not only theory conceived as the history of social thought, but also connections with almost any developments in social theory and the philosophy of the social sciences in the last quarter-century. The agency–structure debates might as well not have taken place. Kuhn, Hesse, Rorty – they all laboured in vain. The new theoretical movement is beyond notice. (For that matter, so are the profound misgivings about the direction American sociology has taken voiced by the leading proponent of causal modelling, Blalock (1984).) Most tellingly of all, Coleman seems unaware that the very notion of the foundations of social science could be controversial. Significantly, his book was respectfully reviewed in the leading American journals and ignored altogether in the British ones.

The detachment of theorists' theory from research practice seems to have done mainstream American sociology – Turner and Turner's 'impossible science' (1990) – no favours. Their thesis is that American sociology has, since the 1950s, sold itself to the foundations, to agencies of the federal and state governments, and to prospective

students on a false prospectus – basically a natural-science-type prospectus – on which it has all too conspicuously proved unable to
deliver. They are particularly interesting on the poisoned legacy of the
1960s. They argue that sociologists enjoyed huge increases in federal
funding for research and in student numbers in the 1960s and 1970s
before they had resolved fundamental questions about what their
discipline could and should be and do. The reorganized ASA became
an umbrella organization for enormously diverse activities.

> The result was an almost complete inability to consolidate symbolic
> resources around either a sense of a common professional community
> – as the founders of American sociology tried to do – or a common
> corpus and storehouse of knowledge. And when the period of decline
> in funding, student enrollments, ASA membership, and eventually
> Ph.D. production began in the mid 1970s, sociology did not have the
> organizational resources, such as centralized administration and con-
> trol, nor the symbolic resources, such as common professional identi-
> fication, consensus over a knowledge base, and prestige within the
> academic or lay community, to cope with the decline. (Turner and
> Turner, 1990, pp. 139–40)

Obsession with quantitative research techniques is simply not
enought to integrate the discipline.

Each of the Turners has responded differently to the continuing
plight of American sociology. Jonathan is the gnostic sectarian who
cannot come to terms with post-empiricism. 'The relativistic,
solipsistic, particularistic, anti-positivistic, and meta-istic (to invent a
word) character of theory is no longer a challenge to debate', he tells
us, but, rather, 'Increasingly, it is something to be ignored' (Turner,
1990, p. 389). The fifty or so true believers in 'the realization of
Comte's original vision for a "social physics"' are invited to abandon
the mainstream of sociological theory. (I am reminded of the old joke
about the English, 'Fog in Channel: Continent cut off'.) Stephen is the
sardonic *flâneur* self-exiled in a philosophy department. Looking at
American sociology, he sees too much contentment with comfortable
niches, too few students, too little connection with society, and too
little prospect of theoretical integration.

I believe that the majority of American sociologists, and the minority of American theorists, who still pursue an empiricist conception of
sociology will find that their holy grail continues to elude them. But
sociology is an impossible science only for those who subscribe to an
impossible conception of science. Unfortunately, subscribers include
politicians, publics and purseholders. As a consequence, Smelser

(1988) expects his fellow American sociologists to go on trying to give donor agencies and government officials what they expect irrespective of whether that strategy 'is, in the end, effective or self-defeating' (p. 15). Even so I think Turner and Turner underestimate the long-term persuasiveness of post-empiricism and the new theoretical movement, and the numbers who will eventually be touched by it in their research practice. I also note with interest calls for the redirection of sociology in America. I have in mind Gans's call for more 'public sociologists', by which he means not popularizers of other people's work but researchers, analysts and theorists in their own right who have the commitment and the skills to engage the interest of the educated lay public – or, as I would prefer, to initiate and sustain a dialogue with lay publics (Gans, 1988). He gives Riesman as the prime example. I also think Marris is right to call upon sociologists to pay more attention to their role as story-tellers. He argues that influential research mostly tells a story with a moral. Furthermore,

> if research is mostly persuasive as story telling, the researcher is responsible for the moral interpretation of the findings – the beginning and ending, the issues chosen as central, and the way they are resolved, are no longer merely conveniences of marshalling evidence, or steps toward demonstrating a solution, but the unfolding of a drama whose moral implications are crucial to the persuasiveness of the research. (Marris, 1990, p. 76)

To make researchers alone responsible for the moral interpretation of their findings is to treat their readers as moral dopes; but Marris's suggestion that sociologists should cultivate the skills of story-tellers who point up moral issues is well judged. I suspect that he has identified at least part of the success of works like Bellah et al.'s *Habits of the Heart* (1985) and Wilson's *The Truly Disadvantaged* (1987), each of which addresses aspects of the moral condition of America.

In sum American sociological theory is alive and well, but may have more impact on sociology in general outside America than within it. In the long term, American sociology generally will probably come right, but it is questionable whether in the short term it offers many positive lessons for sociological communities elsewhere.

In Britain, as in America, sociology expanded greatly in the 1960s and early 1970s without having first secured the disciplinary integration coveted by Turner and Turner. This expansion was, however, not so great as to make possible the fragmentation of sociology into countless self-sustaining specialties – the introverted nicheism which Turner and Turner so deplore in America – and seems not to have impeded concerted responses to the cutbacks of the early 1980s. There are some separatist tendencies in the sociology of health and illness (the largest specialty in Britain) and in ethnomethodology but they are very much the exception and not the rule. Most British sociologists are, without doubt, less accomplished in quantitative social research methods than their American counterparts (something which has long worried the publicly funded Economic and Social Research Council (e.g. ESRC, 1987)), but they are probably better informed, by choice and necessity, about developments in different sociological traditions – analytical, hermeneutic and historical – and different specialties. The war of the schools is now a distant, if often fond, memory. Departments are cohesive. Student demand for sociology – long falling until the mid-1980s – is now climbing sharply. The high point of political hostility to sociology has passed. Membership of the British Sociological Association is at an all-time high. None of this is to deny, of course, that serious problems remain. In particular the chronic and wearying underfunding of higher education in Britain in general, and the location of sociology among the least favoured group of disciplines in particular, has, in the context of the current rapid expansion of higher education, put sociology teachers under great strain and limited time and money for research. It has also restricted provision for in-service training, the updating of equipment and much else besides. Research institutes of the size now familiar in Germany are also conspicuous by their absence (Weymann, 1990). British sociology is, however, in better shape than seemed possible in the early 1980s – partly because it is not wedded to an impossible conception of science. Compared with its American counterpart, it could perhaps be best described as poor but honest.

It is notable that the circumstances of British sociology do seem to have sustained work in theory which has been copious in volume, high in quality and rich in diversity. My list of theory writers includes Martin Albrow, Margaret Archer, Michèle Barrett, Zygmunt Bauman, Ted Benton, Tom Bottomore, Percy Cohen, Ian Craib, Norbert Elias, David Frisby, Mike Gane, Anthony Giddens, Geoffrey Hawthorne, David Held, Richard Kilminster, Derek Layder, Steven Lukes, Stephen Mennell, Nicos Mouzelis, William Outhwaite, Ray Pawson, John Rex, Paul Rock, W. G. Runciman, Andrew Sayer, Liz Stanley, John Thompson, Bryan Turner and John Urry. Others with different interests will think differently and the names will multiply – which is precisely the point. Why has sociology in Britain provided so encouraging an environment for theorists? One factor is surely that British sociology has from the 1960s, the decade of its academic take-off, been less the cumulative science sought by Merton and Turner in America and more a set of discourses. Open to both the empirical and statistical traditions of American sociology and the theoretical and philosophical traditions of European sociology, it has had the singular fortune to be the meeting point for the sociologies of the world.

Post-empiricist knowledge cumulation and decline

Alexander and Colomy have developed what Colomy (1990a, 1990b) calls a 'post-positivist model of knowledge cumulation and decline' (see also Alexander, 1982, and Alexander and Colomy, 1992). I want to propose some amendments to it, re-label it post-empiricist, but otherwise endorse it.

Following Alexander (1982, p. 40), Colomy sets out 'the continuum of social scientific thought' (see figure 6.1). At one end is the metaphysical environment of science (non-empirical), and at the other the physical environment of science (empirical). As one moves from the metaphysical to the physical pole one passes, in order of decreasing generality and increasing specificity, presuppositions, ideological orientations, models, concepts, definitions, classifications, laws, complex and simple propositions, methodological assumptions and observational statements – ten items in all. Although he represents the continuum horizontally, Colomy refers to the ten items as levels – a vertical metaphor – and then makes three points. First, sociology (and presumably other social sciences, too, given the claim for a continuum of social scientific thought) 'is carried out at different levels of generality and is conducted through distinctive modes of discourse' (Colomy, 1990a, p. xix); second, 'in the history of social thought the options at each level have been limited' (p. xix); and third, although no intrinsic relationship exists between levels, social scientists usually presume a linkage because social science practice unfolds within powerful theoretical traditions which stipulate them.

This scheme is attractive in so far as it blurs the distinction between theory proper (the real thing) and metatheory (a seductive diversion from the real thing) by referring to social science as discourse which properly embraces the referents of both. It is unattractive in so far as it proposes a metatheoretical structure based on unambiguous and

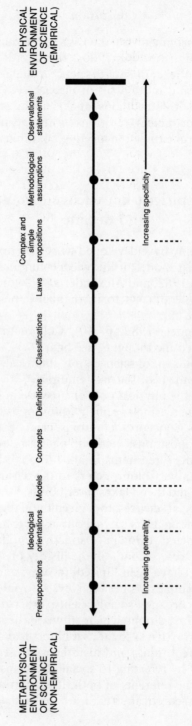

Figure 6.1 Alexander's continuum of social scientific thought

Source: Adapted from Alexander (1982), p. 40

stratified distinctions between concepts, definitions, classifications and laws – to take the middle four levels as an example. Alexander and Colomy's mistakes are to assume a quasi-foundational continuum/layering of social thought instead of the shifting clustering of components of social thought, and to posit the mediation of empirical reality instead of the constitution of society and the person. They make social thought much tidier than it is or ever can be. As a consequence Alexander also refers to theoretical and empirical logics – the former neglected since the decline of Parsonianism in America left the field clear for positivism – as two different processes both of which are indispensable to science, a distinction which threatens to reintroduce into sociology as discourse the unprofitable dualism of theory and evidence.

Colomy (1990a) argues that, thanks to the founding influence of intellectually charismatic figures, 'Social reality . . . is mediated by the discursive commitment of traditions, and social scientific formulations are channelled within relatively standardized, paradigmatic forms' (p. xix). Traditions afford both generalized discourse and research programmes. They can often be traced to an intellectually charismatic founder. Their theoretical cores resist change, but they are otherwise subject to elaboration, proliferation and revision. Elaboration and proliferation are true to the tradition; revision acknowledges, sometimes implicitly, strains within it, and offers reformulations accordingly. Reconstruction, on the other hand, explicitly questions elements of the tradition and opens up to alternatives offered by other traditions. Alexander and Colomy's own reconstruction of Parsonian functionalism as neo-functionalism provides an example. Traditions can also be abandoned and revived. When this happens it is not so much that they have been falsified as that they have become 'delegitimized in the eyes of the scientific community' (p. xix).

In Alexander and Colomy's model, the 'primary motor of social scientific growth is conflict and competition between traditions' (Colomy, 1990a, p. xx). Most estimates of progess can only be estimates of progress within a tradition relative to others. Elaboration, proliferation, revision and reconstruction have to do with closeness of fit to the original tradition; 'They do not describe the degree of real advance' (p. xx). (Colomy does not say how 'real advance' is constituted and justified.) Disciplinary communities change theoretical positions in response to shifts in 'scientific sensibility' which pose different questions and prompt different modes of discourse. In turn,

> Disciplines should not be understood as being organized primarily by
> specialties defined by their empirical objects of investigation and
> divided into middle-range subfields like deviance, stratification, or
> political sociology. The deep structure of a discipline consists of the
> networks and literatures produced by the contact between empirical
> objects, ongoing traditions and new disciplinary movements. (p. xx)

Instead of 'deep structure', Colomy would, I think, have done better
to speak of 'dynamic structure' – the combination of factors which
generate stability and change. He might also have confirmed that
'empirical objects' are 'constituted empirical objects' and he ought
also to have added in 'applications'. With those amendments, however, change in a discipline or specialty can be understood as the
product of contacts between old and new objects of inquiry, old and
new thinking, and old and new applications, and knowledge cumulation and decline can be understood in terms of the growth and loss of
support for a generalized discourse and its accompanying research
programmes within a scientific community. One might also add that
whether change amounts to 'progress' or 'real advance' is also something which can be justified only through dialogue within a scientific
community.

Practical sociology: a social science that works

Two themes run through this book above all others. The first is that
the quest for sure foundations, whether epistemological, conceptual or real – as in the pursuit of theory proper, deductive-
nomologicalism, definitive reconstructionism and the establishment
of a categorial system, strong scientific realism, etc. – has not just
failed, but failed irretrievably. The social engineering and the exclusively instrumental reason associated with some versions of the quest
have also, of necessity, failed to deliver much of what was expected of
them. The product of modelling social science on different conceptions of natural science, they are misconceived, whether grand in scale
or ambition like Parsons, middling like Merton, or small like the
theories Warshay discusses. This is, however, most definitely not to
charge that legions of able and industrious men and women have
laboured for decades and produced nothing of value. Quite apart
from what we might treat in the long run as their necessary but
instructive failures, sociologists of various positivist, empiricist and
realist persuasions have, on the contrary, come up with a huge
number of substantive theories, concepts, research methods, empiri-

cal findings, interpretations and applications which are, or have been, of great social value. It is just that there is no way of connecting them all to yield a single integrated and cumulating body of law and evidence; it is in connection with that project, and that project only, that all those sociologists have laboured in vain. In sum, what could be called the theory-building orientation in sociology has exhausted whatever potential it might once have had.

The second theme is that the linguistic and hermeneutic turns, and anti-foundational and post-empiricist philosophies of science, have supported alternative ways of doing social science which are consistent with the ontologies of the social defined within the agency–structure debate and with the double-hermeneutic and the connections identified between social scientific and lay and other discourses. They also facilitate convergences between social science and moral inquiry and open up the possibility of procedures for the rational assessment of values, and they encourage cognitive and practical ambitions which are realistic. In sum, what could be called the constitution-of-society orientation in sociology has great cognitive potential and avoids giving hostages to political fortune. It affords a pragmatic sociology, one whose practitioners are alive to the conditions and the limits of what they can do and one which enhances the capacity of citizens to engage effectively with the changing social milieus in which they move. (There are affinities here with what R. H. Brown (1989) calls 'sociology for civic competence'.) A pragmatic sociology does not promise what it cannot deliver, but it also knows the social value of what it can deliver. It succeeds by persuasion, by informing the reasoning of agents.

Given the positive and constructive character of this second orientation, is its triumph assured? In the longer term, its prospects would seem very good as ever more sociologists can be expected to take a realistic view of what sociology is and can be – hence the unfashionable optimism I admitted to in the Introduction. In the short term, however, it faces considerable obstacles. First, its adoption is intolerably *dis*orientating to colleagues habituated to the first, or theory-building, orientation. Second, politicians, publics and purseholders largely expect a social *science* worthy of the name and the funding to produce knowledge as reliable and incontestable as that they attribute, however simplistically, to the natural sciences. (That post-empiricist philosophy of science has undermined empiricist natural science, too, seems as yet to have made no difference.) Hence Smelser's dilemma, mentioned above, according to which sociologists in America continue to be locked into delivering to government and other funders what some may have come to recognize is undeliverable.

For the post-empiricist reconstruction of theory and application to succeed, sociologists have to persuade publics, politicians and purseholders that sociology is rational even as it is contestable, that there are learnable and justifiable principles and techniques which inform both different discourses and communication between them and different kinds of research design, practice and analysis. They have also to convey that sociology is necessary: that in differentiated and changing societies there are always understandings to be reached and connections to be made, and that the principles and techniques that make sociology a set of discourses, a discipline, and not an activity in which anything goes, also ensure that it has a contribution to make to the reflexivity of contemporary societies different from anything poets, prophets and pundits can offer. This re-presentation and repositioning of sociology will be difficult and protracted, but on its success the future strength of the discipline depends.

Notes

Chapter 1 Introduction: Theory, Metatheory and Discourse

1 I have used the revised and enlarged second edition of Merton's *Social Theory and Social Structure* published in 1957. There is an earlier version of the essay, 'The bearing of sociological theory on empirical research', which lists the types of work which have gone by the name of theory, in the first edition of 1949. Engel's law of consumption is my example of an empirical generalization, not Merton's. The two 'Continuities' essays mentioned later in the paragraph appear for the first time in the second edition.

2 The term has subsequently been used, and the claim endorsed, by Jonathan Turner (1989a); also see Wacquant (1993). For a brief elaboration see ch. 6, pp. 152–3.

3 Although I argue that in principle postmodernism/ity introduces additional considerations to those associated with anti-foundationalism and post-empiricism, in practice what gets discussed is often similar. See, for example, Seidman and Wagner (1992).

4 Neither Ritzer, nor his contributors, confine themselves to his narrow definition of metatheorizing as 'the systematic study of the underlying structure of sociological theory' (1992b, p. 7). Ritzer, himself, broadens metatheorizing to include the debates on the paradigmatic status of sociology, the micro–macro and agency–structure linkages and the modelling of social science on natural science, and his contributors add issues as diverse as the value of classical theory, concept standardization, reflexivity and postmodernity and theory. I doubt whether sociological theory has any single underlying structure but will return to the issue in ch. 6.

5 For a discussion of five clearly distinguishable uses of the term 'discourse' in the social sciences, including Foucault's, see Cousins and Hussain (1984), ch. 4; and for a review of the similarities and dissimilarities between different conceptions of discourse and ideology, see Purvis and Hunt (1993).

Chaper 2 Concept Formation: Contest and Reconstruction

1 I should dearly like to claim 'the shakers and the shapers' as my own; alas, it was suggested to me by Ray Pawson.

2 For the record, Swanton develops her point in response to criticism of Lukes made by Barry (1975), not Clarke.

3 It is not Kuhn but Feyerabend who identifies incommensurability with the impossibility of translation. See for example the discussion of incommensurability in his *Against Method* (1975), ch. 17.

4 A spy tells me that the thought police staged a counter-coup at the 1994 World Congress of Sociology in Bielefeld.

Chapter 3 The Constitution of Society: Agency and Structure

1 The 'constitution' of society here refers to both process and outcome, the making of society and its make-up. It also alludes to both society as an object of inquiry constituted by social scientists and society as pre-constituted by ordinary men and women. For an extended discussion of the uses of 'constitution' in philosophy and social thought, see Outhwaite (1983), ch. 3.

2 Layder (1994) was published too late for me to take its content systematically into account, but it does include extensive coverage of the micro–macro issue and of four of the five figures I have chosen to concentrate on, the exception being Bhaskar.

3 David Jary has put it to me that Elias is 'suggestive but promissory'.

4 Each of the elements of Giddens's theory of structuration mentioned in this paragraph is discussed later in the chapter.

5 'Recursive' has, I think, been taken from mathematics where recursion formulae indicate the subsequent terms in a series; the formula $x.x+1.x+2...$, for example, indicates that the series 3.4.6 can be continued 9.13.18.

6 For an argument that there are circumstances in which it is appropriate to maintain the dualism of subject and object – notably where actors have a theoretical relation to objects (of reflection, monitoring, evaluation, criticism, etc.) or a strategic relation to objects (in which they are confronted, manipulated, used, reformed, transformed, etc.), see Mouzelis (1992), ch. 2. For a reply see the Introduction to the Second Edition of *New Rules* (1993) where Giddens claims always to have acknowledged that individuals in all forms of society 'distance themselves', to use Mouzelis's expression, from rules and resources, but then goes on to enlarge on institutional reflexivity as a special feature of modernity.

Chapter 4 Values in Social Science: Decisions, Justifications and Communities

1 The Family Expenditure Survey Report for 1989 indicates that the average real annual disposable income of the poorest 20% of households fell from

£3,442 in 1979 to £3,282 in 1989, at 1989 prices; in the same period the figure for the average of all households rose from £10,561 to £13,084 (Townsend, 1991, p. 1). According to the *Guardian*, 1 July 1993, the HMSO publication *Households Below Average Income 1979–1990/91* reveals that the decline worsened significantly in 1990–91.

2 In the elaboration of his theory, Rawls does try to cover the cases of international and intergenerational justice, but, arguably, not convincingly. See Barry (1989), pp. 183–203.

3 Lukes (1982) gives reasons for what I merely assert. For replies, see Habermas (1982, 1991).

4 In *Moral Consciousness and Communicative Action* Habermas refers only to three redeemable claims to validity: (propositional) truth, (normative) rightness and truthfulness. The first two are redeemable discursively. The third is redeemable only by acting consistently: 'A person can convince someone that he means what he says only through his actions, not by giving reasons' (1983, p. 59).

5 To be consistent with the distinction between morality and ethical life, Habermas should now refer to his 'discourse theory of morality'. He persists with 'discourse ethics' because the term has become established usage (Habermas, 1991, p. vii).

6 For an overview of American feminist contributions to sociological theory, see Chafetz (1988).

7 I make no claim that these are the only examples which bring out the issues under discussion here. Other possibilities include Dahl (1970) on democracy after the revolution and Giddens (1990) on utopian realism.

Chapter 5 Models of Applied Social Science: Engineering, Enlightenment, Interaction and Dialogue

1 There is an echo of this in the mission of the Central European University, which has been established since 1989 with an endowment from the financial speculator George Soros to provide postgraduate education in social sciences and humanities for men and women from all the post-communist countries in East-Central Europe and the former Soviet Union. It is expected that students will return to posts in the reformed universities and ministries in their countries and play a key role in the transformation towards democracy and a market economy. Durkheim wanted to educate the educators; the Central European University wants to educate the transformative change agents.

2 Much of Horowitz's venom is directed at Zetterberg (1962), then also at Columbia. Zetterberg promoted not the sociologist as social engineer but the sociologist as social physician diagnosing social ills and prescribing remedies. See Bryant (1976), ch. 9, on 'the new sociology'.

3 This is clearly a topic for further research. Nelson et al. (1987) note research which suggests that 'In business, policymaking market research information appears to be used instrumentally rather than conceptually'

(p. 574) and speculate whether there is a difference between decision making in the private sector where profit is king and the public sector where there are more constituencies to satisfy.

Chapter 6 Conclusion: Impossible and Possible Sociology

1 I allude here to a distinction between theorists' theory and researchers' theory, which is broader than Menzies's distinction between theoreticians' theory and researchers' theory (Menzies, 1982). Menzies's distinction is between theory-building, or the pursuit of what, in ch. 1, echoing Boudon, I called 'theory, proper', and researchers' theory, which settles for establishing such limited connections between phenomena as the complexity and messiness of the social world permit. My version of the 'theory gap' contrasts the broad range of theoretical concerns – conceptual, analytical, hermeneutic, critical, 'metatheoretical', etc. – of self-styled theorists with the narrow theoretical focus of empirical researchers for whom theory refers only to hypotheses for test, and the labelling of connections confirmed by test, within discrete areas of inquiry – in short to (the littlest of) what Warshay (1975) calls 'little theories'. My contrast emphasizes the size of the theory gap between these two types of sociology but does not suppose that they are the only two types in America. The number of empirical researchers so characterized is, however, very large.

References

Abell, Peter (1987) *The Syntax of Social Life*, Oxford: Clarendon Press.
—— (1990) 'Methodological Achievements in Sociology over the Past Few Decades', in Bryant and Becker (1990), ch. 6.
Adriaansens, Hans P. M. (1980) *Talcott Parsons and the Conceptual Dilemma*, London: Routledge & Kegan Paul.
Alcoff, Linda and Potter, Elizabeth (eds) (1993) *Feminist Epistemologies*, New York: Routledge. Introduction by the editors.
Alexander, Jeffrey C. (1982) *Theoretical Logic in Sociology*, vol. 1. *Positivism, Presuppositions, and Current Controversies*, Berkeley: University of California Press.
—— (1988) 'The New Theoretical Movement', in Smelser (1988), pp. 77–101.
Alexander, Jeffrey C. and Colomy, Paul (1992) 'Traditions and Competition: Preface to a Postpositivist Approach to Knowledge Cumulation', in Ritzer (1992a), ch. 2.
Alexander, Jeffrey C., Giesen, Bernhard, Münch, Richard and Smelser, Neil J. (1987) *The Micro–Macro Link*, Berkeley: University of California Press.
Alpert, Harry (1938) 'Operational Definitions in Sociology', *American Sociological Review*, vol. 3, pp. 855–61.
Archer, Margaret S. (1982) 'Morphogenesis versus Structuration: On Combining Structure and Action', *British Journal of Sociology*, vol. 33, pp. 455–83.
—— (1988) *Culture and Agency: The Place of Culture in Social Theory*, Cambridge: CUP.
Baritz, Loren (1960) *The Servants of Power: A History of the Use of Social Science in American Industry*, Middletown CT: Wesleyan UP.
Barnes, Barry (1974) *Scientific Knowledge and Sociological Theory*, London: Routledge & Kegan Paul.
—— (1981) 'On the Conventional Character of Knowledge and Cognition', *Philosophy of the Social Sciences*, vol. 11, pp. 303–33.

—— (1982a) 'On the Extensions of Concepts and the Growth of Knowledge', *Sociological Review*, vol. 30, pp. 23–44.

—— (1982b) *T. S. Kuhn and Social Science*, London: Macmillan.

—— (1992) 'Realism, Relativism and Finitism', in D. Raven, L. van Vucht Tijssen and J. de Wolff (eds) *Cognitive Relativism and Social Science*, New Brunswick NJ: Transaction, ch. 8.

Barry, Brian (1975) 'The Structure of Power', *Government and Opposition*, vol. 10, pp. 250–4.

—— (1989) *A Treatise on Social Justice*, vol. 1 *Theories of Justice*, London: Harvester-Wheatsheaf.

Bauman, Zygmunt (1979) 'The Phenomenon of Norbert Elias', *Sociology*, vol. 13, pp. 117–25.

—— (1987) *Legislators and Interpreters: On Modernity, Post-Modernity and Intellectuals*, Cambridge: Polity.

—— (1989) 'Hermeneutics and Modern Social Theory', in Held and Thompson (1989), ch. 2.

Becker, Henk A. (1990) 'Achievement in the Analytical Tradition in Sociology', in Bryant and Becker (1990), ch. 2.

Becker, Howard S. (1953) 'Becoming a Marihuana User', *American Journal of Sociology*, vol. 59, pp. 235–42.

Bellah, Robert, Madsen, Richard, Sullivan, William M., Swidler, Ann and Tipton, Steven M. (1985) *Habits of the Heart: Middle America Observed*, New York: Harper & Row.

Benhabib, Seyla (1987) 'The Generalized and the Concrete Other', in S. Benhabib and D. Cornell (eds) *Feminism and Critique*, Minneapolis: University of Minnesota Press.

van Bentham van den Bergh, Godfried (1971) 'The Structure of Development: An Invitation to the Sociology of Norbert Elias', *ISS Occasional Papers*, no. 13, The Hague: Institute of Social Studies.

Benton, Ted (1977) *Philosophical Foundations of the Three Sociologies*, London: Routledge & Kegan Paul.

Berger, Peter and Luckmann, Thomas (1967) *The Social Construction of Reality*, London: Allen Lane.

Berger, Peter and Pullberg, Stanley (1966) 'Reification and the Sociological Critique of Consciousness', *New Left Review*, no. 35, pp. 56–71.

Bergmann, Gustav (1964) *Logic and Reality*, Madison W. I.: University of Wisconsin Press.

Bernstein, Richard (1971) *Praxis and Action*, Philadelphia: University of Pennsylvania Press.

—— (1983) *Beyond Objectivism and Relativism*, Oxford: Blackwell.

Bhaskar, Roy (1975) *A Realist Theory of Science*, 2nd edn, Brighton: Harvester, 1978.

—— (1979) *The Possibility of Naturalism*, Brighton: Harvester.

—— (1986) *Scientific Realism and Human Emancipation*, London: Verso.

Biderman, Albert D. (1970) 'Information, Intelligence, Enlightened Public

Policy: Functions and Organization of Societal Feedback', *Policy Science*, vol. 1, pp. 217–30.

Blaikie, Norman (1993) *Approaches to Social Inquiry*, Cambridge: Polity.

Blalock, Hubert M. Jr (1969) *Theory Construction*, Englewood Cliffs NJ: Prentice-Hall.

—— (1984) *Basic Dilemmas in the Social Sciences*, Beverly Hills CA: Sage.

Blau, Peter M. (1975a) 'Parameters of Social Structure', in his (1975b), ch. 12.

—— (ed.) (1975b) *Approaches to the Study of Social Structure*, London: Open Books.

Bloor, David (1976) *Knowledge and Social Imagery*, London: Routledge & Kegan Paul.

Blumer, Herbert (1942) 'Rejoinder' (to Lundberg, 1942), *American Journal of Sociology*, vol. 47, pp. 743–5.

—— (1954) 'What Is Wrong with Social Theory?', *American Sociological Review*, vol. 19, pp. 3–10.

Boden, Deirdre (1990) 'The World as It Happens: Ethnomethodology and Conversation Analysis', in Ritzer (1990b), ch. 7.

Bogner, Artur (1986) 'The Structure of Social Process: A Commentary on the Sociology of Norbert Elias', *Sociology*, vol. 20, pp. 387–411.

Bottomore, Thomas B. (1975) 'Structure and History', in Blau (1975b), ch. 10.

Boudon, Raymond (French 1970) 'Theories, theory and Theory', in his *The Crisis in Sociology: Problems of Sociological Epistemology*, London: Macmillan, 1980, ch. 7. Translation by H. H. Davis.

—— (French 1982) 'Theory', in R. Boudon and F. Bourricaud, *A Critical Dictionary of Sociology*, London: Routledge, 1989, pp. 409–15. Translation by P. Hamilton.

—— (1984) *La Place du désordre*, Paris: Presses Universitaires de France.

Bourdieu, Pierre (French 1972) *Outline of a Theory of Practice*, Cambridge: CUP, 1977. Translation by R. Nice.

—— (French 1979) *Distinction: A Social Critique of the Judgement of Taste*, London: Routledge & Kegan Paul.

—— (French 1980) *The Logic of Practice*, Cambridge: Polity, 1990. Translation by R. Nice.

—— (French 1984) *Homo Academicus*, Cambridge: Polity, 1988. Translation by Peter Collier.

Bourdieu, Pierre and Passeron, Jean-Claude (1970) *Reproduction in Education, Society and Culture*, London: Sage, 1977. Translation by R. Nice.

Bourdieu, Pierre and Wacquant, Loïc J. D. (1992) *An Invitation to Reflexive Sociology*, Cambridge, Polity.

Bourricaud, François (French 1977) *The Sociology of Talcott Parsons*, Chicago: University of Chicago Press, 1981. Translation by Arthur Goldhammer.

Braverman, Harry (1974) *Labor and Monopoly Capital: The Deregulation of Work in the Twentieth Century*, New York: Monthly Review Press.

Brodbeck, May (1968) 'Explanation, Prediction and Imperfect Knowledge', in her (ed.) *Readings in the Philosophy of the Social Sciences*, New York: Macmillan.

Brown, Richard Harvey (1989) *Social Science as Civic Discourse: Essays on the Invention, Legitimation, and Uses of Social Theory*, Chicago: University of Chicago Press.

Brown, Richard K. (1987) 'Norbert Elias in Leicester: Some Recollections', *Theory, Culture and Society*, vol. 4, pp. 533–9.

Bryant, Christopher G. A. (1976) *Sociology in Action: A Critique of Selected Conceptions of the Social Role of the Sociologist*, London: Allen & Unwin.

—— (1985) *Positivism in Social Theory and Research*, London: Macmillan.

—— (1991) 'Theory, Metatheory and Discourse: Reflections on Post-Empiricism', Paper presented to the ASA Annual Conference, Cincinnati, August 1991.

—— (1992) 'Sociology Without Philosophy? The Case of Giddens's Structuration Theory', *Sociological Theory*, vol. 10, pp. 137–49.

—— (1994) 'Economic Utopianism and Sociological Realism: Strategies for Transformation in East-Central Europe', in C. G. A. Bryant and E. Mokrzycki (eds), *The New Great Transformation? Change and Continuity in East-Central Europe*, London: Routledge, ch. 4.

Bryant, Christopher G. A. and Becker Henk A. (eds) (1990) *What Has Sociology Achieved?*, London: Macmillan.

Bryant, Christopher G. A. and Jary, David (eds) (1991) *Giddens' Theory of Structuration: A Critical Appreciation*, London: Routledge.

Bulmer, Martin (1982) *The Uses of Social Research: Social Investigation in Public Policy-Making*, London: Allen & Unwin.

—— (1990) 'Successful Applications of Sociology', in Bryant and Becker (1990), ch. 7.

Burman, Patrick (1988) *Killing Time, Losing Ground*, Toronto: Wall & Thompson.

Cain, Maureen (1990) 'Realist Philosophy and Standpoint Epistemologies or Feminist Criminology as a Successor Science', in L. Gelsthorpe and A. Morris (eds), *Feminist Perspectives in Criminology*, Milton Keynes: Open University Press.

Calhoun, Craig, LiPuma, Edward and Postone, Moishe (eds) (1993) *Bourdieu: Critical Perspectives*, Cambridge: Polity.

Care, Norman S. (1973) 'On Fixing Social Concepts', *Ethics*, vol. 84, pp. 10–21.

Carroll, R. (1982) 'Adequacy in Interpretative Sociology', *Sociological Review*, vol. 30, pp. 392–406.

Chafetz, Janet S. (1988) *Feminist Sociology: An Overview of Contemporary Theories*, Itasca IL: Peacock.

Cherns, Albert (1976a) 'Social Engineering in Britain: The Use of Social Sciences in Social Policy', in his (1976b), ch. 22.

—— (ed.) (1976b) *Sociotechnics*, London: Malaby Press.

—— (1986) 'Policy Research Under Scrutiny', in Heller (1986), ch. 13.

Cicourel, Alvin V. (1964) *Method and Measurement in Sociology*, New York: Free Press.

Clark, Jon, Modgil, Celia and Modgil, Sohan (eds) (1990) *Anthony Giddens: Consensus and Controversy*, London: Falmer Press.

Clarke, Barry (1979) 'Eccentrically Contested Concepts', *British Journal of Political Science*, vol. 9, pp. 122–6.

COCTA (1992) Statement about COCTA attached to letter sent to ISA members.

Coleman, James S. (1972) *Policy Research in the Social Sciences*, Morristown NJ: General Learning Press.

—— (1990) *Foundations of Social Theory*, Cambridge MA: Belknap Press.

Collins, Randall (1981) 'On the Microfoundations of Macrosociology', *American Sociological Review*, vol. 86, pp. 984–1014.

Colomy, Paul (ed.) (1990a) *Functionalist Sociology*, London: Elgar.

—— (1990b) *Neofunctionalist Sociology*, London: Elgar.

Connell, Robert W. (1987) *Gender and Power*, Cambridge: Polity.

Connolly, William E. (1974) *The Terms of Political Discourse*, 2nd edn, Oxford: Martin Robertson, 1983.

Cooley, Charles H. (1902) *Human Nature and Social Order*, New York: Scribner.

Coser, Lewis A. (1971) *Masters of Sociological Thought: Ideas in Historical and Social Context*, New York: Harcourt Brace Jovanovich.

Cousins, Mark and Hussain, Athar (1984) *Michel Foucault*, London: Macmillan.

Crespi, Franco (Italian 1989) *Social Action and Power*, Oxford: Blackwell, 1992. Translation by author.

Crook, Stephen (1991) *Modernist Radicalism and its Aftermath: Foundationalism and Anti-foundationalism in Radical Social Theory*, London: Routledge.

Crothers, Charles (1987) *Robert K. Merton*, Chichester: Ellis Horwood.

Dahl, Robert A. (1970) *After the Revolution? Democracy in a Good Society*, New Haven CT: Yale UP.

—— (1971) *Polyarchy: Participation and Opposition*, New Haven CT: Yale UP.

—— (1976) *Modern Political Analysis*, 3rd edn, Englewood Cliffs NJ: Prentice-Hall.

Dahrendorf, Ralf (1958) 'Out of Utopia', *American Journal of Sociology*, vol. 64, pp. 115–27.

—— (German 1965) *Society and Democracy in Germany*, London: Weidenfeld & Nicolson, 1968. Translation by author.

Dainton, Frederick (1971) 'The Future of the Research Council System', in *A Framework for Government Research and Development*, Cmnd 4184, London: HMSO.

Dandeker, Christopher (1989) *Surveillance, Power and Modernity*, Cambridge: Polity.

Derrida, Jacques (French 1972) *Margins of Philosophy*, Brighton: Harvester. Translation by A. Bass.

Dodd, Stuart C. (1939) 'A System of Operationally Defined Concepts for Sociology', *American Sociological Review*, vol. 4, pp. 619–34.

—— (1942) *Dimensions of Society: A Quantitative Systematics for the Social Sciences*, New York: Macmillan.

Donnison, David (1972) 'Research for Policy', in M. Bulmer (ed.) *Social Policy Research*, London: Macmillan, 1978, ch. 2.

Dubin, Robert (1969) *Theory Building: A Practical Guide to the Construction and Testing of Theoretical Models*, New York: Free Press.

Durkheim, Emile (French 1895) *The Rules of Sociological Method*, included in *The Rules of Sociological Method: and Selected Texts on Sociology and its Method*, London: Macmillan, 1982. Introduction by S. Lukes; translation by W. D. Halls.

—— (French 1897) *Suicide: A Study in Suicide*, London: Routledge & Kegan Paul, 1952. Introduction by G. Simpson; translation by J. A. Spaulding and G. Simpson.

Durkheim, Emile and Mauss, Marcel (French 1903) *Primitive Classification*, London: Cohen & West, 1963. Introduction and translation by R. Needham.

Eckberg, Douglas L. and Hill (Jr), Lester (1979) 'The Paradigm Concept and Sociology: A Critical Review', *American Sociological Review*, vol. 44, pp. 925–37.

Elias, Norbert (German 1939) *The Civilizing Process*, vol. 1 *The History of Manners*, and vol. 2 *State Formation and Civilization*, Oxford: Blackwell, 1978 and 1982.

—— (German 1968) 'Introduction' to the 2nd German edn of *The Civilizing Process*, appendix to vol. 1 of translation, pp. 221–63.

—— (German 1970) *What is Sociology?*, London: Hutchinson, 1978. Translation by S. Mennell and G. Morrisey.

—— (1982) new author's endnotes to vol. 2 of translation of *The Civilizing Process*.

ESRC (1987) *Horizons and Opportunities in the Social Sciences*, London: ESRC.

Eubank, E. E. (1931) *The Concepts of Sociology*, Boston: D. C. Heath.

Feyerabend, Paul (1975) *Against Method*, London: New Left Books.

Foucault, Michel (French 1966) *The Order of Things*, London: Tavistock, 1970.

—— (French 1969) *The Archaeology of Knowledge*, London: Tavistock, 1972. Translation by A. M. Sheridan Smith.

—— (1981) 'Questions of Method: An Interview with Michel Foucault', *Ideology and Consciousness*, no. 8, pp. 3–14.

—— (1982) 'The Subject and Power', Afterword to H. L. Dreyfus and P. Rabinow, *Michel Foucault: Beyond Structuralism and Hermeneutics*, Hassocks: Harvester.

Frisby, David and Sayer, Derek (1986) *Society*, London: Tavistock.

Gallie, William B. (1956) 'Essentially Contested Concepts', *Proceedings of the Aristotelian Society*, new series vol. 56, pp. 167–98; revised in his *Philosophy and the Historical Understanding*, London: Chatto & Windus, 1964.

Gambetta, Diego (1982) *Were They Pushed Or Did They Jump?*, Ph.D. thesis, University of Cambridge.

Gans, Herbert J. (1988) 'Sociology in America: The Discipline and the Public', in his (1990), Appendix B.

—— (ed.) (1990) *Sociology in America*, London: Sage.

Garfinkel, Harold (1967) *Studies in Ethnomethodology*, Englewood Cliffs NJ: Prentice-Hall.

—— (1988) 'Evidence for Locally Produced, Naturally Accountable Phenomena of Order', *Sociological Theory*, vol. 6, pp. 103–9.

Geertz, Clifford (1973) *The Interpretation of Cultures*, New York: Basic Books.

Gelsthorpe, Loraine (1992) 'Response to Martyn Hammersley's Paper "On Feminist Methodology"', *Sociology*, vol. 26, pp. 213–18.

Gerth, Hans H. and Mills, Charles Wright (eds) (1948), *From Max Weber: Essays in Sociology*, London: RKP. Introduction and translation by the editors.

Giddens, Anthony (1973) *The Class Structure of the Advanced Societies*, London: Hutchinson.

—— (1976) *New Rules of Sociological Method*, London: Hutchinson.

—— (1977) *Studies in Social and Political Theory*, London: Hutchinson.

—— (1979) *Central Problems in Social Theory: Action, Structure and Contradiction in Social Analysis*, London: Macmillan.

—— (1981) *A Contemporary Critique of Historical Materialism*, vol. 1, *Power, Property and the State*, London: Macmillan.

—— (1982a) *Profiles and Critiques in Social Theory*, London: Macmillan.

—— (1982b) 'Reason Without Revolution: Habermas's *Theorie des Kommunikativen Handelns*', *Praxis International*, vol. 2, pp. 318–38.

—— (1984) *The Constitution of Society*, Cambridge: Polity.

—— (1985) 'Marx's Correct Views on Everything: With Apologies to Kolakowski', *Theory and Society*, vol. 14, pp. 167–74.

—— (1987) *Social Theory and Modern Sociology*, Cambridge: Polity.

—— (1989) 'Reply to my Critics', in Held and Thompson (1989) ch. 12.

—— (1990) *The Consequences of Modernity*, Cambridge: Polity.

—— (1991) 'Structuration Theory: Past, Present and Future', in Bryant and Jary (1991), ch. 8.

—— (1992) *The Transformation of Intimacy: Sexuality, Love and Eroticism in Modern Societies*, Cambridge: Polity.

—— (1993) 'Introduction to the Second Edition' of *New Rules of Sociological Method*, Cambridge: Polity.

Giddens, Anthony and Turner Jonathan H. (eds) (1987) *Social Theory Today*, Cambridge: Polity.

Gilligan, Carol (1982) *In a Different Voice: Psychological Theory and*

Women's Development, Cambridge MA: Harvard UP.

—— (1983) 'Do the Social Sciences Have an Adequate Theory of Moral Development?, in Haan et al. (1983), ch. 2.

Glaser, Barney G. and Strauss, A. (1965) *Awareness of Dying*, Chicago: Aldine.

—— (1967) *The Discovery of Grounded Theory*, Chicago: Aldine.

Goffman, Erving (1974) *Frame Analysis: An Essay on the Organization of Experience*, Harmondsworth: Penguin, 1975.

Gordon, Colin (ed.) (1980) *Michel Foucault: Power/Knowledge*, Hassocks: Harvester.

Goudsblom, Johann (1977a) *Sociology in the Balance: A Critical Essay*, Oxford: Blackwell. Revision of Dutch edn of 1974 translated by the author.

—— (1977b) 'Responses to Norbert Elias's Work in England, Germany, the Netherlands and France', in P. R. Gleichman et al. (eds) *Human Figurations: Essays for Norbert Elias*, Amsterdam: Amsterdam Sociologisch Tijdschrift.

Gouldner, Alvin W. (1970) *The Coming Crisis of Western Sociology*, London: Heinemann, 1971.

Grathoff, Richard (ed.) (1978) *The Theory of Social Action: The Correspondence of Alfred Schutz and Talcott Parsons*, Bloomington IN: Indiana UP.

Gray, John (1977) 'On the Contestability of Social and Political Concepts', *Political Theory*, vol. 5, pp. 331–48.

Gurvitch, Georges (1958) 'Les Structures sociales', in his (ed.) *Traité de Sociologie*, Paris: Presses Universitaires de France.

Gustavsen, Bjorn (1986) 'Social Research as Participative Dialogue', in Heller (1986), ch. 10.

Haan, Norma, Bellah, Robert N., Rabinow, Paul and Sullivan, William M. (eds) (1983) *Social Science as Moral Inquiry*, New York: Columbia UP.

Habermas, Jürgen (German 1962) *The Structural Transformation of the Public Sphere*, Cambridge: Polity, 1989. Translation by T. Burger with F. Lawrence.

—— (German 1963) 'Dogmatism, Reason, and Decision: On Theory and Praxis in Our Scientific Civilization', in his *Theory and Practice*, London: Heinemann, 1974. Translation by J. Viertel.

—— (German 1968) *Knowledge and Human Interests*, London: Heinemann, 1972. Translation by J. J. Shapiro.

—— (1970) 'Towards a Theory of Communicative Competence', in H. P. Dreitzel (ed.) *Recent Sociology no 2: Patterns of Communicative Behavior*, New York: Collier-Macmillan, 1970, ch. 5.

—— (German 1973a) *Legitimation Crisis*, London: Heinemann, 1976. Translation by T. McCarthy.

—— (1973b) 'Wahrheitstheorien', in H. Fahrenbach (ed.) *Wirklichkeit und Reflexion: zum sechzigsten Geburtstag für Walter Schulz*, Pfüllingen: Neske.

—— (German 1976) 'What is Universal Pragmatics?', in his *Communication and the Evolution of Society*, London: Heinemann, 1979, ch. 1.

—— (German 1981) *The Theory of Communicative Action*, vol. 1 *Reason and the Rationalization of Society*, London: Heinemann, 1984; vol. 2 *The Critique of Functionalist Reason*, Cambridge: Polity, 1987. Introductions to, and translations of, both volumes by T. McCarthy.

—— (1982) 'A Reply to My Critics', in Thompson and Held (1982), ch. 12.

—— (German 1983) *Moral Consciousness and Communicative Action*, Cambridge: Polity, 1990. Introduction by T. McCarthy. Translation by C. Lenhardt and S. W. Nicholsen.

—— (German 1990) 'Morality, Society, and Ethics: An Interview with Torben Hviid Nielsen', addition to the English edn of Habermas (1991).

—— (German 1991) *Justification and Application: Remarks on Discourse Ethics*, Cambridge: Polity, 1993. Introduction and translation by C. Cronin.

Hagstrom, Warren O. (1965) *The Scientific Community*, New York: Basic Books.

Hammersley, Martyn (1992) 'On Feminist Methodology', *Sociology*, vol. 26, pp. 187–206.

Hankiss, Elmer (1990) 'In Search of a Paradigm', *Daedalus*, no. 119, pp. 183–214.

Harding, Sandra (1993) 'Rethinking Standpoint Epistemology: What is "Strong Objectivity"?', in Alcoff and Potter (1993), ch 3.

Harré, Rom and Secord, Paul F. (1972) *The Explanation of Social Behaviour*, Oxford: Blackwell.

Hart, Herbert L. A. (1961) *The Concept of Law*, Oxford: Clarendon.

Hart, Hornell (1943) 'Some Methods for Improving Sociological Definitions', an abridged report of the Sub-Committee on Definition of the Committee on Conceptual Integration, *American Sociological Review*, vol. 8, pp. 333–42.

Harvey, Lee (1982) 'The Use and Abuse of Kuhnian Paradigms in the Sociology of Knowledge', *Sociology*, vol. 16, pp. 85–101.

Hechter, Michael (ed.) (1983) *The Microfoundations of Macrosociology*, Philadelphia: Temple UP.

Held, David and Thompson, John B. (eds) (1989) *Social Theory of Modern Society: Anthony Giddens and His Critics*, Cambridge: CUP.

Heller, Frank (ed.) (1986) *The Use and Abuse of Social Science*, London: Sage.

Hempel, Carl G. (1965) 'Fundamentals of Taxonomy' (1959), revised in his *Aspects of Scientific Explanation: and Other Essays in the Philosophy of Science*, New York: Free Press, ch. 6.

Hesse, Mary (1974) *The Structure of Scientific Inference*, London: Macmillan.

—— (1978) 'Theory and Value in the Social Sciences', in C. Hookway and P. Pettit (eds) *Action and Interpretation: Studies in the Philosophy of the Social Sciences*, Cambridge, CUP, ch. 1.

—— (1980) *Revolutions and Reconstructions in the Philosophy of Science*, Brighton: Harvester.

Horowitz, Irving L. (1963a) 'Establishment Sociology: The Value of Being Value-Free', in his (1968), ch. 10.

—— (1963b) 'Sociology for Sale', in his (1968), ch. 11.

—— (1968) *Professing Sociology: Studies in the Life Cycle of Social Science*, Chicago: Aldine.

—— (ed.) (1979) *Constructing Policy*, New York: Praeger.

Hoy, David (1985) 'Jacques Derrida', in Q. Skinner (ed.) *The Return of Grand Theory in the Human Sciences*, Cambridge: CUP.

Ingham, Geoffrey K. (1984) *Capitalism Divided? The City and Industry in Britain*, London: Macmillan.

James, William (1890) *Principles of Psychology*, 2 vols, New York: Holt.

Janowitz, Morris (1971) *Sociological Models and Social Policy*, New York: General Learning Press.

—— (1972) 'Professionalization of Sociology', *American Journal of Sociology*, vol. 78, 1972–73, pp. 105–35.

Jarvie, Ian C. (1972) *Concepts and Society*, London, Routledge & Kegan Paul.

Jenkins, Richard (1982) 'Pierre Bourdieu and the Reproduction of Determination', *Sociology*, vol. 16, pp. 270–81.

—— (1992) *Pierre Bourdieu*, London: Routledge.

Johnson, Harry M. (1981) 'Foreword' to Bourricaud (1977).

Kalleberg, Ragnvald (1992) 'A Constructive Turn in Sociology', *ISO Rapportserie*, no. 19, Oslo: University of Oslo.

—— (forthcoming) 'Action Research as Science and Profession in the Discipline of Sociology', in S. Toulmin and B. Gustavsen (eds) *Beyond Theory: Changing Organizations Through Participative Action Research*, Assen and Maastricht: Van Gorcum.

Kangiesser, S. (1976) 'Sprachliche Universalien und diachrone Prozesse', in K. O. Apel (ed.) *Sprachpragmatik und Philosophie*, Frankfurt: Suhrkamp.

Kariel, Henry (1973) 'Neither Sticks Nor Stones', *Politics and Society*, vol. 3, pp. 179–99.

Keat, Russell and Urry, John (1975) *Social Theory as Science*, London: Routledge & Kegan Paul.

Knorr-Cetina, Karin D. and Cicourel, Aaron V. (eds) (1981) *Advances in Social Theory; Toward an Integration of Micro- and Macro-Sociologies*, London: Routledge & Kegan Paul.

Kohlberg, Lawrence (1963) 'The Development of Children's Orientation toward a Moral Order: 1. Sequence in the Development of Moral Thought', *Vita Humana*, vol. 6, pp. 11–33.

—— (1969) 'Stage and Sequence: The Cognitive Developmental Approach to Socialization', in D. A. Goslin (ed.) *Handbook of Socialization Theory and Research*, New York: Rand McNally.

—— (1971) 'From Is to Ought: How to Commit the Naturalistic Fallacy and Get Away with It in the Study of Moral Development', in T. Mischel (ed.)

Cognitive Development and Epistemology, New York: Academic Press, pp. 151–235.

—— (1981) *The Philosophy of Moral Development*, San Francisco: Harper Row.

Kolakowski, Leszek (1975) *Husserl and the Quest for Certitude*, New Haven CT: Yale University Press.

van Krieken, Robert (1990) 'The Organisation of the Soul: Elias and Foucault on Discipline and the Self', *Archives européennes de sociologie*, vol. 31, pp. 353–71.

Kuhn, Thomas S. (1962) *The Structure of Scientific Revolutions*, published as *International Encycopedia of Unified Science*, vol. 2, no. 2, Chicago: University of Chicago Press.

—— (1970a) 'Postscript – 1969' to 2nd edn of Kuhn (1962), Chicago: University of Chicago Press, pp. 174–209.

—— (1970b) 'Reflections on my Critics', in Lakatos and Musgrave (1970), pp. 231–78.

—— (1974) 'Second Thoughts on Paradigms', in F. Suppé (ed.) *The Structure of Scientific Theories*, Urbana IL: University of Illinois Press, pp. 459–99.

—— (1977) *The Essential Tension: Selected Studies in Scientific Tradition and Change*, Chicago: University of Chicago Press.

Lakatos, Imre and Musgrave, Alan (eds) (1970) *Criticism and the Growth of Knowledge*, Cambridge: CUP.

Lane, Jan-Erik with Stenlund, Hans (1984) 'Power', in Sartori (1984b), ch. 7.

Lassman, Peter (1980) 'Value-Relations and General Theory: Parsons' Critique of Weber', *Zeitschrift für Soziologie*, vol. 9, pp. 100–11.

Latour, Bruno and Woolgar, Steve (1979) *Laboratory Life: The Social Construction of Scientific Facts*, Beverly Hills CA: Sage.

Layder, Derek (1986) 'Social Reality as Figurations', *Sociology*, vol. 20, pp. 367–86.

—— (1994) *Understanding Social Theory*, London: Sage.

Lazarsfeld, Paul F. (1968) *Latent Structure Analysis*, Boston: Houghton Mifflin.

Lazarsfeld, Paul F. and Rosenberg, Morris (eds) (1955) The Language of Social Research: A Reader in the Methodology of Social Research, Glencoe IL: Free Press.

Lee, Raymond L. M. (1992) 'The Structuration of Disenchantment: Secular Agency and the Reproduction of Religion', *Journal for the Theory of Social Behaviour*, vol. 22, pp. 381–401.

Lengermann, Patricia M. and Niebrugge-Brantley, Jill (1990) 'Feminist Sociological Theory: The Near Future Prospects', in Ritzer (1990b), ch. 12.

Lieberson, Stanley (1985) *Making It Count*, Berkeley CA: University of California Press.

Lindblom, Charles E. and Cohen, David K. (1979) *Usable Knowledge: Social Science Problem Solving*, New Haven CT: Yale UP.

Longino, Helen (1993) 'Subjects, Power and Knowledge: Description and

Prescription in Feminist Philosophies of Science', in Alcoff and Potter (1993), ch. 5.

Lukes, Steven (1974a) *Power: A Radical View*, London: Macmillan.

—— (1974b) 'Relativism: Cognitive and Moral', *Proceedings of the Aristotelian Society*, supplementary vol. 48, pp. 165–89.

—— (1982) 'Of Gods and Demons: Habermas and Practical Reason', in Thompson and Held (1982), ch. 7.

Lundberg, George A. (1929) *Social Research: A Study in Methods of Gathering Data*, New York: Longmans, Green & Co.

—— (1936a) 'Quantitative Methods in Social Psychology', *American Sociological Review*, vol. 1, pp. 38–60.

—— (1936b) 'The Thoughtways of Contemporary Sociology', *American Sociological Review*, vol. 1, pp. 703–23.

—— (1939) *Foundations of Sociology*, New York: Macmillan.

—— (1942) 'Operational Definitions in the Social Sciences', *American Journal of Sociology*, vol. 47, pp. 727–43.

Lyotard, Jean-François (French 1979) *The Postmodern Condition: A Report on Knowledge*, Manchester: Manchester University Press. Foreword by F. Jameson; translation by G. Bennington and B. Massumi.

McCarthy, Thomas (1978) *The Critical Theory of Jürgen Habermas*, London: Hutchinson.

McCrone, David (1992) *Understanding Scotland: The Sociology of a Stateless Nation*, London: Routledge.

Macdonald, Kenneth I. (1976) 'Is "Power" Essentially Contested?', *British Journal of Political Science*, vol. 6, pp. 380–2.

MacIntosh, Norman B. and Scapens, Robert W. (1990) 'Structuration Theory in Management Accounting', *Accounting, Organizations and Society*, vol. 15, pp. 455–77.

MacIntyre, Alasdair (1967) *Secularisation and Moral Change*, Oxford: OUP.

—— (1973) 'The Essential Contestability of Social Concepts', *Ethics*, vol. 84, pp. 1–9.

—— (1981) *After Virtue: A Study in Moral Theory*, London: Duckworth.

Malinowski, Bronislaw (1922) *Argonauts of the Western Pacific*, London: Routledge & Kegan Paul.

Marris, Peter (1990) 'Witnesses, Engineers or Storytellers? Roles of Sociologists in Social Policy', in Gans (1990a), ch. 5.

Martineau, Harriet (1853) (ed.) *The Positive Philosophy of Auguste Comte*, 2 vols, London: Chapman. 'Freely translated and condensed' by the editor from A. Comte, *Cours de philosophie positive*, 6 vols, Paris: Bachelier, 1830–42.

Martins, Herminio (1972) 'The Kuhnian "Revolution" and its Implications for Sociology', in T. D. Nossiter et al. (eds) *Imagination and Precision in the Social Sciences*, London: Faber and Faber.

Marx, Karl (German 1845) 'Theses on Feuerbach', in K. Marx and F. Engels, *Collected Works*, vol. 5, 1845–47, London: Lawrence & Wishart, 1976.

—— (German 1852) 'The Eighteenth Brumaire of Louis Bonaparte', in his and F. Engels, *Selected Works*, Moscow: Foreign Languages Publishing House, 1962, vol. 1, pp. 247–344.

—— (German, written 1857–58) *Grundrisse*, Harmondsworth: Penguin, 1973. Foreword and translation by M. Nicolaus.

Masterman, Margaret (1970) 'The Nature of a Paradigm', in Lakatos and Musgrave (1970), pp. 59–89.

Mellor, Phillip A. (1993) 'Reflexive Traditions: Anthony Giddens, High Modernity and the Contours of Contemporary Religiosity', *Religious Studies*, vol. 29, pp. 111–27.

Mennell, Stephen (1989) *Norbert Elias: Civilization and the Human Self-Image*, Oxford: Blackwell.

—— (1990) 'The Sociological Study of History: Institutions and Social Development', in Bryant and Becker (1990), ch. 4.

—— (1992) 'Afterword' to 2nd edn of his (1989).

Menzies, Ken (1982) *Sociological Theory in Use*, London: Routledge & Kegan Paul.

Merton, Robert K. (1957a) 'The Bearing of Sociological Theory on Empirical Research', in his (1957d), ch. 2.

—— (1957b) 'Continuities in the Theory of Reference Groups and Social Structure', in his (1957d), ch. 9.

—— (1957c) 'Continuities in the Theory of Social Structure and Anomie', in his (1957d), ch. 5.

—— (1957d) *Social Theory and Social Structure*, rev. edn, Glencoe IL: Free Press.

—— (1972) 'Insiders and Outsiders', *American Journal of Sociology*, vol. 78, pp. 9–47.

—— (1984) 'Socially Expected Durations: A Case Study of Concept Formation in Sociology', in W. W. Powell and R. Robbins (eds) *Conflict and Consensus: A Festschrift for Lewis A. Coser*, New York: Free Press, pp. 262–83.

Merton, Robert K. and Lazarsfeld, Paul F. (1954) 'Friendship as Social Process: A Substantive and Methodological Analysis', in M. Berger, T. Abel and C. H. Page (eds) *Freedom and Control in Modern Society*, New York: Van Nostrand, pp. 18–66.

Merton, Robert K. and Lerner, Daniel (1951) 'Social Scientists and Research Policy', in D. Lerner and H. D. Lasswell (eds) *The Policy Sciences*, Princeton NJ: Stanford UP.

Mills, Charles Wright (1959) *The Sociological Imagination*, New York: OUP.

Mouzelis, Nicos (1992) *Back to Sociological Theory: The Construction of Social Orders*, London: Macmillan.

Mulkay, Michael (1971) *Functionalism, Exchange and Theoretical Strategy*, London: Routledge & Kegan Paul.

Myrdal, Gunnar (1944) *An American Dilemma*, New York: Harper.

Nelson, Carnot E. (ed.) (1987) *Utilization of Social Science Information by*

Policymakers, special issue of *American Behavioral Scientist*, vol. 30, no. 6, July/August.

Nelson, Carnot E., Roberts, Jeanne, Maederer, Cynthia M., Wertheimer, Bruce and Johnson, Beverly (1987) 'The Utilization of Social Science Information by Policymakers', in Nelson (1987), pp. 569–77.

On, Bat-Ami Bar (1993) 'Marginality and Epistemic Privilege', in Alcoff and Potter (1993), ch. 4.

Oppenheim, Felix (1981) *Political Concepts: A Reconstruction*, Oxford: Blackwell.

Outhwaite, William (1983) *Concept Formation in Social Science*, London: Routledge & Kegan Paul.

—— (1987) *New Philosophies of Social Science: Realism, Hermeneutics and Critical Theory*, London: Macmillan.

—— (1990) 'Agency and Structure', in Clark, Modgil and Modgil (1990), ch. 6.

Parsons, Talcott (1937) *The Structure of Social Action*, Glencoe IL: Free Press.

—— (1951) *The Social System*, London: Routledge & Kegan Paul.

—— (1963a) 'On the Concept of Influence' (with rejoinder to comments), *Public Opinion Quarterly*, vol. 27, pp. 37–62 and 87–92.

—— (1963b) 'On the Concept of Political Power', *Proceedings of the American Philosophical Society*, vol. 107, pp. 232–62.

—— (1974) 'A Retrospective Perspective', in Grathoff (1978), pp. 115–24.

Parsons, Talcott and Shils, Edward A. (eds) (1951) *Towards a General Theory of Action*, Glencoe IL: Free Press.

Pawson, Ray (1989) *A Measure for Measures: A Manifesto for Empirical Sociology*, London: Routledge.

Peel, John D. Y. (1971) *Herbert Spencer: The Evolution of a Sociologist*, London: Heinemann.

Phillips, Derek L. (1986) 'Preface' to M. L. Wardell and S. P. Turner (eds) *Sociological Theory in Transition*, Boston: Allen & Unwin.

—— (1992) 'Relativism, Morality, and Feminist Thought', in Diederick Raven, Lieteke van Vucht Tijssen and Jan de Wolf (eds) *Cognitive Relativism and Social Science*, New Brunswick NJ: Transaction, ch. 14.

Poole, Ross (1991) *Morality and Modernity*, London: Routledge.

Popper, Karl (1944) *The Poverty of Historicism*, London: Routledge & Kegan Paul.

Purvis, Trevor and Hunt, Alan (1993) 'Discourse, Ideology, Discourse, Ideology, Discourse, Ideology . . .', *British Journal of Sociology*, vol. 44, pp. 473–99.

Ramazanoglu, Caroline (1992) 'On Feminist Methodology: Male Reason Versus Female Empowerment', *Sociology*, vol. 26, pp. 207–12.

Rasmussen, David M. (1990) *Reading Habermas*, Oxford: Blackwell.

Rawls, John (1958) 'Justice as Fairness', *The Philosophical Review*, vol. 57, pp. 164–97.

—— (1971) *A Theory of Justice*, Cambridge MA: Harvard UP.

—— (1975) 'Fairness to Goodness', *Philosophical Review*, vol. 8, pp. 536–54.

Rich, R. F. (1978) 'The Pursuit of Knowledge', *Knowledge*, vol. 1, pp. 6–30.

Rickert, Heinrich (German 1902) *The Limits of Concept Formation in Natural Science: A Logical Introduction to the Historical Sciences*, Cambridge: CUP, 1986. Introduction and abridged translation by G. Oakes.

Ricoeur, Paul (1971) 'The Model of the Text: Meaningful Action Considered as Text', *Social Research*, vol. 38, pp. 529–62.

Riesman, David (1950) *The Lonely Crowd: A Study of the American Character*, New Haven CT: Yale UP.

Riggs, Fred W. (1984) 'Development', in Sartori (1984b), ch. 3.

Riley, Patricia (1983) 'A Structurationist Account of Political Culture', *Administrative Science Quarterly*, vol. 28, pp. 414–37.

Ritzer, George (1990a) 'The Current Status of Sociological Theory', in his (1990b), ch. 1.

—— (ed.) (1990b) *Frontiers of Social Theory: The New Syntheses*, New York: Columbia UP.

—— (ed.) (1992a) *Metatheorizing*, Newbury Park CA: Sage.

—— (1992b) 'Metatheorizing in America: Explaining the Coming of Age', in his (1992a), ch. 1.

Roberts, John and Scapens, Robert W. (1985) 'Accounting Systems and Systems of Accountability: Understanding Accounting Practices in their Organizational Contexts', *Accounting, Organizations and Society*, vol. 10, pp. 443–56.

Roethlisberger, Fritz J. and Dickson, William J. (1939) *Management and the Worker*, Cambridge MA: Harvard UP.

Rojek, Chris (1986) 'Problems of Involvement and Detachment in the Writings of Norbert Elias', *British Journal of Sociology*, vol. 37, pp. 584–96.

Rorty, Richard (ed.) (1967) *The Linguistic Turn: Recent Essays in Philosophical Method*, Chicago: University of Chicago Press.

—— (1980) *Philosophy and the Mirror of Nature*, Princeton NJ: Princeton University Press.

—— (1982) *The Consequences of Pragmatism*, Minneapolis: University of Minnesota Press.

—— (1983) 'Method and Morality', in Haan et al. (1983), ch. 7.

Rose, Arnold M. (1962) 'A Systematic Summary of Symbolic Interaction Theory', in his (ed.) *Human Behavior and Social Processes*, London: Routledge & Kegan Paul.

Rothschild, Lord (1971) 'The Organisation and Management of Government R & D', in *A Framework for Government Research and Development*, Cmnd 4184, London: HMSO.

Rowbotham, Sheila (1989) *The Past Is Before Us: Feminism in Action since the 1960s*, London: Pandora.

—— (1992) *Women in Movement: Feminism and Social Action*, New York: Routledge.

Sartori, Giovanni (1970) 'Concept Misinformation in Comparative Politics', *American Political Science Review*, vol. 44, pp. 1033–53.

—— (1984a) 'Guidelines for Concept Analysis', in his (1984b), ch. 1.

—— (ed.) (1984b) *Social Science Concepts*, Beverly Hills C. A. and London: Sage.

Sartori, Giovanni, Riggs, Fred W. and Teune, Henry (1975) 'Tower of Babel: On the Definition and Analysis of Concepts in the Social Sciences', *International Studies Association Occasional Papers*, no. 6.

Sayer, Andrew (1984) *Method in Social Science: A Realist Approach*, London: Hutchinson.

von Schelting, Alexander (1934) *Max Webers Wissenschaftslehre*, Tübingen: Mohr/Siebeck.

Schlick, Moritz (1930) 'The Turning Point in Philosophy', in A. J. Ayer (ed.) *Logical Positivism*, London: Allen & Unwin, 1959, pp. 53–9.

Schutz, Alfred (1945) 'On Multiple Realities', in his *Collected Papers*, vol. 1, The Hague: Nijhoff, 1973, pp. 205–79.

—— (1953a) 'Common-sense and Scientific Interpretation of Human Action', in his ibid., pp. 3–47.

—— (1953b) 'Concept and Theory Formation in the Social Sciences', in his ibid., pp. 48–66.

Scott, Robert A. and Shore, Arnold R. (1979) *Why Sociology Does Not Apply: A Study in the Use of Sociology in Public Policy*, New York: Elsevier.

Seidman, Steven and Wagner, David G. (eds) (1992) *Postmodernism and Social Theory: The Debate over General Theory*, Oxford: Blackwell.

Shilling, Christopher (1992) 'Reconceptualising Structure and Agency in the Sociology of Education: Structuration Theory and Schooling', *British Journal of the Sociology of Education*, vol. 13, pp. 69–87.

Shils, Edward (1961) 'The Calling of Sociology', in T. Parsons et al. (eds), *Theories of Society*, vol. 2, Glencoe IL: Free Press.

Shotter, John (1983) ' "Duality of Structure" and "Intentionality" in an Ecological Psychology', *Journal for the Theory of Social Behaviour*, vol. 13, pp. 19–43.

Skjervheim, Hans (1973) *Ideologianalyse, dialektikk, sosiologi*, Oslo: Pax Forlag.

Smelser, Neil J. (ed.) (1988) *Handbook of Sociology*, Beverly Hills C. A. and London: Sage. Introduction by editor.

Spybey, Tony (1984) 'Traditional and Professional Frames of Meaning', *Sociology*, vol. 18, pp. 550–62.

Stanley, Liz (ed.) (1990) *Feminist Praxis: Research, Theory and Epistemology in Feminist Sociology*, London: Routledge.

Stanley, Liz and Wise, Sue (1983) *Breaking Out: Feminist Ontology and Epistemology*, London: Routledge & Kegan Paul. 2nd edn, *Breaking Out Again*, with new preface, London: Routledge, 1993.

Stehr, Nico (1982) 'Sociological Languages', *Philosophy of the Social Sci-*

ences, vol. 12, pp. 45–57.

Stinchcombe, Arthur (1968) *Constructing Social Theories*, New York: Harcourt Brace Jovanovich.

Stockman, Norman (1983) *Antipositivist Theories of the Sciences: Critical Rationalism, Critical Theory and Scientific Realism*, Dordrecht (Netherlands): Reidel.

Stouffer, Samuel A. et al. (1949) *The American Soldier*, 2 vols (vol. 1 *Adjustment During Army Life* by Stouffer, E. A. Suchman, L. C. DeVinney, S. A. Star and R. M. Williams Jr; vol. 2 *Combat and Its Aftermath* by Stouffer, A. A. and M. H. Lumsdaine, R. M. Williams Jr, I. L. Janis, Star and L. S. Cottrell Jr), Princeton NJ: Princeton UP.

Swanton, Christine (1985) 'On the Essential Contestedness of Political Concepts', *Ethics*, vol. 95, pp. 811–27.

Sztompka, Piotr (1986) *Robert K. Merton: An Intellectual Profile*, London: Macmillan.

—— (1991) *Society in Action: The Theory of Social Becoming*, Cambridge: Polity.

—— (ed.) (1994) *Agency and Structure: Reorienting Social Theory*, Yverdon (Switzerland): Gordon & Breach.

Taylor, Charles (1971) 'Interpretation and the Sciences of Man', *Review of Metaphysics*, vol. 25, pp. 3–51.

—— (1983) 'Political Theory and Practice', in C. Lloyd (ed.) *Social Theory and Social Practice*, Oxford: Clarendon.

Thomas, Patricia (1985) *The Aims and Outcomes of Social Policy Research*, Beckenham: Croom Helm.

Thomas, William I. and Znaniecki, Florian (1918–20) *The Polish Peasant in Europe and America*, 5 vols, Boston: Gorham Press.

Thompson, John B. (1989) 'The Theory of Structuration', in Held and Thompson (1989), ch. 3.

Thompson, John B. and Held, David (eds) (1982) *Habermas: Critical Debates*, London: Macmillan.

Tijssen, I. (1988) *Kwaliteit Noordt Tot Meer Gebruik*, doctoral thesis, Catholic University of Nijmegen.

Tocqueville, Alexis de (French 1835 and 1840) *Democracy in America*, 2 vols, New York: Harper & Row, 1966.

Touraine, Alain (1965) *Sociologie de l'action*, Paris: Le Seuil.

—— (French 1973) *The Self-Production of Society*, Chicago: University of Chicago Press, 1977. Translation by D. Coltman.

Townsend, Peter (1991) *The Poor Are Poorer: A Statistical Report on Changes in the Living Standards of Rich and Poor in the United Kingdom 1979–1989*, Bristol: Department of Social Policy and Planning, University of Bristol.

Turner, Jonathan H. (1987) 'Analytical Theorizing', in Giddens and Turner (1987), pp. 156–94.

—— (1989a) 'Sociology in the United States', in A. Genov (ed.) *National*

Traditions in Sociology, Beverly Hills C. A. and London: Sage.

—— (ed.) (1989b) *Theory Building in Sociology: Assessing Theoretical Cumulation*, Newbury Park CA and London: Sage.

—— (1990) 'The Past, Present and Future of Theory in American Sociology', in Ritzer (1990b), ch. 14.

Turner, Jonathan and Turner, Stephen (1990) *The Impossible Science: An Analysis of American Sociology*, Newbury Park CA and London: Sage.

van de Vall, Mark (1986) 'Policy Research: An Analysis of Function and Structure', in Heller (1986), ch. 14.

Wacquant, Loïc J. D. (1993) 'Positivism', in T. Bottomore and W. Outhwaite (eds) *Blackwell Dictionary of Twentieth Century Thought*, Oxford: Blackwell, pp. 495–8.

Wagner, David G. (1984) *The Growth of Sociological Theories*, Beverly Hills C. A. and London: Sage.

Waismann, Friedrich (1945) 'Verifiability', *Proceedings of the Aristotelian Society*, supplementary vol. 19, pp. 119–50.

Wallace, William (1988) 'Towards a Disciplinary Matrix in Sociology', in Smelser (1988), pp. 23–76.

—— (1990) 'Standardizing Basic Concepts in Sociology', *American Sociologist*, vol. 21, pp. 352–8.

Warshay, Leon H. (1975) *The Current State of Sociological Theory: A Critical Interpretation*, New York: McKay.

Webber, David J. (1987) 'Legislators' Use of Policy Information', in Nelson (1987), pp. 612–31.

Weber, Max (German 1903–6) *Roscher and Knies: The Logical Problems of Historical Economics*, New York: Free Press, 1975. Introduction and translation by G. Oakes.

—— (German 1904) ' "Objectivity" in Social Science and Social Policy', in his (1949), ch. 2.

—— (German 1906) 'The Logic of the Cultural Sciences', in his (1949), ch. 3.

—— (German 1919a) 'Politics as a Vocation', in Gerth and Mills (1948), ch. 4.

—— (German 1919b) 'Science as a Vocation', in Gerth and Mills (1948), ch. 5.

—— (German 1922) *Economy and Society: An Outline of Interpretive Sociology*, Berkeley and Los Angeles: University of California Press, corrected edn, 2 vols, 1978. Edited by G. Roth and C. Wittich; introduction by G. Roth; various translators.

—— (1949) *The Methodology of the Social Sciences*, Glencoe IL: Free Press. Foreword by E. A. Shils; translation by E. A. Shils and H. Finch.

Weinberg, Elizabeth A. (1992) 'Perestroika and Soviet Sociology', *British Journal of Sociology*, vol. 43, pp. 1–10.

Weiss, Carol H. (1976) 'Evaluation Research in the Political Context', in Cherns (1976b), ch. 19.

—— (ed.) (1977) *Using Social Research in Public Policy-Making*, Lexington

MA: D. C. Heath. Introduction by editor, pp. 1–22.

—— (1979) 'The Many Meanings of Research Utilization', *Public Administration Review*, vol. 39, pp. 426–31.

—— (1980) 'Knowledge Creep and Decision Accretion', *Knowledge: Creation, Diffusion, Utilization*, vol. 1, pp. 381–404.

—— (1983) 'Ideology, Interests and Information: The Basis of Policy Decisions', in D. Callahan and B. Jennings (eds) *Ethics, the Social Sciences, and Policy Analysis*, New York: Plenum Press, ch. 9.

—— (1986) 'Research and Policy-Making: A Limited Partnership', in Heller (1986), ch. 15.

Weiss, Carol H. with Bucuvalas, Michael (1980) *Social Science Research and Decision-Making*, New York: Columbia UP.

Wells, Richard H. and Picou, J. Steven (1981) *American Sociology: Theoretical and Methodological Structure*, Washington: University Press of America.

Weymann, Ansgar (1990) 'Sociology in Germany: Institutional Development and Paradigmatic Structure', in Bryant and Becker (1990), ch. 11.

White, Stephen K. (1988) *The Recent Work of Jürgen Habermas: Reason, Justice and Modernity*, Cambridge: CUP.

Whittington, Richard (1992) 'Putting Giddens into Action: Social Systems and Managerial Agency', *Journal of Management Studies*, vol. 29, pp. 693–712.

Whorf, Benjamin L. (1956) *Language, Thought and Reality: Selected Writings*, Cambridge MA: MIT Press.

Wiley, Norbert (1990) 'The History and Politics of Recent Sociological Theory', in Ritzer (1990b), ch. 15.

Willer, David and Willer, Judith (1973) *Systematic Empiricism: A Pseudoscience*, Englewood Cliffs NJ: Prentice-Hall.

Williams, Robin (1990) 'From Cognitive Style to Substantive Content: Programmatics and Pragmatics in the Development of Sociological Knowledge', in Bryant and Becker (1990), ch. 3.

Willis, Paul (1977) *Learning to Labour*, Farnborough: Saxon House.

Wilson, William J. (1987) *The Truly Disadvantaged: The Inner City, the Underclass and Public Policy*, Chicago: University of Chicago Press.

Winch, Peter (1958) *The Idea of a Social Science*, London: Routledge & Kegan Paul.

Wittgenstein, Ludwig (German 1921) *Tractatus Logico-Philosophicus*, London: Routledge & Kegan Paul (1961). Introduction by B. Russell; translation by D. F. Pears and B. F. McGuinness.

—— (German 1930) *Philosophical Investigations*, 2nd rev. edn, Oxford: Blackwell, 1958. Translation by G. E. M. Anscombe.

Wolfe, Alan (1989) *Whose Keeper? Social Science and Moral Obligation*, Berkeley: University of California Press.

Wrong, Dennis (1961) 'The Over-Socialized Conception of Man', *American Sociological Review*, vol. 26, pp. 185–93.

Yates, Joanne and Orlikowski, Wanda J. (1992) 'Genres of Organizational Communication: A Structurational Approach to Studying Communication and Media', *Academy of Management Review*, vol. 17, pp. 299–326.

Zaslavskaya, Tatyana I. (1987) '*Perestroika* and Sociology', *Social Research*, vol. 55, pp. 267–76.

Zetterberg, Hans L. (1962) *Social Theory and Social Practice*, New York: Bedminster Press.

Zijderveld, Anton C. (1972) 'The Problem of Adequacy: Reflections on Alfred Schutz's Contribution to the Methodology of the Social Sciences', *Archives européennes de sociologie*, vol. 13, pp. 176–90.

Index